From Darw

Women as Transi

GW01017711

# Studies on Cultural Transfer

# and Transmission

## VOLUME 1

*Series ISSN*
1879-7350

*Series editor*
Petra Broomans
Faculty of Arts
University of Groningen
P.O. Box 716
NL-9700 AS  Groningen
p.broomans@rug.nl
www.petrabroomans.net

*Series publisher*
Barkhuis
Zuurstukken 37
NL-9761 KP Eelde
info@barkhuis.nl
www.barkhuis.nl

All volumes in the series can be purchased
via your academic bookseller
or directly from the publisher

# From Darwin to Weil

*Women as Transmitters of Ideas*

edited by

PETRA BROOMANS

Barkhuis
Groningen
2009

Cover design: Coltsfootmedia, Nynke Tiekstra, Noordwolde
Book design: Barkhuis

ISBN 9789077922644

# Table of Contents

# Preface

In 2004 the project 'Scandinavian literature in Europe: the influence of language politics, gender and aesthetics', was started as part of the research program Autonomy and the 'new' Independence in the Arts of the Groningen Research School for the Study of the Humanities (GRSSH). The first workshop of the project about language politics was organized in 2005 and resulted in the book *The Beloved Mothertongue. Ethnolinguistic Nationalism in Small Nations. Inventories and Reflections* (2008). In October 2006 the second workshop 'The Making of a Profession. Women as Cultural Transmitters in the Dutch-speaking region and Scandinavia 1880-1950', was held in Groningen and was supported by the Groningen Research School for the Study of Humanities. Scholars belonging to various disciplines from Belgium, The Netherlands and the Scandinavian countries participated in the workshop.

The workshop dealt with the role of women cultural transmitters in the Dutch-speaking region and Scandinavia 1880-1950. The purpose of the workshop was threefold: 1. to discuss the concept of 'cultural transmitter' 2. to discuss this concept from a gender perspective 3. to investigate the importance of ideologies women cultural transmitters themselves entertained, concerning the reception of literature of small language areas like the Dutch-speaking region and Scandinavia. The essays in this volume, the first in the series Studies on Cultural Transfer and Transmission (CTaT), are based on contributions to the workshop. In the essays, especially the topic women as transmitters of ideas in the period concerned, was elaborated, hence the title *From Darwin to Weil. Women as Transmitters of Ideas.*

Why Studies on Cultural Transfer and Transmission? I regard cultural *transfer* as an one-way activity, a text is translated from one language into another, cultural *transmission* is in my opinion reciprocally, cultural and literary information is shared. Both actions are objects of study in CTaT.

I would like to thank my co-organizers of the workshop Ester Jiresch (University of Groningen) and Marta Ronne (University of Uppsala). I am also grateful to Marijke Wubbolts for helping organize the workshop and Ester Jiresch for helping me with the index.

Julia Harvey of the Language Center at the University of Groningen I would like to thank for a fruitful discussion about the meaning of 'transfer' and 'transmission'.

Petra Broomans

# Introduction:
# Women as Transmitters of Ideas

Petra Broomans

The profession of cultural transmitter was one that was shaped by women in an active way in the nineteenth century. As Margaret H. McFadden showed in her book *Golden Cables of Sympathy. The Transatlantic Sources of Nineteenth-Century Feminism* (1999), women used networks to establish contacts in different personal and commercial fields in the nineteenth century, including the field of translation.[1] Women translators, as McFadden labels them, spread 'the network of ideas and works.'[2] Here McFadden uses the term 'network' in a virtual way, designating an abstract entity. However, it goes without saying that women cultural transmitters also used *concrete* networks, materialized in terms of people and institutions, to establish contacts, both personal and professional. In the twentieth century, the profession of cultural transmitter developed into a more efficient profession, parallel to the development of the literary field and the growth of the translation market.

Two main purposes of this book are firstly to discuss the concept of 'cultural transmitter', specifically from a gender perspective, and secondly to investigate the role of cultural transmitters in spreading ideas through the introduction, writing about and translation of literature. While the focus is on Scandinavia and the Dutch-speaking region in the nineteenth and twentieth centuries, the positions and activities of the cultural transmitters discussed can be 'translated' into other language areas.

How should we define a 'cultural transmitter'? There are various descriptions of the kind of work that might be undertaken and while cultural transmitters are usually linked to translation work, they can combine various roles. Around 1900 they were already active as literary agents, publishers, journalists, reviewers, journal editors, or literary historians.

---

[1] Margaret H. McFadden, *Golden Cables of Sympathy. The Transatlantic Sources of Nineteenth-Century Feminism* (Lexington, 1999), pp. 208–210.

[2] *Ibidem*, p. 208.

There are also examples of authors who were active as translators. An example is the Swedish author Ola Hansson (1860–1925), who lived in Germany and who, together with his wife Laura Marholm (1854–1928), introduced Scandinavian literature to Germany.[3] The Hansson-Marholm duo, a 'literary gangster duo' as the Danish critic Georg Brandes called them (see the article by Ebba Witt-Brattström in this volume), is not unique. There were many translator couples. Together with her husband William Howitt, the writer Mary Howitt (1799–1888) translated, German and Scandinavian authors into English.[4] Of course, there were and are many who only translated, and these people were often forgotten, seldom being mentioned in a publisher's catalogue or included in literary histories. However, it was also possible for a writer of a text not to be mentioned, but only the translator, so that it was unclear who was who. Translations, of course, are very important, with the act of translation itself being a form of reception which can be of significance for the success of an author abroad.[5]

In the following working definition of the term 'cultural transmitter' I have encompassed various positions of the cultural transmitter. Furthermore, the description reflects the development of the cultural transmitter during the nineteenth and twentieth centuries.

A cultural transmitter basically works within a particular language and cultural area. She/he often takes on various roles in the field of cultural transmission: translator, reviewer, critic, journalist, literary historian, scholar, teacher, librarian, bookseller, collector, literary agent, scout, publisher, editor of a journal, writer, travel writer, or counsellor. Transmitting another national literature and its cultural context to one's own national literature and cultural context is the central issue in the work of a cultural transmitter. Transmission often reflects a bilateral situation. Even the transmission of one's own literature takes place. The motivation can be aesthetically, ideologically, politically and/or economically based.[6]

---

[3] See Inger Månesköld-Öberg, *Att spegla tiden – eller forma den. Ola Hanssons introduktion av nordisk litteratur i Tyskland 1889–1895* (Göteborg, 1984).

[4] McFadden, *Golden Cables of Sympathy*, p. 209.

[5] Månesköld-Öberg, *Att spegla tiden – eller forma den*, p. 30.

[6] I have elaborated this working definition on the basis of previous articles (e.g.

Some roles could be fulfilled by women in the nineteenth century, such as reviewer; other roles were developed in the twentieth century. Today women also work as scouts and earn a living spotting foreign authors for publishers. The Frankfurt Book Fair, the meeting place for the 'industry's experts',[7] is a good example of how trade and networking have become important tools for women cultural transmitters as well for women writers in the twenty-first century.

Meeting and networking at huge events such as book fairs or in a more intimate context is not an entirely new phenomenon, as women were using such networks, meeting each other, discussing and transmitting ideas much earlier. They wrote letters to each other, they read books written by other women, they travelled abroad and they met in their respective homes and salons. This invisible history has been revealed and investigated in the last twenty years in studies such as Brian Dolan's *Ladies of the Grand Tour* (2001) and *'I have heard about you': Foreign Women's Writing Crossing the Dutch Border: from Sappho to Selma Lagerlöf* (2004). The quotation 'I have heard about you' is from a letter from Anna Maria van Schurman (1607–1678) to Lady Dorothy Moore (c.1613/1617–1664).[8] It shows that learned women knew of and communicated with each other.

The discovery or rediscovery of women writers and women cultural transmitters in the twentieth century was to a certain extent possible

---

2006, 2008). 'Om vårt sätt att forska i kulturförmedling. Exempel: Marie Herzfeld (1855–1940)', in: Sven H. Rossel, et al. eds, *Der Norden im Ausland - das Ausland im Norden. Formung und Transformation von Konzepten und Bildern des Anderen vom Mittelalter bis heute.* (= Wiener Studien zur Skandinavistik Vol. 15) (Vienna, 2006), p. 203. Petra Broomans, 'The Concept of Ethnolinguistic Nationalism and Cultural Transfer. The Reception of Scandinavian Literature in Flanders and the Netherlands', in: Petra Broomans, et al. eds, *The Beloved Mothertongue. Ethnolinguistic Nationalism in Small Nations. Inventories and Reflections.* (= Groningen Studies in Cultural Change Vol 23) (Leuven, 2008) p. 40.

[7] See <http://www.buchmesse.de/en/fbf/general/> (accessed 8 November 2009).

[8] See Mirjam de Baar, '"God has chosen you to be a crown of glory for all women!". The international network of learned women surrounding Anna Maria van Schurman', in: Suzan van Dijk et al. eds, *'I have heard about you': Foreign Women's Writing Crossing the Dutch Border: from Sappho to Selma Lagerlöf* (Hilversum, 2004), pp. 108-135. De Baar dates Schurman's letter to c. 1640.

because, in the days of Schurman, men and women of letters across Europe started to compile lists of names of women who had remarkable skills in fields such as arts or science. Such a list was called 'gynaeceum', after the Greek word for women's room. The genre was popular in the seventeenth and eighteenth centuries. Most of the lists were in Latin and were international. As Marianne Alenius states, it was not yet the time for nationally oriented surveys.[9]

In the nineteenth century, when the genre of national literary history was developing, the aim of presenting the efforts of women writers again came to the fore. It might be said that the genre of the 'gynaeceum' was continued in a nationalized form. Bibliographies and surveys of women writers were published, such as the bibliography *Qvinnan inom svenska litteraturen; bibliografiskt försök af två damer* (1873) by Karin Adlersparre (1851–1895) and Elvira Huss, which was complied for the world fair in Vienna in 1873. It was followed by *Kvinnan inom svenska litteraturen intill år 1893*[10] (1893) and the *Lexikon deutscher Frauen der Feder* (1898).[11] These surveys were often made against the backdrop of

[9] Marianne Alenius, 'Om alla slags berömvärda kvinnopersoner. Gynaeceum – en kvinnolitteraturhistoria' in Elisabeth Møller Jensen et al., eds, *I Guds namn. 1000–1800* (Höganäs, 1993), p. 219. ('About all kinds of famous women. Gynaeceum – a women's literary history' in 'In the name of God', translation pb.)

[10] Sigrid Leijonhufvud och Sigrid Brithelli, *Kvinnan inom svenska litteraturen intill år 1893. En bibliografi: utarbetad med anledning af världsutställningen i Chicago* (Stockholm, Rediviva, 1978 [1893]). See for a detailed historical description of the Swedish bibliographies from 1873 and 1893: Anna Nordenstam, *Begynnelser. Litteraturforskningens pionjärkvinnor 1850–1930* (Stockholm, 2001), pp. 114–122. See for a meta-literary historical context, Broomans, 'In the name of God and the Father. Scandinavian women's literary history from a meta-literary historical point of view', in S. van Dijk, L. van Gemert and S. Ottway, eds, *Writing the history of women's writing. Toward an international approach*, Koninklijke Nederlandse Akademie van Wetenschappen Verhandelingen, Afd. Letterkunde, Nieuwe Reeks, deel 182 (Amsterdam, 2001b), pp. 125–134.

[11] Sophie Pataky, *Lexikon deutscher Frauen der Feder. Eine Zusammenstellung der seit dem Jahre 1840 erschienenen Werke weiblicher Autoren, nebst Biographien der Lebenden und einem Verzeichnis der Pseudonyme* (Berlin, 1898). A facsimile appeared in 1971. The text is also available on the internet: <http://www.archive.org/stream/lexikondeutsche01patagoog/lexikondeutsche01patagoog_djvu.txt>.

the world fairs, which became prominent in the second half of the nineteenth century and were designed to present national cultures and introduce visitors to new developments in fields such as science, technology and culture. The world fairs can be regarded as 'laboratories of modernization' and as 'prototypical "culture industries"' – in the Frankfurt school sense of the term – that hastened the reconfiguration of popular culture into mass culture'.[12] The first version of the Swedish bibliography of Swedish and Finland-Swedish women writers was presented at the world fair in Vienna in 1873. It was compiled as a contribution to the promotion of Sweden. One of the themes of the Vienna World Fair concerned participating countries providing an insight into women's labour, as well as women's cultural, historical and literary efforts within their nation.[13] An important aim of the bibliography was to present Swedish women writers abroad. Perhaps this is the reason why translations of works of Swedish women writers were also included in the bibliography. They demonstrated that the writer concerned had been acknowledged by foreign readers.[14] Sophie Adlersparre (1823–1895), editor of the journal *Tidskrift för hemmet* (The Journal of Domestic Life), stepmother of Karin Adlersparre, and initiator of the bibliography of 1873, wrote the introduction, which is in fact the first Swedish women's literary history.

Women such as Sophie Adlersparre worked outside institutions such as universities, academies and political institutions as well as in conjunction with them. In addition to these 'male domains' they used national and international women's associations, journals and networks, and acted as transmitters of knowledge about the position of women in their home countries.

---

[12] Robert W. Rydell and Nancy Gwinn, eds, *Fair Representations. World's Fairs and the Modern World* (Amsterdam, 1994), p. 1.

[13] Ruth Nilsson and Karin Westman Berg, 'Studier i den första svenska bibliografin över kvinnliga författare', in: Hermelin, C., Lewandowski, J., Lönnqvist, H., eds, *Kvinnliga författare 1893-1899. Biobibliografi över svensk och finlandssvensk skönlitteratur* (Stockholm, 1892), p. 13.

[14] See also Suzan van Dijk's comments on the mention of translations in the survey *Dictionnaire historique, littéraire et bibliographique des Françaises [...]* (1804) by Fortunée Briquet (1782–1815). Van Dijk, 'Foreword: Foreign women's writing as read in the Netherlands', p. 16.

The visualization of women in various fields in the arts and sciences with the help of surveys and bibliographies can be regarded as an important step towards the participation of women within the academic institutions. Around 1900, women gained entry to universities and in the first decades of the twentieth century they started to work as scholars and write PhD theses. The long and difficult road to acknowledgment and employment at universities is described in various studies, such as that by Nordenstam on women in the field of Swedish literary historiography (2001), Mineke Bosch's *Het geslacht van de wetenschap. Vrouwen en hoger onderwijs in Nederland 1878-1948 (The Gender of Science. Women and higher education in the Netherlands*, 1994) and Bonnie G. Smith's *The Gender of History. Men, Women, and Historical Practice* (1998). In this period of increasing visibility within the academy prior to the second feminist wave in the 1960s and 1970s, women became both subjects and objects in relation to the goal of demonstrating that they were capable of scientific work. They had already started to reflect on and contextualize their own position.

Along with the second feminist wave in the twentieth century, women's studies and gender studies became new disciplines at the universities and research into the 'forgotten' woman writer developed rapidly. Important studies in the 1970s include Elaine Showalter's *A Literature of their Own. British women novelists from Brontë to Lessing* (1977) and *The madwoman in the attic. The woman writer and the nineteenth-century literary imagination* (1979) by Sandra M. Gilbert and Susan Gubar. These studies inspired women scholars in other language areas to map unknown and forgotten women writers and to explore a new field of study. In addition, books about individual writers and many women's literary histories have been published since the 1980s.

In Scandinavia, a strong tradition in writing women's literary histories has developed. The pioneering work of Adlersparre had many successors, the five-volume *Nordisk kvinnolitteraturhistoria* (Scandinavian women's literary history) being one example. This major project, on which about 100 scholars cooperated, was published between 1993 and 1999.[15] In the Netherlands, *Met en zonder lauwerkrans. Schrijvende vrouwen uit de vroegmoderne tijd 1550-1850: van Anna Bijns tot Elise van Calcar* appeared in 1997. The above-mentioned study '*I have heard about*

---

[15] See Broomans, 'In the name of God and the Father', pp. 125–134.

*you'* can be regarded as one of the spin-offs from these kind of studies.

As mentioned in the working definition of the cultural transmitter, writers also operate as cultural transmitters. Many women writers were active as cultural transmitters, and in several studies the 'lost' woman translator has also been investigated. The research on forgotten women writers and lost translators has generated another type of research; a 'meta literary historiography' and a 'meta cultural transfer and transmission historiography'. An example of the first is Margareth Ezell's critical discussion of English women's literary histories in *Writing Women's Literary History* (1993). An example of 'meta cultural transfer and transmission historiography' is to be found in *Translating and gender. Translating in the 'Era of Feminism'* (1997) by Luise von Flotow. In this book Von Flotow analyses the efforts that were made to make lost women translators visible.[16] Von Flotow discusses a number of works, including *Silent but for the Word. Tudor Women as Patrons, Translators, and Writers of Religious Works*, edited by Margaret Patterson Hannay (1985), and *Oppositional Voices: Women as Writers and Translators of Literature in the English Renaissance* (1992) by Tina Krontiris. These studies cover national histories of the lost woman translator. A transnational cultural transfer and transmission history has not yet been written. However, some general characteristics of the phases in the history of women cultural transmitters can be identified.

When reading studies on lost women cultural transmitters in England during the English Renaissance in the sixteenth century, it becomes clear that the area in which women could translate was religion. As Von Flotow states, in studies on forgotten women translators, these women, though they were politically vulnerable, were regarded as 'subversives' because 'they dared to publish work in an essentially hostile environment'.[17] In this respect, the image of the silent muse and invisible translator changed into an active and subversive one. With Von Flotow, one could say that studies such as *Silent but for the Word* and *Oppositional Voices* are of the programmatic kind, their aim is 'to establish a history of resistant women'.[18]

---

[16] Louise von Flotow, *Translating and gender. Translating in the 'Era of Feminism'* (Manchester/Ottawa, 1997), pp. 66–76.

[17] *Ibidem*, p. 69.

[18] *Ibidem*.

The same pattern is apparent in Scandinavia. As described in the first volume of the Scandinavian women's literary history, *I Guds namn* (1993), women were writing in the name of God, and used religious texts and translations to make their own voice heard. Learned women in Scandinavia lived and acted within the same conventions as their 'sisters' in England, and Scandinavian women's literary history can also be seen as programmatic. Here women are presented as heroines, and feminist literary historical politics are combined with a romantic genius plot *à la* Hayden White and a focus on originality *à la* Harald Bloom.[19]

In the seventeenth century the combination of women's writing/ translating and religion was also common, one example being the Frenchwoman Antoinette Bourignon (1616–1680), who was known for her religious writing, and whose production was enormous compared to other male and female writers of the time. She is a fine example of a learned woman who communicated with other women and who used her networks, meeting, for one, Anna Maria van Schurman in Amsterdam in 1668. Bourignon was always looking for dialogue and the exchange of ideas, including with her critics.[20] Bourignon's works were translated into German, Dutch and Latin. She made strong efforts to broaden her public and therefore needed translators, one of whom Mirjam de Baar discusses in her article on Bourignon: Eleonora von Merlau (1644–1724).[21] Von Merlau was, like Bourignon, very religious and a member of the circle of pietists in Frankfurt am Main. Bourignon heard of her through a disciple, Pierre Poiret (1646–1719), and obviously regarded Von Merlau as a suitable translator. Von Merlau subsequently translated a work by Bourignon into German. Here we have an example of how women writers and translators networked within the realm of religion and helped each other spread ideas.[22]

---

[19] Broomans, 'In the name of God and the Father', p. 133.

[20] Mirjam de Baar, 'Prophetess of God and prolific writer. Antoinette Bourignon and the reception of her writings', in: Suzan van Dijk et al., eds, *'I have heard about you': Foreign Women's Writing Crossing the Dutch Border: from Sappho to Selma Lagerlöf* (Hilversum, 2004), p. 139f.

[21] *Ibidem*, p. 141f.

[22] Peter Burke remarks in a short paragraph that women in the seventeenth century were 'relatively prominent' in the field of translation, but that they all were 'amateurs'. Burke, *Lost (and Found) in Translation: A Cultural History of Translators*

Although there were women who acted in the political arena during the seventeenth century, such as Queen Christina of Sweden (1626–1689) and the Danish countess Leonora Christina (1621–1698), in relation to literature and translation, it is especially in the eighteenth century that women started to write about and translate political and military topics. An example of a Scandinavian women who translated a text on military history is the Norwegian Birgitte Lange, who in 1747 translated Don Antonio de Solis's book on the conquest of Mexico: *Historie om Conqvêten af Mexico* (1684). In her correspondence she depicts herself as a young girl who had wanted to read but had been trapped in a conflict between her longing for learning and the traditional occupations of women.[23] The translation of a political and military text can thus be regarded as a deliberately subversive act during a time when women were not supposed to write on such topics. In the eighteenth century, more women chose to express their political ideas, for example the Swedish writer Hedvig Charlotte Nordenflycht (1718–1763),[24] who was very active in the political debate in Sweden and who wrote military poems. An example of language politics is to be found in the introduction and afterword to the novel *Den beklædte sandhed* (The concealed truth) by the Danish writer Anna Margrethe Lasson (1659–1738), inspired by Madeleine de Scudéry's novel *Artamène ou Le grand Cyrus*. Lasson pleads a case for the Danish language and states that she is writing out of love for her mother tongue. She also wanted to show that women were capable of writing novels, and thus did so herself.[25] Thus, women wrote for the nation as well for their own sake.

---

*and Translating in Early Modern Europe* (Wassenaar, 2005), p. 11.

[23] Torill Steinfeld, 'Fra salmeoversettelser til det borgerlige familiedrama', *Norsk kvinnelitteraturhistorie. Bind 1 1600–1900* (Oslo, 1988), p. 29.

[24] See Petra Broomans, 'The Self-Fashioning of Hedvig Charlotta Nordenflycht', in: Inger M. Olsen and Sven H. Rossel, eds, *Female Voices of the North II. An Anthology*. Wiener Texte zur Skandinavistik (WTS). Band 3 (Vienna, 2006), pp. 27–51.

[25] Anne-Marie Mai, 'Det danska språkets innerliga älskarinna. Om Anna Margrethe Lasson', in: Elisabeth Møller Jensen et al., eds, *I Guds namn. 1000–1800* (Höganäs, 1993), pp. 341–347.

In the eighteenth century, women started to travel to a greater extent and they also wrote about their travels.[26] A famous example is of course Mary Wollstonecraft (1759–1797), who was a journalist, critic and philosopher. Her major work is *A Vindication of the Rights of Woman* (1792), but her *Letters written during a short residence in Sweden, Norway and Denmark* (1796) were very popular. Her travelogues were translated into several languages,[27] and she was also a translator herself. Wollstonecraft translated works from French and German, including *Elements of Morality, for the Use of Children; with an Introductory Address to Parents* in 1790 by Christian Salzmann (1744–1811).[28] Thus, Wollstonecraft was not only a transmitter of revolutionary and feminist ideas, but also of ideas about the education of children.

As McFadden described in her study *Golden Cables of Sympathy*, the nineteenth century was an era in which it was no longer that unusual for women to travel and write about their experiences, as the Swedish writer Fredrika Bremer (1801–1865) did about her journeys to North America and Cuba between 1849 and 1851. Her travel letters were published in Sweden in 1853 and translated by Mary Howitt into English in the same year. Howitt translated many books by Bremer and, as mentioned above, also the works of many other Scandinavian authors. Her contemporary, the Norwegian writer Camilla Collett (1813–1895) travelled with her father in the 1830s and again on her own in the 1860s (see the contribution by Janke Klok).

In the second chapter of her study *"Behind Inverted Commas"*, Susanne Stark provides a survey of nineteenth-century women who translated from German into English, stressing not only the importance of travelling and learning foreign languages for women cultural transmitters, but also the study of grammar.[29] Stark presents these female cul-

---

[26] See e.g. Brian Dolan, *Ladies of the Grand Tour* (London, 2001).

[27] Petra Broomans, 'Mary Wollstonecraft in Scandinavia; her letters in the Netherlands', in: Suzan van Dijk et al., eds, *'I have heard about you': Foreign Women's Writing Crossing the Dutch Border: from Sappho to Selma Lagerlöf* (Hilversum, 2004), pp. 248–253.

[28] Janet Todd, *Mary Wollstonecraft, a revolutionary life* (London, 2000), pp. 134–137.

[29] Susanne Stark, *"Behind inverted commas". Translation and Anglo-German Cultural Relations in the Nineteenth Century* (Clevedon, 1999), pp. 31–61.

tural transmitters as women who, by translating, could write 'without being exposed to the demands of independent authorship'.[30] Stark remarks that translation might have been 'a specifically female flight from public recognition'[31] for women cultural transmitters in the nineteenth century. Despite the fact that they did not attempt to assume a male role, 'they have nonetheless inadvertently slipped into the mode of literary professionalism'.[32] Stark sees a clear paradox in the act of translation: 'on the one hand, there is its subsidiary, reproducing and self-denying character; yet, its creative, thoroughly professional and assertive dimension also has to be given credit'.[33] Moreover, to translate from modern languages was much more profitable than translating from Greek, and during the nineteenth century the commercial aspect of translation became a self-evident part of the process. According to Stark, the women cultural transmitters in her material:

> ... were neither mute nor transparent but fully aware of the power of their mediating role. For they themselves chose the texts they wished to make known in their own country, connected their name with them and to a certain extent recreated them, thereby following their own taste. ... Many of the female translators engaged in professional discussion and referred to one another.[34]

Although Stark thus depicts women cultural transmitters as active and assertive professionals, she states that they could also undervalue their work, considering themselves as mere servants of the author of the original text. Nevertheless, in the nineteenth century the spectrum broadened, with the arrival of the profession of literary translation. Women, who did not yet have access to an academic education, took advantage of the fact that they had often learned many modern foreign languages, and thus started to translate.

One of the major events in the history of translation in the nineteenth century was the translation of *Uncle Tom's Cabin, or Life among*

---

[30] *Ibidem*, p. 34.

[31] *Ibidem*, p. 37.

[32] *Ibidem*, p. 39.

[33] *Ibidem*, p. 43.

[34] *Ibidem*, p. 56.

*the Lowly* (1852) by Harriet Beecher Stowe (1811–1896) into many languages. The novel is an example of how literature became a vehicle for a moral cause.[35] Engagement also played a leading role for women cultural transmitters in Europe who were attracted to the progressive literature of the Modern Breakthrough (1870–1890) in Scandinavia (see also the contribution by Ester Jiresch in this volume). One of these women was Philippine Wijsman (1837–1907), who can be regarded as a self-made translator who obtained several positions in the field of cultural transmission, acting as a literary agent, essayist, writer and translator.[36]

Her favourite author was Anne Charlotte Leffler (1849–1892), whom she met personally. In her letters to Leffler, it is apparent how the process of negotiation and networking was shaped. Wijsman was often engaged in negotiating royalties. Furthermore, there is also some play going on in the letters, a teasing and pleasing of the author, to obtain what the translator wants – the right to translate a literary work.[37] As such, the translator appears to act as a seducer, taking a masculine position towards the text, which is figured as female, an object of desire.[38]

The seduction of the author by the translator can be seen against the backdrop of a tension between the text and the translation. The author/text symbolizes originality and authority, while the translation was often regarded as secondary, a reproduction, a copy, even as false.[39]

The question, also brought up by Stark, of whether or not women translators felt themselves as merely useful tools for the reproduction of the admired text of a beloved author, or as active mediators who made their own choices, is still under discussion. Through the ages women

---

[35] See Irene Visser, 'American women writers in the Dutch literary world 1824–1900', in: Suzan van Dijk, *'I have heard about you'*, pp. 281–299.

[36] See for example Petra Broomans and Ester Jiresch, 'Philippine Wijsman: een self-made vertaalster', *Filter. Tijdschrift over vertalen* 13, no. 3 (2006), pp. 31–41.

[37] This was very important during a time when not all countries had signed the Berne Convention for the Protection of Literary and Artistic Works. See <http://www.wipo.int/treaties/en/ip/berne/trtdocs_wo001.html> (accessed 11 December 2009).

[38] See for example Lori Chamberlain, 'Gender and the Metaphorics of Translation', in Lawrence Venuti, ed, *The Translation Studies Reader* (London/New York, 2000), p. 316.

[39] *Ibidem*, p. 315.

translated in the name of God, for the nation, for the sake of an admired text and/or author, to mediate ideas and knowledge, to earn a living, and also for themselves. The nineteenth century became the era of the intellectual, mental and practical preparation of women for their emancipation in the twentieth century and translation played an evident role in this process.

One of the main questions addressed in this volume is how cultural transmitters spread ideas by introducing and translating literature. Cultural transmitters mediate literature, but as is reflected in the term itself, they also mediate culture, and therefore even ideas, sometimes transformed into ideologies. Cultural transmitters are in this case also transmitters of images. They create images and mediate these images, for example in reviews or in the authors they choose to introduce and/ or translate.

An example of how women cultural transmitters manipulated the image of an author for the purpose of ideological propaganda, which also reveals how ideologies can influence reception, is the case of the Norwegian playwright Henrik Ibsen (1828–1906), whose play *A Doll's House* (1879) had a central role in this image building.

Around 1900, women cultural transmitters had different views on Ibsen's way of presenting women in his plays.[40] At first Ibsen's social dramas had 'a liberating influence on Marholm and other women in the 1880s.'[41] In Marholm's opinion, Ibsen later became too closely identified with the women's movement and no longer useful to her polemic against the movement in essays such as *Das Buch der Frauen* (1894–1895) (see Ebba Witt-Brattström's contribution in this volume). In her survey, *Die Skandinavische Litteratur und ihre Tendenzen. Nebst anderen essays*

---

[40] This discussion of image-building by women cultural transmitters in relation to Ibsen is to some extent based on my previous articles on this topic, e.g. Petra Broomans, 'The Inexpressible of the Nature of Woman. Women Cultural Transmitters and Ibsen's Writing About How Women Love', in: F. Helland et al., eds, *The Living Ibsen*. Proceedings – The 11th International Ibsen Conference, 21–27 August 2006. Acta Ibseniana, Centre for Ibsen Studies, University of Oslo, (Oslo, 2007), pp. 399–405.

[41] Susan Carol Brantly, *The life and writings of Laura Marholm*. (= Beiträge zur nordischen Philologie. Schweizerische Gesellschaft für skandinavische Studien) (Basel, 1991), p. 21.

(Trends in Nordic literature and some other essays) from 1898, another cultural transmitter, the Austrian Marie Herzfeld (1855–1940), criticized the urban way of thinking and refuted a rational way of thinking that can lead to nihilism. The author who Herzfeld regarded as a nihilist was Henrik Ibsen. While she praised Ibsen's earlier dramas, she criticized *A Doll's House* and commented that the character of Nora was the step which led Ibsen away from the aesthetic. It is striking that Marholm and Herzfeld criticized Ibsen for his unfaithfulness to what they regarded as true womanhood.

The debate about Ibsen's women protagonists was a European debate. In the Netherlands, cultural transmitters such as Anna de Savornin Lohman (1868–1930) also expressed their opinions. De Savornin Lohman was positive about some of Ibsen's views, but she was negative regarding the final scene of *A Doll's House* and considered that the play proved that Ibsen did not understand women.

> … he [Ibsen] knows that women can be something other than our narrow-minded upbringing has taught us to be. When Ibsen describes a woman who liberated herself from the ties she was bound with and who dared to go in a new direction, in my opinion he connected himself with the yearning for freedom that his poetical characters feel. And at this point he goes too far and becomes a man who does not understand woman – the most delicate aspects of her inner life, the quintessence of her nature, her love.[42]

De Savornin-Lohman's critique can be seen against the backdrop of her views on women's emancipation and love. While she supported equal rights for men and women, she was of the opinion that this had to take into account the natural destiny of women, which was to love their husbands. How a real woman feels and loves could never be understood by a man. For example, the fact that Nora's love dies when she understands who the real Torvald is, is already a error. According to De Savornin-Lohman, a woman's love would never die in this manner, as women love blindly and will always forgive. She considers that another mistake by Ibsen was that he allows Nora to forget her children, which a real wom-

---

[42] Margaretha Maeyboom, 'Een Ibsen-Enquête', *De Nederlandsche Spectator* (1898), pp. 214-217.

an could never do.

De Savornin-Lohman's reaction to *A Doll's House* is also closely connected to the debates on masculinity and femininity around 1900. The debate was significant in the transmission and reception of Scandinavian literature throughout Europe. The 'new woman' had entered the scene, but Scandinavian thinkers such as the Swede Ellen Key (1849–1926) and Laura Marholm criticized radical feminism and formulated an essentialist variant. Notably, many women were active in the field of literary and cultural transmission as translators, intermediaries, reviewers and journalists. It is striking that some of the women who entered these traditionally male professions, and who could themselves be regarded as 'new women', insisted that male and female authors create female characters who submit to their role as wives and mothers.

Thus it is apparent that women cultural transmitters acted in different positions and against the backdrop of various social conventions regarding their proper role. At first they gained some room and a voice of their own within a religious context, venturing into more masculine fields such as military and political history. In the eighteenth and nineteenth centuries they gained a stronger position. They learned foreign languages, travelled and were active in networks. Around 1900, they had also developed into entrepreneurs, negotiating with authors and publishers. As we have seen in the above discussion of the image of Ibsen and the ideological implications, women cultural transmitters also entered the moral field. Aesthetics and translation became a tool in global propaganda about the most desirable female character. Herzfeld, Marholm and De Savornin Lohman were among those who focused on neo-romanticism and a quest for a new woman: a true woman. This was a trend that would last through the first decades of the twentieth century and it was very much inspired by Ellen Key, an essentialist who believed that the nature of a true woman could only be expressed by a woman. In that sense, women cultural transmitters acted as the gatekeepers of a true womanhood.

What role did ideology and gender as well as cultural transfer and transmission play in the works of the cultural transmitters discussed in the articles in this volume?

In the first contribution, 'From our Correspondent in Europe – Camilla Collett (1813–1895) and Cultural Transmission' by **Janke Klok**, we encounter the Norwegian writer Collett, who came from a liberal home and received a good education, enabling her to become a salon hostess. As a young girl she travelled through Europe and wrote about her experiences. When she married, she felt that her public life had come to an end, but after the death of her husband she started travelling and writing again and experimented with short prose. In her article, Klok demonstrates how Collett used her writings about her journeys in Europe and her visits to the European literary salons to mediate ideas. As a core example, Klok analyses Collett's writings from Berlin in 1863, demonstrating that Collett was a cultural transmitter who mediated her ideas about the writer's task, which she thought was to give the common people an opportunity to understand and enjoy literature and arts. The innovative manner in which she looked for a way to express herself and to find a proper genre is also discussed. Klok comes to the conclusion that the answer partly lies in Collett's travelogues, and she makes the point that her literary travel writings, the ideas transmitted through them and Collett's own place in the European cultural network are still barely mentioned today. Thus, she argues that it is time to add the image of Colette as a national heroine, along with her activities as a correspondent and her innovative form of travel writing, to this history.

In their article, 'Virginie Loveling (1836–1923) as a Cultural Mediator: From Translating Klaus Groth to Manipulating Charles Darwin', **Liselotte Vandenbussche, Griet Vandermassen, Marysa Demoor and Johan Braeckman** take the production of the Flemish writer Virginie Loveling (1836–1923) as a case study to illustrate the wide range of practices a cultural transmitter may be involved in. They divide her activities as cultural transmitter into two phases. In the first phase, Loveling worked as a translator, essayist and literary critic and this phase of her professional activities can be regarded as 'an example of cultural transfer in the strict sense, importing and commenting on the cultural production from abroad'. In the second phase, Loveling wrote novels, short stories and folkloric work. According to the authors, in this phase of her professional life, Loveling can still be seen as a cultural transmitter because she mediated aspects of evolutionism in her prose. In their careful reading of Loveling's novels and short stories, Vandenbussche, Vandermassen, Demoor and Braeckman explain clearly how she integrates Darwin's ideas about natural and sexual selection. In her narratives, they find that she both follows conventional gender constructions and also deviates from them. The analysis shows that in Loveling's work both men and women are affected by determinism, neither being able to escape their fate. The male characters often end up powerless, confronting multiplicity and fragmentation. The authors conclude that as a cultural transmitter Loveling criticizes the principle of separate male and female spheres in her work of various genres. Her life as an independent woman is reflected in the untraditional depictions of masculine and feminine subjectivities. However, as is apparent in the works of other women writers around 1900, alternative stories are still difficult to imagine.

A possible alternative story was propagated by her contemporary Laura Marholm (1854–1928). In her contribution, 'Laura Marholm (1854–1928): Nordic Cultural Transmission with a Heterosexual Vengeance', **Ebba Witt-Brattström** demonstrates how in 1895 the German-Baltic, Danish-speaking critic and translator Laura Marholm ushered in a new era in the European discussion of gender issues. Through her analyses of Nordic authorships, Marholm introduced the idea of fictional works as the basis of a training course in cultural representations of gender. As Loveling had done in relation to her fictional characters, Marholm focused on both male and female writers in her literary criticism. In 1895 she published two books: *Wir Frauen und unsere Dichter*, which consisted of studies of the construction of masculinity in the works of August Strindberg and others, and *Das Buch der Frauen. Zeitpsychologische Porträts*, which discussed three Scandinavian 'modern women' types. Witt-Brattström discusses the feminist and essentialist approach of Marholm in these books and in other key texts, and shows that Laura Marholm's ideas were to a great extent based on Nordic literature. Marholm, though, was critical of a degenerate Scandinavian emancipation, as it was presented in the literary texts of the Modern Breakthrough. She sought a new definition of 'femininity', and in her New Woman Fiction, she tried to construct a passionately heterosexual New Woman. Together with her husband, the Swedish writer Ola Hansson (1860–1925), she 'generated a decadent manifesto literature with gender as an analytic category'. Witt-Brattström presents a fascinating picture of Marholm, a cultural transmitter who shaped images of authors, one of the most spectacular in literary history being she and Hansson's 'making' of Strindberg: 'der Dichter des Weiberhasses'.

Marholm was a central figure in the debate on the 'new woman'. In the Netherlands, this debate also engaged many women writers and cultural transmitters, one of whom was Margaretha Meyboom. In the contribution by **Ester Jiresch**, 'Margaretha Meyboom (1856–1927) – "Cultural Transmitter", Feminist or Socialist?', the role of Meyboom as cultural transmitter is discussed. Meyboom is one of the cultural transmitters who was active in the mediation of Scandinavian literature in the Netherlands around 1900. Literature of the Modern Breakthrough, a movement which criticized the social structure (c.1870–1890), was especially popular among translators, who transmitted modern ideas such as those of feminism and equality from the North. Jiresch's main question is how Meyboom should be characterized. Following Meyboom through her life and work, she focuses on her literary, feminist and social achievements. Meyboom was very outspoken in her opinion about the possibilities and responsibilities of women concerning domestic work and for women's right to do work of their choice. Jiresch also describes Meyboom's views in relation to the debate about unmarried and economically independent women. One of the works to which many people involved in this debate referred was Laura Marholm's *Das Buch der Frauen*. Meyboom herself was an independent woman and in her articles she insisted on the right to self-determination and for individuals to shape their own lives. According to her, a love of fellow human beings and especially work could also make women happy. In this respect she stood opposed to De Savornin-Lohman. At the end of her article, Jiresch discusses the term 'cultural transmitter' and comes to the conclusion that Meyboom was not only a cultural transmitter on a literary level but also a transmitter of modern socialist and feminist ideas. She combined the translation of progressive literature with writing about emancipation and socialism.

In addition to feminism and socialism, religion forms another factor of influence in the transmission of culture and literature. In the following article, 'Catholicism as Stepping Stone to Authorship. The Contribution of Women to the Flemish Catholic Periodical *Dietsche Warande en Belfort*', **Geraldine Reymenants** shows that religion can also be a motor behind the literary and cultural activities of women writers. The position of women was relatively strong in the *Dietsche Warande en Belfort*. Two women were members of the editorial board, Marie Elisabeth Belpaire (1853–1948) was the owner and financer of the periodical and more than ten percent of the contributions were written by women. Compared to other literary and cultural periodicals in Flanders, these figures are high. Reymenants describes the context in which women engaged in the Flemish Catholic literary field and shows that the contribution of women was influenced by the orthodox position of *Dietsche Warande en Belfort* in the literary field and by the fact that it presented an ideology that was both Catholic and pro-Flemish. Reymenants analyses the reception of women's writing in *Dietsche Warande en Belfort* and comes to the conclusion that the reception was contradictory. While high moral standards in the content of their work led to the approval of women writers, aesthetically their contributions were regarded as unsatisfactory: 'beautiful thoughts in bad verse'. In the second part of her article, Reymenants discusses Belpaire's position as a cultural transmitter, revealing that Belpaire did not hide her ideological and Catholic views on literature. Reymenants concludes her thorough examination with the claim that Belpaire used her strong position in the *Dietsche Warande en Belfort* to propagate her Catholic principles, supporting women writers who transmitted Catholic and pro-Flemish ideas in particular, although she also supported women such as Virginie Loveling, who was not Catholic. Furthermore, Belpaire functioned as a bridge between women writers and the male-dominated literary field.

In the final article, 'Decoding a Genius Mind. The French Philosopher Simone Weil (1909–1943) and the Swedish Critic Margit Abenius (1899–1970): a Case of Cultural Transmission', **Marta Ronne** investigates the introduction of Weil's work to Sweden by Margit Abenius, known in Swedish literary history as a critic. Ronne regards Margit Abenius' introduction of Simone Weil's writings to Sweden as a case of cultural transmission. She focuses on the process of cultural transmission as well as on the role of the female cultural transmitter, paying attention to the circumstances of Abenius's discovery of Weil and her early work on Weil's writings. She also discusses the possible motives behind Abenius' attempt to understand Weil's philosophy and transmit this to Swedish readers. To gain a better understanding of Weil's philosophy, Abenius first began to translate Weil from the French into Swedish, but later she used professional translators and instead wrote the prefaces to the translations. Ronne argues that the definition of a 'cultural transmitter' should thus be modified because the case of Abenius shows that a transmitter 'may obtain different positions in relation to the same object'. Abenius acted as a translator of Weil's work, as an editor and as a critic. Did Abenius herself benefit from the introduction of Weil? Ronne concludes that in this respect Abenius built an international network of translators, editors and bibliographers and that they regarded her as an important mediator of Weil's ideas in Northern Europe during the 1950s, which gave her substantial cultural capital as a woman.

## Conclusion

The discussion of the concept of 'cultural transmitter' from a gender perspective reveals that religion, nation, womanhood and entrepreneurship are important aspects to be incorporated into any definition of a cultural transmitter. Moreover, the historical background must also be further elaborated. A transnational and comparative history of the role of women cultural transmitters has not yet been written. At a meta-textual level, the hidden and subversive voice of the woman translator must be included and scrutinized. In some contexts, however, one has to be careful not to romanticize about the 'lost' translator. The combination of a professional approach and esteem for the author is complicated and tense.

Regarding the importance of women cultural transmitters mediating ideas through translation, we can conclude that they played a vital role. In the life and works of the women cultural transmitters discussed, the paradox of an active yet servile position remains. Religious, political and economic structures played guiding roles in the lives of many women cultural transmitters. Therefore, they dealt with feminism and sociopolitical issues (Meyboom and Marholm), sexual politics (Marholm), the practice of translation (to earn money/Meyboom), the role of women in society and how women were raised (Meyboom and Collett), the position of women writers and critics (Collett and Belpaire) and religion (Belpaire). Examples of other fields in which women cultural transmitters were involved are science (Loveling) and philosophy (Abenius), not only by way of translation, but also by writing about it, as both Loveling and Abenius did. The case of Abenius shows how translation could also become a form of self-education, in her case to gain greater understanding of Weil's philosophy. This volume thus demonstrates that women were not only transmitters of literature, culture and ideas, but were also engaged in the transmission of knowledge in philosophy and science, fields that had long been forbidden to women. In this respect, in the nineteenth century and the first half of the twentieth century, mediation was still a subversive act.

# From our European Correspondent – Camilla Collett (1813–1895) and Cultural Transmission

In this article I will focus on Camilla Collett's occupation as a foreign correspondent and the preconditions for this job, which was quite new for her time. Amongst contemporary writers, she has few colleagues in Norway in this field, only a writer such as Aasmund Olavsson Vinje (1818–1870) comes to mind.[1] What made Camilla Collett a frequent guest at European literary salons? How had she been educated? Where did she work and what were her working conditions? What knowledge and information does Camilla Collett include in her essays 'home' and what does Collett's correspondence tell us about her aesthetics and her writing programme?

*New ideas on education*

Camilla Collett's (née Wergeland) connections with middle-class salons and foreign visitors can be traced back to her earliest years. Her maternal grandparents and her parents belonged to the wealthy middle class, which in the late eighteenth and early nineteenth centuries welcomed visitors of all types and nationalities to their homes. Foreign artists gave concerts, and the first dramatic companies performed their plays. The place of action is Christiansand, in southern Norway, which became extremely affluent in around 1800 due to illegal piracy during the Napoleonic wars. Camilla vividly remembered her first four years in

---

[1] He recorded his impressions and observations during his travels to Britain and published them in the weekly *Dølen: eit vikublad,* which he edited in the period 1858 – 1870. They were published in book form in English as *A Norseman's views of Britain and the British,* (Edinburgh, 1863), and thereafter in Norwegian as *Bretland og Britarne* (Kristiania, 1873).

this town, at least, that is the picture she presents to her readers in her
memoirs, *I de lange Nætter* (1863). She relates memories of the house of
her infancy and toddler years, the streets, the decoration of the rooms.
Camilla's father provides us with a picture of the women at these Norwegian salons. He was interested in general in the new bourgeois fashions
in contact and manners at that time and more in particular in the role
played in them by women.[2] He writes about balls and concerts, to which
the gentlemen took the ladies, and about the eight performances that
the dramatic societies organized in the bourgeois salons every winter. At
that time Norway had no theatres and all dramatic activities were held in
the homes of well-to-do citizens. Nicolai Wergeland was not really satisfied with what he saw – in his opinion the gentleman's society organized
too many meetings to which women were not invited, and there was
too much discussion about clothing and meals and too little about literature, theatre, music and sculpture.[3] His ideal was a salon where men
and women could practise friendship, the art of conversation and the
fine arts, as was common in other European cities. The male-dominated
social life in Christiansand operated at the expense of women, in Wergeland's opinion, and they became good-natured, phlegmatic, reserved and
not very entertaining as a result. They were not interested in politics and
displayed little knowledge, he later added, with the rider that it probably
wasn't possible to be anything else in a city where there were no schools
for girls. Nicolai Wergeland's observation that public life in a Norwegian
city was dominated by men matches observations by foreign visitors
about Norwegian cities, for example Bergen.[4] In 1795, during a journey
through Scandinavia, Mary Wollstonecraft met the phlegmatic women
Wergeland described in Tønsberg, another town in the South of Norway,
and wrote about them in *Letters written during a short residence in Swe-*

---

[2] See also Torill Steinfeld, *Den unge Camilla Collett. Et kvinnehjertes historie* (Oslo,
   1996) on the era of tact, on breeding and the loss of self – often two sides of the
   same coin – and on decorum. These in fact led to tactlessness, which Steinfeld
   believed recurred in the next generation, pp. 41-44.

[3] *Ibidem*, pp. 19-28.

[4] In Christiania and Trondheim the situation was somewhat different, and women
   were admitted to the social life. Anne Scott Sørensen, ed, *Nordisk salonkultur. Et
   studie i nordiske skønånder og salonmiljøer 1780–1850* (Odense, 1998), pp. 103-
   106.

On the threshold of her education. The young Camilla painted by her father Nicolai Wergeland. Miniature on ivory.

*den, Norway and Denmark* (1796).[5] Against this background, it's understandable that Nicolai Wergeland had different ideas for his daughter. His ideas on her education were directed towards qualifying her to run a literary salon like those common in continental European cities. In her biography, Steinfeld mentions the character Corinne – the mother of all salon hostesses – from the novel from 1808 by Madame de Staël as one of Wergeland's sources of inspiration. After a few years being taught by her brothers' tutor,[6] at the age of twelve Camilla was sent to the girl's school run by Miss Pharo in Christiania, at the time the largest teaching institute for girls in the town. The education was mainly directed towards turning her into a competent housewife: humility, patience and modesty were the important virtues they taught, alongside embroidery

---

[5] Wollstonecraft referred to their phlegm and ignorance in a more positive way: she describes the women as unaffected, with a simple, loveable attitude and a playfulness. Mary Wollstonecraft, *Letters written during a short residence in Sweden, Norway and Denmark* (Wilmington, 1796), p. 86. Wollstonecraft's description, which usually fits a child rather than a grown woman, and her positivism can be understood from a romantic perspective. She thought the Norwegian people were less developed than other Europeans and were closer to nature.

[6] At their new home at Eidsvoll, c. 70 km away from Christiania.

and sewing and some tuition in the fine arts, with the duty to please
high on the list of priorities. Camilla Wergeland hated it and the only
thing she got out of it was a few dear friends. Emilie Diriks, with whom
she later maintained an intensive correspondence, is the best known of
these. The lessons in Christiania did not conform to the ideas of Nicolai
Wergeland about the education of his daughter and so he looked for
something else. He found it at Christiansfeld in North Schleswig (now
South Jutland, Denmark), established in 1772 by Danish Hernhutters
after the Dutch model at Zeist.[7] In Christiansfeld in 1827 the girls' and
boys' schools were attended by pupils from all over Europe, and also
from further afield, for example the West Indies where Denmark had
colonies. Steinfeld has researched the educational wishes expressed by
Wergeland for his daughter. Camilla had to follow all the subjects, with
particular attention to German and French. English was not necessary –
the latter on condition that she spent extra time on French. Singing and
playing the piano, drawing and painting were also considered important. More practical matters such as mental arithmetic, spelling in Danish, knowledge of the Bible and handwork are not mentioned. Camilla's
stay at Christiansfeld got off to a bad start. Her preparatory education

---

[7] The Hernhutters – who arose out of the Moravian Brethren (Unitas Fratrum)
– acquired their name from the German settlement of Hernhut, which they established in 1722 under the leadership of Nicolaus Ludwig von Zinzendorf. The
Hernhutters viewed everyone – rich or poor, young or old, male or female – as
equal. They set great store by missionary work, education and training (for both
boys and girls), and each community was self-sustaining. The first Dutch Hern-
hutter community was established in Zeist, where the building of the settlement
began in 1748. It was an ambitious project, made possible by funds from wealthy
Amsterdam merchants. The settlement consisted of very large buildings for the
unmarried sisters, the widows and unmarried brothers, communal buildings, a
church hall and beautifully laid-out gardens. A unique feature of the Zeist community was the rapid emergence of various traditional businesses, which eventually formed a complete cottage industry. It was this aspect in particular that
inspired the Danish king Christian VII, who paid a visit to the Zeist settlement
after 1766, with his personal physician Struense. He decided that he would like
a similar settlement in Denmark, which led to the building of Christiansfeld in
1772. (See also: http://www.hetutrechtsarchief.nl/thema/tijdbalk/1745; http://
www.christiansfeldcentret.dk/00038/ )

was insufficient, she suffered badly from homesickness, she was teased, and the pupils did not get enough to eat. The strict straitjacket of life under the Hernhutters was an enormous contrast with her relatively unrestricted life at Eidsvoll. But, after a period of hunger and sweating it out, Camilla found her feet, made friends and became an active pupil. In Norwegian literary research, the years that Camilla Wergeland spent in Christiansfeld are often treated negatively. However, I agree with Steinfeld that this attitude does not do justice to the training. For the Hernhutters, men and women were much more equal than for many of their contemporaries, and Steinfeld proposes the plausible theory that there was a connection between Camilla Wergeland's years in Christiansfeld and her later feminism.[8]

## Establishing networks

Whatever the case may be, Camilla Wergeland completed the *first step* in her education – her years at two different schools – in Christiansfeld. This education was quite different from that of many of her female contemporaries. Moreover, she made friendships she would keep for the rest of her life, *inter alia* with Adolphine Marie Schmidt, known in Norway as the writer Marie Colban. For Camilla Wergeland, the friendships she made during her time at school, both in Christiania and Christiansfeld, were extremely important. Young women from the bourgeoisie had two possible ways of networking – the most usual way was via family connections, the second was via friendships made in their youth. Unlike many of her contemporaries, Camilla Wergeland did not use her family as the starting point for a wider social network. Her girlfriends from school, on the other hand, did fulfil that role. Emilie Diriks and Adolphine Marie Schmidt were her hubs; via them she met others and thus enlarged her network. One of the people she met was Emilie's sister Caroline Fougstad (née Diriks), who was a well-known salon hostess in Norway at the time. She introduced Camilla Wergeland to the new intellectuals in the town of Christiania, including those running the newspaper *Den Constitutionelle* where she would later, as Camilla Collett, publish the first fruits of her pen.[9] The making and keeping of

---

[8] Steinfeld, *Den unge Camilla Collett*, p. 90.

[9] Anne Scott Sørensen, 'Taste, manners and attitudes – the *bel esprit* and literary

friends and the visits to the middle-class and literary salons in Christiania which resulted from them could thus be called the *second step* in her education on the way to becoming a salon hostess. The *third step* was formed by her visits to foreign cities and salons. Her first trip was to Paris in the spring of 1834, when she was accompanied by her father. They left Christiania in June 1834 and arrived in Le Havre three weeks later. While there they paid the usual visits to friends' families, but later, when in Paris, and against custom, they did not seek out the company of Norwegian compatriots. They lodged at a pension and met people of many different nationalities, including English ladies and the legendary Finnish freedom fighter Maximillian Myhrberg, who brought them into contact with the young Finnish-Swedish soprano Johanna von Schoultz. They became friends and von Schoultz showed Camilla, through her way of life – she was the breadwinner for her family – that there were more ways for a woman to get by than just marriage. The trip to Paris also brought Camilla Wergeland into closer contact with the arts and sights of the city. However, as yet there is no question of any significant salon visits. In August 1834 they travelled back to Norway via Amsterdam and Hamburg. In Amsterdam they first came into contact with what later came to be called 'the residence of a cultured rich man', that of the Russian consul Ivan Brunet. Camilla made friends with his daughter, Madame Blanriez, and they remained in touch. What happened here would repeat itself later – she exceeded in all respects the expectations that contemporary Europeans had of the daughter of a Norwegian country parson.[10] This says something of course about Camilla Wergeland, but equally about the image that Europeans had of Norway and its inhabitants. After Amsterdam the journey continued on to Hamburg, where Camilla caused a stir as a Norwegian guest at the salons. It would be the first of many visits to come.

The story of Camilla Wergeland's training as a salon hostess can be wound up as follows. In 1829, at the age of 16, she made her entrée into the social life of Christiania, where she spent part of each year. At first she frequented the homes of the middle class, but soon, thanks to the

---

salon in the Nordic countries c. 1800', in: Drude von der Fehr et al., eds, *Is there a Nordic feminism?: Nordic feminist thought on culture and society*, (London, 1998), p. 128.

[10] Steinfeld, *Den unge Camilla Collett*, p. 174.

contacts she made in Christiansfeld, her social skills and her appearance, she rose in the social ranks. By the mid-1830s she was also invited to the homes and salons of the Christiania upper class.[11] The mere fact of her arrival in Christiania in July 1835 warranted a mention in the *Morgenbladet* newspaper.[12] She was spoken of as 'den deilige Camilla Wergeland' [the delightful CW[13]] and was a welcome guest in the salon of Caroline Fougstad, who gathered together the new intelligentsia of Christiania. From September 1836 until July 1837 Camilla again visited Hamburg, where she stayed at the Ludwigs', polished her skills in languages and music and drew inspiration from the famous salon hostess Therese von Bacheracht, whom she described as a 'modern Aspasia'.[14] Camilla's appearances at the Hamburger salons established her reputation as the sylph of the north.[15] As well as honing her skills as a salon guest, the second stay in Hamburg also gave her a more frank and outspoken attitude to addressing the public through writing.[16] She had learned that the salons were expanding her world and her opportunities. When she returned to Christiania she practised her *salonfähigkeit* at the literary evenings and soirées organized in the home of Minister Petersen. One could say that she had now completed her education as a salon hostess. But she had done more than this: in Torill Steinfeld's words, she had also created a public through her European salon life.[17] Camilla was aware of this herself. When her life took another turn in 1841 through her pending marriage to Peter Jonas Collett (1813–1851), a conventional man when it came to public life and literary salons who didn't want his wife to maintain any kind of salon life, either as guest or as host, she wrote to the German writer Theodor Mundt that she would now become a housewife and therefore '…tager Afsked med Publicum,

---

[11] *Ibidem*, pp. 92, 107-108.

[12] *Ibidem*, p. 198.

[13] *Ibidem*, p. 201.

[14] *Ibidem*, p. 268.

[15] It was the German writer Theodor Mundt (1808–1861) who introduced this term in his lyrical prose text 'Denkblätter für die nordische Sylphide' about his last encounter with Camilla Wergeland before she travelled home again. (*Ibidem*, p. 287).

[16] Steinfeld, *Den unge Camilla Collett*, p. 360.

[17] *Ibidem*, p. 438.

idet jeg blander mig mellem det.' […bid farewell to the public, as I am becoming part of it].[18]

## The making of a Correspondent

Any person who reached the age of 82 in the nineteenth century certainly outlived most of his or her contemporaries. This is also what happened to Camilla Collett. She lost many of her family and friends long before her own death. Her parents, her good friend Emilie Diriks, her brother Henrik and her husband Jonas all died within 8 years, between 1843 and 1851. In other words, she survived many of her nearest and dearest by over 40 years, two generations. You could almost say that compared to most people from the nineteenth century, she lived three lives. Her first life began in 1813 with her birth and ended in 1841 with her marriage, it was the life of a young girl being trained to become an active participant in public society, in the literary salons in Europe. The second life consists of the 10 years as a married woman, when she founded a household and gave birth to four sons. Not only did she make her debut as a mother, she also wrote her first article for a Norwegian newspaper. In 1842 *Den Constitionelle* published 'Nogle Strikketøisbetragtninger' [Some knitting thoughts], in which Camilla commented on the patronizing attitude of the gentlemen of Christiania towards women. Camilla recognized her new status as an author, in a letter from 1879 to the Norwegian Bohemian writer Henrik Jæger (1854-1919) she wrote that the friends she met in the street greeted her as an author the day after her article had been published.[19] The article was the first of many, on many different subjects, in a style that was quite new for her time, light and associative, lively and informal. It is a style that Henrik Jæger called 'livlig, lun passiar' [lively, warm, conversational] and that Torill Steinfeld traced back to the art of conversation in the literary salons.[20] In 1851 the married life of Camilla came to an end with the death of Peter Jonas Collett and her third life began, her widowhood. Again her education bore fruit. She had acquired knowledge and built a network, she had also formed a clear picture of what a woman's life entailed – a

---

[18] *Ibidem*, pp. 362-364.

[19] Ellisiv Steen, *Camilla Collett om seg selv* (Oslo, 1985), p. 58.

[20] Steinfeld, *Den unge Camilla Collett*, p. 365.

very negative one. 'Is this the life for which I was born? For this decaying idleness, this dead end for all my abilities and powers...'. As a woman swimming against the current, Collett rejected this prospect and forged her own path. She decided to become a professional writer. Since early childhood she had written letters, many of which she later published. Publishing personal letters was an important project for Collett – she regarded them as vital documentation of women's lives, lives that all too often remained anonymous. In this respect, the motto 'the personal is political' of the women's movement which was to emerge over a century later could have been written for her. The style of her era gave her first letters a flowery and veiled character – the word 'tact' is often used in relation to the period of the bourgeois culture of the early nineteenth century.[21] Over time her writing became more direct and livelier, almost certainly under the influence of reading (Georges Sand was one of her favourites) and, as pointed out above, of numerous conversations in the different literary salons where style had always been an important issue. She eventually acquired a reputation as one of the best prose writers of her era, and younger contemporaries, such as the well-known Norwegian novelist on bourgeois life Alexander Kielland (1849–1906), came to regard her as their great example. The famous Norwegian fairy tale collector and language innovator Per Christen Asbjørnsen (1812–1885) asked her to become his language consultant.[22] In 1837 she had made her debut as an author for the public, be it a limited public, with impressions of a journey to a European city, her first contribution as a foreign correspondent you could say. She called it *Otte dage i Hamburg* [Eight days in Hamburg] and it was published in a handwritten periodical, 'Forloren Skilpadde' [Mock Turtle], that she edited and distributed with her friend Emilie Diriks in the autumn of 1837.[23] Such handwritten peri-

---

[21] People wanted to show that they were civilized in all respects and achieved this in particular by displaying a good command of current etiquette and a high degree of self-control.

[22] Like his partner Asbjørnsen, Jørgen Engebretsen Moe (1813-1882), when rewriting Norwegian folktales, introduced both the idiom and vocabulary of the Norwegian vernacular into the Danish that was customary for written language in Norway at that time.

[23] Steinfeld, *Den unge Camilla Collett*, p. 318. 'Otte dage i Hamburg' was published in book form in 1913 when editor H. Eitrem included them in *Samlede verker.*

odicals were very popular at the time. Steinfeld has traced this tradition
back to Diderot and the period 1750–1760, and Collett's contemporaries
Wergeland (who was also her brother) and Welhaven often 'published'
works within this genre.[24] In those early days of Norwegian prose fiction,
many different names were invented and applied to short prose as well
as novels. Examples of names used by writers and publishers include
'skisser, billeder, betraktninger, blader, føljetonger, fortellinger, bon-
defortellinger, erindringer, artikler, brev, tilegnelser, brudstykker af en
dagbok', etc. [sketches, images, thoughts, pages, serials, tales, peasant's
tales, memoirs, articles, letters, dedications, diary extracts, etc.], and
many more examples of names could be added. Collett was very creative
in finding new names and appears to have had a slight preference for
genre descriptions that referred to women's everyday experience. *Forloren Skilpadde*, the title of her handwritten periodical, is also the name
of a famous dish of the time.[25] One of her early pieces she called *Brudstykker af en Fruentimmers Dagbog* [Fragments of a Woman's Diary][26]
and her first article in the printed paper *Den Constitutionelle* in 1842
bore the title *Nogle Strikketøisbetragtninger* [Some knitting thoughts].
This plethora of genre names offers a good starting point for a discussion of the prose genre in Norwegian literature that emerged in the nineteenth century. Many of the genre names refer to the fact that the world
is being shown through the eyes of the chronicler: images, sketches,
thoughts, memories, letters, and diaries. These letters and diary extracts
often concern fictional or at least selected and edited letters and diary
entries. The workings of this principle can be seen, for example, in Mary
Wollstonecraft's approach. She wrote down the impressions of her journey to Scandinavia in 1795 in the form of letters a year after her return.

---

*Mindeutgave. Tredje Bind*, pp. 321-347 .

[24] Steinfeld, *Den unge Camilla Collett*, p. 279.

[25] 'Forloren skilpadde' [Mock Turtle Soup] is a traditional Danish dish that is still
popular today. The ingredients include a calf's head, vegetables, fishballs, meatballs and hard boiled eggs. It took a long time to prepare and was often a group
effort, with one woman preparing the meatballs and another the fishballs, and
involving considerable lively interaction.

[26] Almost certainly an allusion to the short story 'Brudstykker af en Landsbydegns
Dagbog' [*The Diary of a Parish Clerk and Other Stories*] (1824), by Steen Steensen
Blicher (1782-1848).

Collett used a similar method for her debut piece 'Otte dage i Hamburg', in which she recorded her impressions of Hamburg back home in Eidsvoll. In view of her wide reading, it is highly likely that Collett was familiar with and had drawn inspiration from Wollstonecraft's book. Once Collett had become a professional writer and moved regularly around Europe, less time would elapse between the observation and the writing of the text, and her short prose developed more and more in the direction of literary travel letters or essays, as they are now referred to in Norwegian literary historiography. The nineteenth-century search for new names for her writings, by Collett as well as others, illustrates the fact that the genre was still under development in those days.[27]

The same can be said about the profession of literary correspondent, which hardly existed at all in Norway at that time. Camilla Collett and Aasmund Olavsson Vinje (1818–1870) were pioneers in this field. To what extent they were inspired by their famous predecessor Joseph Addison (1672–1719), who published *The Spectator* and has been called 'the father of British journalism', is not clear. After her husband's death, Camilla Collett entered the arena of the European city as a true spectator. She travelled around and wrote home, from Paris, Rome, Munich, Berlin, Copenhagen and Stockholm. And every now and then she came to Christiania. It was a restless life without a family or home base, much of which was spent at railway stations, in countless guesthouses and in the streets of the big cities. Everywhere she went, she carried a black case in which she kept her sketches and notes. Her writing activities became her *raison d'être*. Her workspace could be a cold room in a guesthouse, a train compartment or ship's cabin, or a table in a café. Her language is provocative, humorous, vital and subtle, but between the lines her seriousness and honesty shines through, as well as her attempts to express her impressions and opinions as best she can. It is interesting how literary scholars have attributed contradictory qualifications to Collett's suitability for the job of foreign correspondent. Elisiv Steen thinks she was supremely qualified for the work. 'She spoke German fluently, French somewhat less fluently, and had a great knowledge of literature

---

[27] It also illustrates the fact that publishers over a very long period hesitated to use the term novel. In Norway, the novel was considered to be a second-rate genre until the 1880s.

Camilla Collett,
1860, a few years
before she wrote her
letters from Berlin.
Photographer
unknown.
Photo courtesy of
Gyldendal Norsk
Forlag, Oslo.

and history'.[28] This article demonstrates that she was indeed well trained for the job. Liv Bliksrud, on the other hand, paints a different picture – like others before her she refers to Collett as totally unpractical and much too absent-minded to be a successful traveller. She kept losing things, such as train tickets and her purse, regularly fell and was even run over.[29] These qualifications, however, are not necessarily incompatible. Tone Selboe calls her persistent rather than unpractical and points out that Collett was well aware of the clumsy image that she had.[30] In

---

[28] Steen, *Camilla Collett om seg selv*, p. 94.

[29] Liv Bliksrud, ed, *Norske essayister. Camilla Collett. Essays* (Oslo, 1993), p. 9.

[30] Tone Selboe, *Litterære vaganter. Byens betydning hos seks kvinnelige forfattere*, (Oslo, 2003), pp. 17-18.

Colletts – ironical? – observation that a poetic person can't be practical, there may lie another answer. Perhaps she cultivated her impracticalness because it made her a poetic person, a literary woman. One thing is sure – Collett sent home a series of interesting travel letters. Another thing that is certain is that Collett led the relatively lonely life of an outsider – she became a city walker, a *flâneur* – Tone Selboe calls her a 'literary wanderer'.[31] And from this position she observed, wrote home and fulfilled the role of cultural transmitter.

## Camilla Collett and cultural transmission

Collett sent her literary travel letters to the journal *Illustreret Nyhedsblad* [Illustrated News magazine], which was published by the Norwegian author Jonas Lie (1833–1908). They were later published in the volumes *Sidste Blade [Last Leaves] I-III* (1868–73), *Fra de Stummes Leir [From the Camp of the Mutes]* (1877) and *Mod Strømmen [Against the Current] I-II* (1879–1885). What knowledge and information does Camilla Collett include in her travel letters 'home'? And what does Collett's literary correspondence tell us about the 'public house' of Norway? Let me illustrate some aspects by discussing Collett's travel letters from one of the Capital City's in Europe, Berlin, where Collett began her career as a foreign correspondent, sending reports from distant locations for publication back home.

The author shows that she had reflected at length on the genre. When her first travel letters were collected in 1868 in the publication *Sidste Blade. Erindringer og Bekjendelser [Første række]*, she wrote in the preface – formulated as a letter to Mrs Amalie Munch – that the travel 'descriptions' [*reiseskildringer*], as she called her pieces, would certainly provoke considerable reaction because they revealed too much of the person who had written them. This latter aspect was a conscious choice on her part. She writes that it is precisely this that makes travel writing what it is, and she offers the reader a blueprint for the genre. Travel writing is a 'special hybrid of autobiography and other, impersonal texts'.[32]

---

[31] *Ibidem*, pp. 9-15.

[32] 'en slem Mellemting mellem saadan Autobiografi og al anden upersonlig Digtning', H. Eitrem, ed, *Camilla Collett, Samlede verker. Mindeutgave. Andet bind* (Kristiania/Kjøbenhavn,1913), p. 58.

Collett believed that the author must be present in a travel piece, must reveal something about him or herself through the texts. This requirement for self-testimony that Collett placed on the genre relates to her innovative view of literature in general, which was prompted by her awareness that the reading public had changed. No longer did authors address themselves to a fairly small and trusted readership that was unlikely to misinterpret the text. 'That was in the good old days, when people lived together in peace. Authors wrote only innocent, pleasant pieces and their readers rewarded them by not making a fuss'.[33] But the world had changed: authors were now being read by new readers, by a new audience that did not always know what the author intended because they lacked a shared prior knowledge and shared circumstances. She argued that not every reader would correctly interpret the author's tone, mood or outlook in a text unless these were explicitly highlighted. 'It is not from literature that one should draw conclusions about the author (…); it is through the author that one should acquire a better understanding of the author and his or her work'.[34] And in order to be better understood, authors themselves must reveal themselves through their texts. She also stressed the importance of publishing life stories by and about authors, preferably while they were still alive. Collett could appreciate that authors might be hesitant about life stories – it is not easy to 'undress' oneself in public, as she puts it, and she viewed autobiography as the most far-reaching example of this. [35] Nevertheless, she preferred a small amount of autobiographical detail to the best biographies written after an author's death. Collett's thoughts on the need for 'life stories' to provide knowledge and understanding of literature are what make the travel writings, as she conceived them, a special genre. We could call it a hybrid form that enables authors to reveal something of themselves without having to broadcast all their intimate details. Her viewpoint

---

[33] 'Det var i de gode, gamle Dage, hvor man levede i den dybeste Fred med hverandre. Digteren skrev blot uskyldige, behagelige Ting, og Publikum lønnede dem med ikke personlig at bekymre sig om dem.' Collett, *Samlede verker. Mindeutgave. Andet bind*, p. 60.

[34] 'Det er ikke fra Digtningen, man skal slutte hen paa Digteren (…); men det er gjennem Digteren, man skal tilegne sig Digtningen og lære at forstaa den ret.' *Ibidem*, p. 59.

[35] *Ibidem.*

placed particular demands on the genre. It was not enough for authors to report on what they saw abroad; this should be accompanied by an account of the author's own perceptions. Collett called on writers, like the gods of poetry, to reconsider their relationship to the masses and to descend from the clouds of Mount Olympus and wander through the streets in the guise of ordinary mortals.[36] As of old, they should offer 'the flower of their minds' to the new public. More than that, they should give 'the interpretation of this through their own self'.[37] Collett saw the poet as the guardian of the 'Mind', of poetry, a romantic vision. And she linked this guardianship to an educating function; she believed that it was the author's task to explain poetry. The way the latter should be done was by using their own perception of the world to clarify their writings. In this regard she bestowed a second task on authors, not least of all women authors: they need to explain the spirit of the text through their personal perception of the everyday. This second task is accompanied by her views on public life, with its dual aspect. On the one hand, authors – and in particular women authors – become public figures: 'Because from the moment a woman steps into the public arena here, she no longer has a private life, nor any place to hide.'[38] On the other hand, Collett called on the public to treat their authors – whom she compares to gifted children – with care: 'Has the [public] ever considered that it too has an obligation, just as a good, warm family has an obligation to its especially talented children, not to frighten them off?'[39] Collett's reflections on the place and role of the author in modern society, her view of the interaction between authors and the public, not to mention her belief that the new public could achieve a greater understanding if authors made them participants in the author's own perception of the world around them – these all serve to make her both romantic and surprisingly modern. Romantic in the sense that it is the author's job to articulate the poetic and to educate the 'people', and modern in her belief that an author should

---

[36] *Ibidem*, p. 61.

[37] 'Blomsten af sin Aand', 'Tydningen dertil i sit eget selv', *Ibidem*.

[38] 'Thi en Kvinde, der hos os træder offentlig op, har fra det Øieblik intet Privatliv mere, ingen Fold, hvori hun kan skjule sig.' *Ibidem*.

[39] 'Har det [publikum] nogensinde tænkt, at det ogsaa havde den [forpligtelse], som en god, humantsindet Familie har ligeoverfor eiendommelig begavede Børn, den ikke at skræmme dem?' *Ibidem*.

do so explicitly, that literature does not speak for itself but needs to be explained. And the form that she chose for this purpose – articulating an individual perception of the world, of the everyday world – is the same one selected by authors of the age we now know as modernism. She linked internal experience (individual perception) to that of the external world. It is not what people experience that is the essential thing, but their perception of that experience. It is a modern writer's creed that she applied and refined in her travel correspondence.

Collett was correct in her prediction that her subjective texts would provoke considerable reaction. She was reviled by the likes of Bjørnstjerne Bjørnson (1832–1910) and Georg Brandes (1842–1927) and admired by people like Henrik Ibsen (1828–1906) and Hans Jæger (1854–1910). It may be overbold to assert that her admirers were among the innovative minds of her time and her detractors among the conservative, although this assertion may warrant further investigation. Whatever the case, the Danish philosopher Harald Høffding (1843–1931) showed a keen understanding of her writing project when, in 1878, he said of her oeuvre that 'she had given herself in her work by giving the poetry of her life'.[40] This is precisely what Collett does in her travel correspondence – she puts her readers in touch with their own poetry by offering them the poetry of her own life. And here 'the poetry of her own life' should be interpreted literally as offering glimpses of what she experienced during her travels and the thoughts and dreams that accompany this. She thus reveals herself to be a cultural mediator on different levels: she assigned an educational function to literature and believed the poet has a duty to explicitly ensure that literature fulfils that function. And she made her audience part of her experiences elsewhere in Europe. A cultural mediator par excellence! The fact that she also brought so much reflection to the genre of travel correspondence ties in perfectly with this purpose.

## Berlin through Collett's eyes

What does Collett tell the reader about Berlin? What does she tell the readers of her day about herself and how she perceives the places she visits? And what does that teach the present-day reader about her view

---

[40] '(…) hun har i sine Værker givet sig selv, idet hun har givet sit Livs Poesi'. Bliksrud, *Norske essayister*, p. 10.

With his statue In the Storm (1911), the Norwegian sculptor Gustav Vigeland (1869-1943) depicted the older Camilla Collett alone against a fierce wind. The statue can be found in the Palace Park in Oslo. Photograph by Rolf Steinar of the upper part of the statue.

of the Norway of her time? I will address these questions below, based on three travel letters. These are the first three travel pieces that she sent from Berlin in the autumn of 1863.

Collett opens her first letter from Berlin, dated 24 October 1863, with a general observation about travelling Norwegians who in increasing numbers are writing letters home. She expresses the collective expectation of those at home that the new and colourful experiences of the travellers will not produce lengthy treatises. Nothing could be further from the truth. Unlike the English, she writes, travelling Norwegians cannot let themselves go. They never forget that they are Norwegians bound by invisible threads to 'Mother Norway' (Collett is consistent in her use of Mother Norway rather than the more customary 'fatherland'). Whatever they see, do and buy, their first thought is how they will talk about it back home, how they will show it off or present it as a gift. The travelling Norwegians whom Collett describes make us think of the clichéd image of the Japanese tourist, forever taking photos and not knowing where they have been until they are home again. Collett closes the passage with the comment that she herself is just such a Norwegian traveller and correspondent – someone who experiences nothing grand, who doesn't consort with the likes of duchesses, princesses, scholars and great artists. From her very first sentences, she adopts the role of correspondent and a Norwegian identity.[41]

Because Collett doesn't experience anything grand, nor consort with the great, the reader should not expect from her any grand cultural, historical, topographical or literary works. It is not in the nature of 'this correspondent' to concern herself with such questions as why Berlin is located where it is and by whom it was first established.[42] She will focus instead on what is near at hand and commonplace, on what she sees on her regular trips, on foot or by omnibus, along *Unter den Linden* to the centre of town. In other words, Collett creates a small and manageable world and makes of her travel perceptions something that the reader can identify with. It is an approach that produces impressions of the Berlin *Alltag* that are at times hilarious, at times piteous. Collett accompanies them with philosophical considerations or a political message.

---

[41] Collett, *Samlede verker. Mindeutgave. Andet Bind*, pp. 64-65.

[42] *Ibidem*, p. 65.

One such example is her description of a trip by omnibus on a day that it is carrying some 'distinguished' passengers – a mother and child, and a woman who runs a market stall and has the gift of the gab. It is a delightful sketch of a blissful mother who for fifteen whole minutes can forget about her grape-eating offspring, a market woman who won't allow herself to be browbeaten by the public at large, in particular a lieutenant, and who retaliates with 'sharp Berlin quickness' and calmly feeds her hen, and an omnibus conductor who, with kindly care for his 'family of passengers', steers everything in the right direction.[43] The hilarious spectacle ends with Collett's comment that social intercourse keeps people in a good mood. In the minor 'class struggle' taking place in the omnibus, her sympathies lie with the market woman.

From the omnibus Collett sees a coachman, who becomes the next subject of her observations. She compares the lonely coachman, whose solitary position on the coach-box and whose exploitation by the vehicle's owner have turned him into a disagreeable person, with his antithesis, the lovable conductor. Collett shows compassion for the coachman and his lot, and for the lot of his horse, which is spurred on by his 'master' the coachman, just as the coachman is spurred on by his master. On her journey from the upper to the lower levels of society, Collett ends with the Berlin cart dogs, which are kept hungry to make them perform better. Once again there is a market woman, this time the owner of the dog cart. Collett's sympathy now rests not with the market woman, but with the weaker of the two – the dog. Collett describes the woman as growling like a dog and she gives the dog a human gaze.

In her second letter from Berlin, which is dated 30 October 1863, Collett refuted the prevailing idea that the people of Berlin were cynical, cunning and cold. The people she met were good-natured. She expressed the number of rude people she met as a percentage: 1%, and she was impressed by the equality between the sexes. Everyone she met on the street – man or woman – was perfectly able to take care of themselves and showed respect and consideration for their fellow road users. Something that struck her particularly was that ladies were able to walk on the streets alone without being addressed by obtrusive passers-by. Collett expressed her admiration for this type of freedom, she immediately added that she had not yet dared to try it herself. She thought this

---

[43] *Ibidem*, p. 67.

freedom could have been a result of the broad, well-lit streets of Berlin, which might serve as a good example for the cities of Scandinavia. An amusing examination of the high degree of rudeness of male city walkers in Scandinavian cities towards their female fellow citizens, who had to resort to carriages to get from A to B, is followed by Collett claiming the streets for herself and her female fellow citizens because 'women who spend all their time in carriages are bored to death'.[44] Her travel letter is concluded by a lyrical description of *Unter den Linden* and the *Brantenburgerthor* and the lively culture of pubs, street cafés and shops she encountered there. She reassures readers who fear that she might write about the museum and the opera because, as she puts it, 'the menu can never equal its dishes'.[45]

A separate story is devoted to her description of a visit to a Berlin museum, which accounts for much of her third missive, dated 17 December 1863. She had pledged that she wouldn't write about visits to museums, so she has broken her promise, which is just as well, today's reader might say, as we are given a unique glimpse of a museum which no longer exists today in its old form. Collett doesn't name the museum she describes, nor did she need to. In her day the Neues Museum (1859), which was linked by a gallery to the Altes Museum (1830), was *the* museum in Berlin.[46] We know that she visited the Neues Museum because of her admiration for Kaulbach's frescos.[47] Commissioned by the Prussian king Friedrich Wilhelm IV, Wilhelm von Kaulbach (1804–1874) painted frescos in the stairwell of the Neues Museum that portrayed history in pictorial form. Kaulbach began in 1847 and completed his work in 1865. The stairwell was officially incorporated into the museum as an exhibition space the following year. The public had had access to the stairwell frescos much earlier, however. Camilla Collett was among the early visitors who admired them in 1863. Her description also reveals

---

[44] *Ibidem*, p. 70.

[45] *Ibidem*.

[46] For the *Verbindungsgalerie*, see http://www.slideshine.de/9102, pp. 11, 17 and 36. Today there are five major museums on the *Museumsinsel* in the Spree in the centre of Berlin: the Alte Nationalgalerie (1876); Prussia's first public museum, the Altes Museum (1830); the Bode Museum (1904); the Neues Museum (1859) and the Pergamon museum (1930).

[47] Collett, *Samlede verker. Mindeutgave. Andet Bind*, p. 72.

that pictures of the frescos were in circulation at that time; she writes that the scenes were familiar to her because she knew them from small reproductions. Collett's story has a special poignancy for today's reader because the stairwell and its frescos were gutted by fire when bombing destroyed much of the museum in 1943 and 1945. As a consequence they can now only be seen in black and white reproductions.[48] Moveable items from the collection had been housed elsewhere in 1939. Collett's description of the frescos shortly before their completion is therefore quite special.

Kaulbach's frescos are not the only artworks in the Neues Museum that Collett describes. She was particularly enthusiastic about several classical statues located in a fairly small room in the museum interior. On every visit, she writes, she was drawn to that room. The pieces displayed there were quite extraordinary – 'the flower of immortal antique art' as she herself describes them.[49] She mentions the Farnese Bull, Apollo Belvedere, the Florentine Venus (as these were antique statues, she may have meant the Medici Venus), the Venus de Milo, the muse Euterpe with her double flute, Diana of Versailles and a sleeping Endymion in a niche on a dais. It is no wonder that the collection made such an impression on Collett. The marble statues that she describes are among the most celebrated from Classical Antiquity. Nowadays they can be found in other major museums in Europe – in Paris, Milan, the Vatican City and Naples. Collett's description puts today's reader on the trail of a period in Europe when these great works of art were found in different locations or perhaps were part of international art exchanges or private collections, such as that of King Friedrich Wilhelm IV. Collett concludes her description with the observation that anyone is able to come and view all this magnificence, provided that their alcoholic refreshments are elegantly concealed.[50] She believes that *the* way to bring a people to enlightenment is to convey to them the proud awareness that they are co-owners of all the artistic wealth that they see. This will help them

[48] For images of the frescos, destroyed by fire, that Kaulbach painted for the Neues Museum in the period 1847–1865, see http://www.projekte.kunstgeschichte.uni-muenchen.de/dt_frz_malerei/41-dt-franz-malerei/studieneinheiten/848_1860_d/6a/gruppe_1/b.htm.

[49] Collett, *Samlede verker. Mindeutgave. Andet Bind*, p. 72.

[50] *Ibidem.*

appreciate the importance of a shared cultural heritage that is essential for shaping a national identity. But above all, it will transform a young 'people' into an adult nation, a civilized collective.

This animated plea for the public ownership of art brings Collett to her own poor country and to its capital, with its mere 60,000 inhabitants. Christiana did not have any such institutes for instruction in national identity, nor any museums or art collections that were accessible to all. In Collett's view, that was a necessary precondition for turning the people of Norway, who in her view were still children, into adults. Once again we are reminded of Mary Wollstonecraft. In her description of the Christiania of 1796, she described how the Norwegian capital and its inhabitants were still in a natural stage, which preceded that of civilization. It is not such a big step from a natural people to a nation of children. We could say that Wollstonecraft and Collett shared a romantic view of peoples in development. In her correspondence, Collett coupled this romantic view with modern ideas about how that development should take place. Preconditions for becoming a civilized person or nation were the combating of exploitation, whether of animals (the dog) or people (the coachman), having people from different classes treat one another with respect, allowing mothers to spend quiet time with their children, permitting men and women to move about freely in the streets (physical movement leads to intellectual movement) and making a country's art treasures public property, accessible to all inhabitants of that country (an early view of public ownership of art). These are the values that Collett conveys in her letters from Berlin to the Norway of her time.[51] The introduction to a later edition of her correspondence shows that where literature is concerned, she believed that it was the author's task to ensure that the message conveyed was clear to the reader – in other words, literary texts also had a didactic function. Her enthusiasm for Kaulbach's frescos, which aimed to present human history, shows that she was also

---

[51] Hilda Merkl and Tone Selboe arrive at the same conclusion. Merkl comments that Collett's travel letters are characterized by social compassion, and serve a didactic purpose (Merkl, H., 'Camilla Collett. Kvinnelig forfatter og kosmopolit i 1870- og 1880-årenes Norge' in: Hareide, ed, *Skrift, kropp og selv: nytt lys på Camilla Collet* (Oslo, 1998). Selboe observes that Collett's observations aim to educate Norway and the Norwegians towards greater freedom and civilization (Selboe, *Litterære vaganter*, p. 21).

responsive to painting that had a didactic function.

All these noble intentions make the conclusion to her third letter from Berlin all the more remarkable. Fully in keeping with her ideals, she is positively disposed toward the spectacle of the 'das gute Berliner-volk' who pass through the rooms of the museum – old and young, poor and well-heeled, sailors, soldiers, craftsmen and workers. They all show respect for the art works around them. But one day a rough working-class woman, dressed in rough attire, enters the museum. Collett doesn't mind so much that she is unable to tell the woman about the precise background to the Farnese Bull sculptural group. She brushes her off with some non-committal remark. But when the woman wants to ad-mire Collett's favourite statue of Endymion, perhaps even touch it, that's going too far. Collett describes how she manages to avert the 'disaster' by sending the woman in another direction with some excuse.[52] It seems that Collett's educational ideals have their limits. And the reader cannot help but gain the impression that Collett herself is well aware of this. She reveals herself to be just an ordinary person like everyone else – or perhaps better still, she addresses herself with a nod and a wink to the readers of her time, who do not include the working-class woman and others of her class. The concluding passage transforms the travel letter into the kind of literature that Collett had in mind – a text that acquires added significance because its author makes herself visible.

## A cultural mediator in every respect

In view of her writing programme, it is not entirely surprising that Col-lett's travel letters offer insights into her political ideals and purposes. What is surprising, however, is that she reveals herself to be a *cultural mediator* on many levels. She does so at the level of her approach to lit-erature, believing it to be the author's task to ensure that the intention of a text is clear. She does so at the level of edifying the people – art should be public property because only then can it serve to bring civilization to all, young or old, rich or poor, men or women. This understanding lends a further depth to Collett's modernity, as does the form that she views as ideal for conveying a text's content to the reader – by combining general observations with the author's perception. It is a plea for the interplay

---

[52] Collett, *Samlede verker. Mindeutgave. Andet Bind*, p. 74.

between the internal and external worlds that reminds us of the work of the later modernists.

Collett's conveying of culture extends even further, crossing the boundaries of time. Her correspondence takes today's reader too on surprising cultural and historical journeys to the Berlin that she visited, to places which in some instances have disappeared and which make us want to find out more, or to follow in her footsteps. Her focus on the small and the everyday offers an alternative look at the city. The result is wonderful descriptions of the Berlin of her day, impressions of its colourful life with its different elements, both ugly and beautiful. These are unexpected bonuses that make her travel letters innovative in both style and content, ensuring that – almost 150 years later – they have lost little of their power. It is therefore all the more remarkable to consider the exhibition, 'Jeg har en koffert i Berlin' [I have a suitcase in Berlin], which ran from November 2007 to February 2008 in Norway's National Library, and the accompanying book. While the curators and authors did devote attention to Collett, they overlooked her texts on Berlin.[53]

Collett is writing short and longer impressions and sketches from different European cities that could have been written by a chronicler of our own time. Her tone is light, her style is modern. She pays a lot of attention to details and places them in historical and philosophical contexts. The specific demand that Collett made on the genre of travel writing and which she herself satisfied, namely that authors should reveal aspects of themselves and should relate their external adventures to an internal perception, together with her focus on and enlargement of everyday events, all lend her texts an almost modernistic character. Furthermore, she shows a perspective on public spaces and public ownership of art that is way ahead of her time. Noticeable is her sensitivity to the lightness, the openness and the cheerfulness of the big European cities. This tells us that public space in Norway must have been quite different in her time, darker, more closed, not as cheerful, and most certainly not suitable for a female city walker. To a 19th-century Norwegian, Collett's travel letters must have been disturbing, agitating or refreshing, offering the reader lots of cultural information. Interestingly, this last aspect still applies to today's reader, who is able to arrive at a new understanding

---

[53] Buchten, D., Christensen, E.S. et al., eds, *"Jeg har en koffert i Berlin". Nordmenn i Berlin rundt 1900 og 2000* (Oslo, 2007).

of the Europe of Collett's time thanks to her precise descriptions and meditations. That her political ideas, particularly her feminism, guided and coloured her gaze is illustrated by the three examples above and is a leading theme running through her oeuvre. All in all she reveals herself as a cultural mediator in every respect.

It is not surprising that Norwegian literary historiographers have paid a lot of attention to her role as a pioneer for women's rights. More surprising is the fact that the travel letters and Collett's place in the European cultural network are hardly mentioned at all. This changed in the 1990s when Torill Steinfeld wrote a new biography (1996) and Liv Bliksrud published and introduced a selection of Collett's correspondence (1993), which she calls essays. In my opinion the latter deserve to be discussed more thoroughly, particularly the definition of the genre. At this point I'm inclined to call them literary travel letters. This discussion of the literary correspondence of Camilla Collett has once again led to the conclusion that the genre of literary history is a genre that is very much orientated to national identity. Despite Collett's many texts about and from abroad, she is still depicted as a national pioneer in the genre of the realistic, contemporary novel, or as a transitional figure between two national, Norwegian, time spans.

Recent knowledge and insights concerning international networks have constructed new images of Camilla Collett, to which I have added another: the image of the literary foreign correspondent, one of the first in Norway.

# Virginie Loveling (1836–1923) as a Cultural Mediator: From Translating Klaus Groth to Manipulating Charles Darwin

Liselotte Vandenbussche, Griet Vandermassen,
Marysa Demoor & Johan Braeckman

Cultural transfer occurs in many different fields and uses a wide variety of means. The career of the Flemish writer Virginie Loveling (1836–1923) is a case in point. Her professional choices illustrate the wide range of practices in which a cultural transmitter can engage. In the early stage of her professional life, we see an example of cultural transfer in the strict sense:[1] Loveling worked as a translator, essayist and literary critic, importing and transforming foreign cultural elements into her native culture. When these mediating and critical activities proved insufficiently remunerative, she gradually stopped translating and reviewing. She then focussed on her own literary production, publishing novels, short stories and folkloric work.

In that later stage of her life, Loveling could still be called a cultural transmitter: not only in her short stories, but even more so in her novels. By integrating and modifying aspects of the evolutionary ideologies that became popular in Western Europe during the last decades of the nineteenth century, Loveling fulfils a mediating role in transmitting ideas from other countries. In her novels, she integrates the mechanisms of natural and sexual selection, and follows traditional, Darwinian court-

---

[1] The concept of 'cultural transfer' was introduced by Michel Espagne and Michael Werner, 'Deutsch-französischer Kulturtransfer im 18. und 19. Jahrhundert. Zu einem neuen interdisziplinären Forschungsprogramm des C.N.R.S.', *Francia* 13 (1985), pp. 502-510; and Espagne and Werner, 'La construction d'une référence culturelle Allemande en France genèse et histoire (1750–1914)', *Annales: Economies, Sociétés, Civilisations* 4 (1987), pp. 969-992.

ship plots, but also deviates from conventional gender constructions.

In this article, we take Loveling's wide-ranging production as a case study to demonstrate the different roles a cultural mediator can assume. Loveling not only transmits complete works as a translator, and introduces authors and ideas in literary reviews and political criticism, she also transfers particular ideas as a novelist, presenting these with a personal twist. After an overview of her particular career choices and their causes, and her slightly awkward attitude towards her role as a cultural transmitter, we will focus on her transfer of evolutionary ideas and her personal interpretation of these issues.

## Cultural transfer: Translations

Virginie Loveling was the youngest of ten children in a well-known liberal and intellectual family in the Dutch-speaking part of Belgium.[2] Her mother, Marie Comparé (1791–1879), was first married to Jacques Fredericq (1778–1824) and later to Herman-Anton Loveling (1806–1846). Her parents were both well-educated and provided Virginie and her favourite sister, Rosalie (1834–1875), with a broad cultural background. Their mother showed a deep interest in philosophy, history and literature, and their father had an excellent command of the main European languages. Loveling taught his young daughters German and introduced them to the art of literature.

When their father committed suicide in 1846, they moved from Nevele to Ghent. They took up residence with their half-brother Cesar Fredericq (1817–1887), who was working there as a doctor. His house was a centre of intellectual intercourse, where the sisters met the intelligentsia of their time. Rosalie and Virginie were introduced to the main debates of the period and were immersed in literature, politics, religion and science. Cesar Fredericq's wife, a French teacher called Mathilde Huet (1827–1865), gave the sisters private lessons in French, geography and history.[3] Until Rosalie's untimely death, the Loveling sisters would write and publish together.

---

[2] Antonin van Elslander, ed, *De 'biografie' van Virginie Loveling* (Ghent, 1963).

[3] Van Elslander, *De 'biografie'*, pp. 18-19.

As adult women, they returned to their home village of Nevele. Even though they were living in the countryside, they still attended the weekly meetings of the *Société littéraire* in Ghent. They also attended all meetings of the congress of the *Société Internationale pour le Progrès des Sciences Sociales* in September 1863. Meanwhile, using their father's grammars and dictionaries, they taught themselves English, Italian, Spanish, and even Danish and Swedish. Rosalie Loveling lived in Nevele until her death in 1875 and Virginie stayed there until 1880. Finally, with her mother having died in 1879, Virginie returned to Ghent.

Before 1870, the Loveling sisters translated German, English and Swedish texts. Their translations were published alongside their poems, which appeared from 1853 onwards in literary periodicals such as *De Eendragt, De Broedermin, Het Nederlandsch Letterkundig Jaerboekje* and *De Toekomst*. In 1864 and 1866, they translated some novellas of the German writer Klaus Groth for *Het Letterkundig Zondagsblad*[4] and *Het Nederduitsch Tijdschrift*.[5] In 1871, a French translation of a Swedish article was published in *La Revue de Belgique*.[6] Because most of their contributions appeared anonymously, few other translations can be clearly assigned to one of the sisters. We can only rely on Virginie Loveling's references in her biographical writings.[7] According to her, translations of German and English prose appeared in *De stad Gent*,[8] and German

---

[4] Rosalie and Virginie Loveling met Klaus Groth (1819–1899) in August 1861. Rosalie Loveling translated his novella *Trina*, which appeared in *Het Letterkundig Zondagsblad* 7 (1864), pp. 11-24.

[5] Virginie Loveling translated the novellas *Detel* and *Anton*, which appeared in *Het Nederduitsch Tijdschrift* (1866), pp. 27-64 and pp. 47-85. Later on translations of *Een Holsteinsche jongen* (a revised version of 'Detel') and *Witen Slachters* (re)appeared in *Nederlandsch Museum* (1880), pp. 174-268 and (1882), pp. 316-348.

[6] V. Loveling, 'De l'Enseignement Populaire dans les trois pays scandinaves', *Revue de Belgique* 3 (1871), pp. 143-149, pp. 213-224, pp. 68-81 and pp. 213-223.

[7] Loveling wrote a short biographical text for Stellwagen in 1895, which was later published by Van Elslander in *De 'biografie'*. She also gave biographical information in her letters to Maurits Basse, who wrote a biography of the sisters: Maurits Basse, *Het Aandeel der Vrouw in de Nederlandsche Letterkunde. Tweede deel* (Ghent, 1921).

[8] Unidentified contributions in *De Stad Gent. Dagblad voor alle klassen* (1859–1889).

and English vulgarizing articles were translated for the *Zondagsblad van Gent*.[9] In 1866, French translations of English and German contributions were published in *Le Travail* and *Le Travailleur Associé*, when Virginie Loveling was staying in Brussels with one of its editors, the advocate Constant Leirens (1813–1886).[10]

*Cultural transfer: Sociology, politics and literature*

After 1870, the Loveling sisters wrote sociological and political articles and literary reviews. Rosalie Loveling's critical activities were rather limited in scope. She published an essay in the pedagogical journal *De Toekomst*, in which she denounced the patronizing way in which elderly or ill people were addressed, and wrote a flaming critique on the quality of girls' education in Flanders.[11] Virginie Loveling published pro-feminist articles in the same journal in 1872 and 1874, in which she emphasized the importance of female agency.[12] In 1892, she wrote a contribution for *Nederlandsch Museum* in which she criticized Cambridge University's sexist practice of conferring degrees on male students only.[13] Between 1876 and 1881, Virginie Loveling also published nine harsh critiques on clericalism in the liberal paper *La Flandre Libérale*.[14] In these anonymous

---

[9] Unidentified contributions in *Zondagsblad van Gent. Gazette voor alle standen* (1855–1874).

[10] The translations from English and German published in the monthly journal *Le Travail. Organe internationale des intérêts de la classe laborieuse / Revue du mouvement coöperatif* (1866–1867) appeared anonymously. This also holds true for the translations in *Le Travailleur Associé. Propagateur international des doctrines coopératives*.

[11] Rosalie Loveling, 'Iets over het onderwijs der vrouw', *De Toekomst* 15 (1871), pp. 411-415; R. Loveling, 'Onbehendige troostwoorden', *De Toekomst* 18 (1874), pp. 216-222.

[12] V. Loveling, 'Moederlijk gezag', *De Toekomst* 16 (1872), pp. 93-94 and 'De keus eener kostschool', *De Toekomst* 18 (1874), pp. 183-184.

[13] V. Loveling, 'The Conferring of Degrees te Cambridge', *Nederlandsch Museum* 18 (1892), pp. 313-320, reprinted in *De Hollandsche Lelie* (1892) and *De Toekomst* 37 (1893), pp. 144-149.

[14] [anonymous], 'L'Infanticide en Chine', *La Flandre Libérale*, 6 January 1876; [anonymous], 'Le bon Dieu détrôné', *La Flandre Libérale*, 7 February 1876;

contributions she satirized the hypocritical practices of the Catholic Church and denounced its tyranny.[15] Meanwhile, she also published literary reviews in *De Toekomst*,[16] *Nederlandsch Museum*[17] and *L'Atheneum belge*.[18] Her last review was published in 1898 in *Tijdschrift van het Willemsfonds*.[19]

---

[anonymous], [untitled], *La Flandre Libérale*, 24 February 1876; W.W., 'Voltaire au Paradis', *La Flandre Libérale*, 23 May 1876; W., 'On nous écrit de M. petit village dans la Flandre Orientale', *La Flandre Libérale*, 3 February 1880; W., 'On nous écrit d'A', *La Flandre Libérale*, 2 March 1880; W. [V. Loveling], 'On nous écrit de Nevele', *La Flandre Libérale*, 12 August 1880; W., 'Le dernier ami', *La Flandre Libérale*, 20 September 1880; W., 'L'école de l'armée', *La Flandre Libérale*, 18 January 1881.

[15] See: Daniël Vanacker, ed, *Virginie Loveling. Sophie* (Ghent, 1990), pp. 13-15 and pp. 26-29.

[16] V. Loveling, 'Het doel van Middelbaar Onderwijs voor meisjes door A.M. De Cock', *De Toekomst* 15 (1871), pp. 385-387; V. Loveling, 'Eenige bemerkingen op sommige strofen van Ledegancks gedicht "De Hut in 't Woud"', *De Toekomst* 18 (1874), pp. 117-121; V. Loveling, 'Iets over Andersens vertellingen', *De Toekomst* 18 (1874), pp. 318-321; V. Loveling, 'Boekbespreking van Louwerse "Voor de kinderkamer, een geïllustreerd maandblad voor het kleine volkje"', *De Toekomst* 28 (1884), pp. 152-154.

[17] V. Loveling, 'Boekbeoordelingen. *Amazone* door C. Vosmaer', *Nederlandsch Museum* 8 (1881), pp. 245-247; V. Loveling, 'Boekbeoordeling. *Studiën over Calderon en zijne geschriften*, door J.J. Putman', *Nederlandsch Museum* 8 (1881), pp. 340-367; V. Loveling, 'J.J. Putman, *Studiën over Calderon en zijne geschriften*', *Atheneum belge* 5 (1882), pp. 102-103.

[18] V. Loveling, 'Klaus Groth, *Drei plattdeutsche Erzählungen*', *Atheneum belge* 4 (1881), pp. 51-52; V. Loveling, 'Teirlinck-Stijns, *Six nouvelles, traduit du flamand par J. Elseni et F. Gueury*', *Atheneum belge* 4 (1881), pp. 109-110; V. Loveling, 'C. Vosmaer, *Amazone*', *Atheneum belge* 4 (1882), p. 233; V. Loveling, '*Lelie- en rozeknoppen. Weekblad voor meisjes*', *Nederlandsch Museum* 9 (1882), pp. 243-249; V. Loveling, 'J.J. Cremer, *Romantische werken*', *Atheneum belge* 5 (1882), pp. 14-16.

[19] V. Loveling, 'Boekbeoordeling van *De schriftlezing. Handschrift en karakter* door H.W. Cornelis', *Tijdschrift van het Willemsfonds* 3 (1898), pp. 190-192.

The sisters' critical activities ran parallel with their literary production. In 1870, they published their first volume of poetry together.[20] Gradually, they also started to publish short stories, which appeared in many Flemish and Dutch periodicals,[21] and they finally stopped publishing poetry and brought out two volumes of novellas together.[22] After Rosalie's death, Virginie Loveling wrote political novels that were highly praised and marked a break with the more romantic literature of the time.[23] She won the prestigious five-yearly state prize for Dutch literature in 1896 for her novel *Een Dure Eed* (*A Solemn Oath*).[24] In the meantime, she published children's literature and other novels. She also travelled abroad to Britain, Italy, France and Australia, and reported on the life and manners in those countries.[25]

Despite this impressive intellectual background and large cultural production, taking up the role of a critic proved not always unproblematic. As we will see, each time Loveling took her first steps in a particular genre, she was confronted with an anxiety to manifest herself or pronounce her ideas. As the dominant nineteenth-century cultural discourse about women held that they were emotional, intuitive and limited in their interests, Loveling literally portrayed herself that way.[26]

---

[20] R. and V. Loveling, *Gedichten* (Groningen, 1870).

[21] Amongst others: *Vlaamsche School, De Toekomst, Nederlandsch Museum, Volkskunde, De Gids, Nederland, Eigen haard, Het leeskabinet, De Hollandsche Lelie, Groot-Nederland* and *De Vlaamsche Gids*.

[22] R. and V. Loveling, *Novellen* (Ghent, 1874) and R. and V. Loveling, *Nieuwe Novellen* (Ghent, 1876).

[23] V. Loveling, *In onze Vlaamsche gewesten: politieke schetsen* (Ghent, 1877) and V. Loveling, *Sophie* (Ghent, 1884).

[24] V. Loveling, *Een dure Eed* (Ghent, s.d. [1892]).

[25] Amongst others: V. Loveling, 'Een wereldlijk hospitaal', *Nederlandsch Museum* 14 (1887), pp. 47-66; V. Loveling, 'Eene catholieke processie in Hannover', *Nederlandsch Museum* 15 (1888), pp. 5-13; V. Loveling, 'Een stierengevecht', *Nederland* 34 (1893), pp. 377-398; V. Loveling, 'Stonehenge', *Leeskabinet* 67 (1902), pp. 127-131; V. Loveling, 'Een soirée bij Busken Huet en een Receptie bij Victor Hugo', *Groot Nederland* 6 (1908), pp. 467-482.

[26] For a detailed illustration of this 'feminine' strategy of the humble servant we refer to Erica van Boven, 'Ver van de literatuur. Het schrijverschap van Ina Boudier-Bakker', *Nederlandse Letterkunde* 2 (1997), pp. 242-257.

*The making of a literary critic?*

From Loveling's early letters to editors and critics who tried to engage her as a literary critic, a stereotypical picture emerges.[27] As a young girl she had often ridiculed well-known literary figures in unpublished satirical poems,[28] and had thus shown herself to be judicious and self-assured. Nevertheless, in her letters to the editor Frans de Cort (1834–1878), who had asked her to write reviews, she apologized for her 'female' incompetence in her letters.[29] She took a rather ambiguous stance towards the critical and mediating role she was asked to fulfil. Loveling asserted that she did not believe that she could ever write satisfactory reviews, because she lacked the composure required to judge honestly and without bias. She wrote to De Cort: 'Like most women we are too selective in our perception and too inclined to approve or reject thoughtlessly'.[30] When the same editor asked for another contribution later on, she answered that she was slightly embarrassed because he had apparently forgotten how little she could offer.[31] Afterwards she told him that she had attempted to write something, although she did not feel herself apt for that task.[32]

Loveling then took refuge in anonymity. If De Cort wanted to publish her contribution, it would be on the condition that she did not have to sign it.[33] When she sent him another review, she wrote: 'I send you another contribution for your periodical; if you wish, you may publish it

---

[27] For a detailed portrayal of Loveling's double-voicedness, we refer to Liselotte Vandenbussche, '"Dat ik de broek aanheb, ziet gij". Het "androgyne" schrijverschap van Virginie Loveling', *Nederlandse Letterkunde* 13 (2008), pp. 69-89.

[28] Between 1846 and 1851 Rosalie and Virginie Loveling wrote satirical poems on the major literary figures of the time. In 1950 they were published by Ger Schmook under the title *Onze Rensen* (Antwerp, Brussels, Ghent and Leuven, 1950).

[29] V. Loveling to Frans de Cort, 2 April 1871, in: Anne Marie Musschoot and Joris van Parys, eds, 'Correspondentie van de gezusters Loveling. Brieven van en aan Frans de Cort', *Mededelingen van het Cyriel Buyssegenootschap* 20 (2004), pp. 75-76.

[30] *Ibidem* (translation lv).

[31] V. Loveling to De Cort, 13 April 1871, in: *Ibidem*, pp. 76-78.

[32] V. Loveling to De Cort, June 1871, in: *Ibidem*, pp. 79-80.

[33] *Ibidem*.

with my name, but if you do not insist, I would be most grateful and it would be an encouragement for me to write more'.[34] This mode of representation also had its effects on the contributions themselves. When Loveling started reviewing, she presented one of her reviews as 'a sort of reflection' on a narrative poem of a fellow poet, and insisted on entitling it 'A few remarks on some stanzas in Ledeganck's poem'.[35] In the accompanying letter, she emphasized that she did not have the ambition to write an overview and only wanted to pronounce judgment on some particular parts.[36] In the review itself she motivated her choice in more professional terms by stressing that Ledeganck's less reviewed or valued work deserved as much attention as his other work.

However, there were also instances in which a different image appeared. Loveling would gradually gain confidence and display a more professional attitude with regard to her cultural contributions. Her former statements can be put into perspective when we consider the other ways in which she presented herself to editors and critics. When she finally agreed to sign her contribution, she self-confidently asked: 'Don't you think it peculiar and preposterous that our readers pay more attention to a writer's name than to the piece itself? Why can't people like or dislike something without knowing who wrote it? Does not the public ever so often like something merely because a renowned author has written it, or vice versa?'[37] In addition to this vision, money also played an important role. When an editor in Holland had offered to publish her work in his periodical, she wrote to her nephew: 'I refused the request twice, and each time the offer is higher or the conditions are better. Before I refuse for the third time, I'll reconsider the affair.'[38]

Apparently, it was not always doubt that could be held accountable

---

[34] V. Loveling to De Cort, 5 February 1872, in: *Ibidem*, p. 80.

[35] V. Loveling, 'Eenige bemerkingen'; cf. V. Loveling, 'Iets over Andersens vertellingen'.

[36] V. Loveling to De Cort, 25 February 1874, in: Musschoot and Van Parys, 'Correspondentie', pp. 85-86.

[37] V. Loveling to De Cort, 18 June 1871, in: *Ibidem*, pp. 78-79.

[38] V. Loveling to Paul Fredericq, 26 December 1877, in: Van Elslander and Musschoot, eds, 'Correspondentie van de Gezusters Loveling. Brieven van en aan Paul Fredericq I', *Mededelingen van het Cyriel Buysse Genootschap* 9 (1993), pp. 76-175, p. 160.

for her reluctance to sign her work or send regular contributions to a periodical. As Loveling grew more experienced, she built up confidence, and when she moved to Ghent to live on her own and thus needed extra money, she even started to look for a permanent position as a translator or literary critic. She did not succeed in her attempt, however, and, after weighing the profits and losses, finally decided to turn to children's stories, folklore, literary reports and, of course, novels, to earn a decent living.

## Growing professionalism

Virginie Loveling was not paid for the translations that were published before 1870. She did not seem to mind because she considered it a pleasant occupation and a good intellectual exercise.[39] When she left the countryside after her mother's death, however, the need for money became an important drive to publish. She focussed not only on prose, but also, and to a greater extent, on reviews and translations. In 1880, Loveling wanted a job that would yield both intellectual satisfaction and a regular income. She longed to earn some money as a correspondent for a journal abroad, by providing translations and summaries, or even by joining the editorial board of a periodical.[40] A couple of months later, she offered to contribute reviews to the chronicle *La Flandre Libérale* (1874–1974). In a letter to her cousin Paul Fredericq (1850–1920) she expressed her regret at the silence on the part of the magazine's editorial board.[41] She considered it quite hostile of them to keep exclusive control over the critical production of Dutch literature and laconically added that she had never heard of any specific qualifications needed to be allowed to write reviews.[42]

---

[39] V. Loveling to Maurits Basse, s.d., University Library Ghent (ULG), Nalatenschap Maurits Basse, Hs III 69, pp. 350-351.

[40] V. Loveling to Paul and Leon Fredericq, 4 February 1880, in: Van Elslander and Musschoot, eds, 'Correspondentie van de Gezusters Loveling. Brieven van en aan Paul Fredericq II', *Mededelingen van het Cyriel Buysse Genootschap* 10 (1994), pp. 31-156, pp. 41-42; V. Loveling to Paul Fredericq, 20 February 1880, in: *Ibidem*, p. 45.

[41] V. Loveling to Paul Fredericq, 20 July 1880, in: *Ibidem*, p. 54.

[42] *Ibidem*.

When none of her efforts turned out well, she ceased her attempts to join the editorial board of a newspaper because of the large investment of time required, and refused to write reviews on a regular basis because of the low financial returns. In a letter to her cousin, she wrote in this respect: 'A chronicle about Dutch literature wouldn't satisfy me that much: reading all those poor books first, and then reviewing them, would cost me too much time, and what is more: I consider them on the whole so substandard, that I wouldn't know what to say about them.'[43] Summaries and translations remained a professional aim in the early 1880s, but only sporadically did she receive an offer to translate a substantial work.

Loveling finally decided to gain some extra money by publishing collections for children, in addition to her irregular contributions to various periodicals. She also shifted her attention to her own novels, which became the main vessels for her to transmit her views on society and life. She exchanged cultural transfer in the strict sense for cultural mediation on a higher level. In her novels and short stories, she integrated scientific ideas of the time and presented them with a personal touch.

*Cultural transfer: Evolutionary theory*

In the last decade of the nineteenth century, Virginie Loveling entered a new stage in her career, appropriately called her 'dark' or 'black' period by one of her first biographers.[44] During that period, she wrote, among other works, the novella 'Meesterschap' ('Mastership', 1898), and the novels *Erfelijk belast* (*The Burden of Heredity*, 1906) and *Een revolverschot* (*A Gunshot*, 1911).[45] In these works, Loveling creates a gloomy universe in which a pessimistic view on life dominates the plot. As suggested by the titles, the characters in these works are haunted by heredity, atavism, death and destruction. However, in some of Loveling's earlier works, such as 'De kwellende gedachte' ('The Haunting Thought', 1876), *Een*

---

[43] V. Loveling to Paul Fredericq, 24 October 1880, in: *Ibidem*, p. 58 (translation lv).

[44] Basse, *Het Aandeel der Vrouw*, p. 135.

[45] Loveling, 'Meesterschap', in: *Jonggezellenlevens en andere novellen* (Aalst, 1907, repr. Antwerp, 1934), pp. 79-153; *Erfelijk belast* (Rotterdam, 1906) and *Een Revolverschot* (Antwerp, 1911).

Virginie Loveling, ca. 1920, From Collection AMVC-Letterenhuis, Antwerpen.

*dure eed* (*A Solemn Oath*, 1892) and *Een idylle* (*An Idyll*, 1893), these issues already appear.[46]

The ideological visions transmitted through those works remind us of the evolutionary theories that became increasingly popular during the last decades of the nineteenth century.[47] Not all references and themes

---

[46] Loveling, 'De kwellende gedachte', in: R. & V. Loveling, *Nieuwe Novellen* (Ghent, 1876, ²1887); Loveling, *Een dure eed* and Loveling, *Een Idylle* (Amsterdam, 1893), repr. Antwerp, 1934).

[47] For a discussion of evolutionary theories in the literary production in the Low Countries, see: 'De biologisering van het wereldbeeld: de doorwerking van Dar-

are strictly Darwinian, but they clearly reflect a naturalistic framework, in which genetic and environmental forces determine human destiny.[48] Metaphors such as 'struggle',[49] 'victory'[50] and 'defeat'[51] are central to her argument. Loveling largely dwells on the struggle between selfish and social instincts, and deals with the danger of powerful, egoistic instincts that become too strong.[52] As in Darwin's theories, there is occasionally room for altruism, but in Loveling's novels kind feelings are finally overcome by the struggle for one's own luck. Men and women are often compared to animals[53] and their lives are sometimes called a bestial ex-

---

wins evolutietheorie in de Nederlandse cultuur', special issue of *Negentiende eeuw* 17 (1993); Mary Kemperink, '"Excelsior" is het devies van de natuur: Darwinisme in de Nederlandse roman (1860-1885)', *Nederlandse letterkunde* 3 (1998), pp. 97-126; Kemperink, 'Jungle en paradijs: Darwinisme in de Nederlandse roman (1885-1910)', *Nederlandse letterkunde* 4 (1999), pp. 1-36; Kemperink, 'Als je voor een dubbeltje geboren bent... Representatie van het lagere volk in de Noord-Nederlandse literatuur van het fin de siècle', *Spiegel der Letteren* 42 (2000), pp. 134-155; Kemperink and Wessel Krul, eds, 'De gedeelde werkelijkheid van wetenschap, cultuur en literatuur', special issue of *Spiegel der letteren* 42 (2000); Harold van Dijk, *"In het liefdeleven ligt gansch het leven". Het beeld van de vrouw in het Nederlands realistisch proza, 1885-1930* (Assen, 2001); Kemperink, *Het verloren paradijs: de Nederlandse literatuur en cultuur van het fin de siècle* (Amsterdam, 2001); 'Darwin & Co. Dubbelnummer over taal, evolutie en literatuur', special issue of *Armada. Tijdschrift voor wereldliteratuur* 8/9 (2002/2003); Patrick Dassen and Kemperink, eds, *The many faces of human evolution in Europe, c. 1860-1914* (Leuven, 2005).

[48] John Dudley, *A man's game. Masculinity and the anti-aesthetics of American literary naturalism* (Alabama, 2004), p. 1.

[49] Loveling, *Idylle*, p. 98; Loveling, 'Meesterschap', p. 124; Loveling, *Revolverschot*, pp. 25, 47, 102, 104, 113, 150 and 159.

[50] Loveling, *Een dure eed*, pp. 174 and 179; Loveling, *Idylle*, p. 34; Loveling, 'Meesterschap', p. 89; Loveling, *Revolverschot*, pp. 79, 82 and 146.

[51] Loveling, *Revolverschot*, p. 96.

[52] Jonathan Smith, '"The Cock of Lordly Plume": Sexual Selection and *The Egoist*', *Nineteenth-Century Literature* 50 (1995: 1), pp. 51-77, p. 54.

[53] *Ibidem*, p. 40; Loveling, 'Meesterschap', p. 124; Loveling, *Erfelijk belast*, pp. 194 and 209; Loveling, *Revolverschot*, pp. 26, 127, 145, 146, 180, 185 and 194.

istence.[54] Loveling speaks of natural, innate characteristics[55] and deals with the power of intuition and instinct.[56] She emphasizes the importance of her characters' descent[57] and stresses the haunting influence of their ancestors.[58] Gothic elements appear in a Darwinian guise now: a new ghost threatens the characters in bestial and atavistic forms.[59] Loveling also raises the issue of eugenics,[60] often associated with evolutionary thinking but not strictly belonging to this framework, and mentions the deliberate choice not to procreate.[61]

Although it is not certain whether Loveling possessed first-hand knowledge of Darwin's work, she was undoubtedly familiar with his ideas. This was not only because they formed part of the 'idées reçues' of many nineteenth-century intellectuals,[62] but even more so because she was an acquaintance of several Flemish intellectuals who studied evolutionism closely. She knew Emile de Laveleye (1822–1897), who was a leading figure in the discussion on 'social Darwinism', Arthur Cornette (1852–1907), who published on Darwinism in the journal *Nederlandsch Museum* (where Loveling also published her work), Julius MacLeod (1857–1919), who was an important popularizer of Darwinian theory in his journal *Natura*, and his wife Fanny Lava (1858–1938), who translated Peter Kropotkin's *Mutual Aid, a factor of evolution*. Loveling also knew the liberal writer and teacher Omer Wattez (1857–1935), who

[54] Loveling, *Erfelijk belast*, p. 72; Loveling, *Revolverschot*, p. 180.

[55] Loveling, 'Meesterschap', p. 90; Loveling, *Revolverschot*, pp. 23, 37 and 55.

[56] Loveling, *Erfelijk belast*, p. 169; Loveling, *Revolverschot*, pp. 100, 102, 127 and 181.

[57] Loveling, *Erfelijk belast*, pp. 150-151 and 189; Loveling, *Revolverschot*, pp. 6 and 107.

[58] Loveling, *Erfelijk belast*, pp. 41, 68 and 131; Loveling, *Revolverschot*, pp. 127, 128, 138, 182 and 195-196.

[59] Lenora Ledwon, 'Darwin's Ghosts: The influence of Darwinism on the nineteenth-century ghost story', *Proteus* 6 (1989), pp. 10-16.

[60] Loveling, *Erfelijk belast*, p. 40: 'Why should such creatures exist, and procreate, and yield generations of illnesses? Why are there no laws forbidding it, why is there no selection, as when breeding useful animals?' (translation lv).

[61] Loveling, *Erfelijk belast*, pp. 42, 135 and 207.

[62] Kemperink, 'Als je voor een dubbeltje geboren bent', p. 135.

wrote a piece on Victor Van Tricht (1842–1896), one of Darwin's Roman Catholic popularizers.[63]

In 1863, Loveling was present at a couple of interventions by Clémence Royer (1830–1902),[64] a Frenchwoman living in Geneva, who had provided the first French translation of Darwin's *Origin of Species* in 1862.[65] Royer attended the congress of the *Société Internationale pour le Progrès des Sciences Sociales* that took place in Ghent in September 1863.[66] She did not talk about her translation, but took part in a debate on literature and ethics, in which she nevertheless mentioned some of her ideas. In her talk about human ethics, she called attention to an 'élément instinctif héréditaire fatal', 'révélatrice innée de la loi héréditaire de l'espèce, de sa loi de la veille, de sa loi d'autrefois' that exists besides a free and rational conscience that all humans must develop themselves.[67] She also described how 'l'animal anthropomorphe, peu à peu s'est fait homme, par une modification successive de ses ancients instincts qui, par une loi d'hérédité, tendent à réapparaître exceptionellement, et sont l'origine de tous nos vices actuels'.[68] In her view, ethics were also a matter of evolution: she added that the 'seule base qu'on puisse admettre à la loi morale [...] c'est l'utilité de l'espèce; tout ce qui peut contribuer à la multiplication de ses formes diverses, à son développement[,] à son extension, à ses progrès, à l'aggrandissement de ses facultés, est moral.'[69]

---

[63] Raf de Bont, *Darwins kleinkinderen. De evolutietheorie in België 1865-1945* (Nijmegen, 2008), pp. 106, 251 and 136-137.

[64] Van Elslander, *De 'biografie'*, pp. 19-20.

[65] Royer supplied her translation with a long anticlerical preface and rewrote 'parts to fit her own ideas – to Darwin's great dismay. Being the major disseminator of Darwinian ideas to a French-speaking audience, she was also highly critical of the male-dominated scientific establishment', in: Griet Vandermassen, Marysa Demoor and Johan Braeckman, 'Close encounters with a new species: Darwin's clash with the feminists at the end of the nineteenth century', in: *Unmapped Countries: Biological visions in nineteenth-century literature and culture*, Anne-Julia Zwierlein, ed (Londen, 2005), pp. 71-81, pp. 75-76.

[66] *Congrès de l'Association internationale pour le Progrès des Sciences Sociales, tenu à Gand, 1862–1863. Annales, portraits, letters* (Ghent, s.d.), pp. 402-449.

[67] *Ibidem*, pp. 423-424.

[68] *Ibidem*, p. 426.

[69] *Ibidem*, p. 443.

In the following part of this paper, we will supplement Loveling's cultural transfer in the strict sense with her transmission of ideas in a broader sense. We will explore how evolutionary thoughts crop up in Loveling's work, how she transmits and subtly transforms these ideas, and how this is linked with her views on the roles of women and men as explored in those works.

## Darwinian themes

### 1. Natural selection

Darwin's theory caused a scientific, moral and cultural revolution in the nineteenth century so large in scope that it has never been equalled.[70] The main reason was Darwin's replacement of God's careful planning, nowadays referred to as 'intelligent design', with the haphazard mechanism of natural selection. All organisms were shown to be the product of a long evolutionary history with no designer present. Loveling literally refers to this mechanism by contrasting 'a little misery-tree', spoiling its vigour by bearing flowers, to the 'phyrrhusplant', a symbol of strength in the kingdom of plants.[71] She also applies the 'survival of the fittest' to human beings, when mentioning: 'Indeed, only the strongest [orphans] grew up in this house'.[72] Organisms and human beings are more or less adapted to their environment and if not, they disappear:

> Maybe he compared both girls, through whose veins the same blood ran, who lived in the same environment and whom fate had created as differently as possible. Created? Wasn't it the stronger body of the first, that had survived the poor food, the lack of care and everything necessary for health and development, while the other, too weak for the struggle, had failed as a poor victim of her class?[73]

In *A Gunshot*, Loveling literally replaces God with nature when she writes: 'As if nature didn't foresee that everything that grows outside can

---

[70] Klaas van Berkel, 'Over het ontstaan van de twee culturen in het negentiende-eeuws Europa', *Spiegel der Letteren* 42 (2000), pp. 83-96, pp. 91-92.

[71] Loveling, *Erfelijk belast*, p. 154.

[72] Loveling, *Dure eed*, p. 18 (translation lv).

[73] Loveling, *Idylle*, pp. 114-115 (translation lv).

endure hardships – like everything that lives inside – without expiring'.[74]
Although the notion of providence is still present, there is no divine
force involved. When Otto, madly in love, reconsiders his decision to
stay single all his life, he tries to persuade himself of the beneficial workings of nature: 'Oh what a fool he was, as if nature did not possess useful
resources, as if she did not continually strive to thwart errors'.[75] Yet he
soon realizes that there is no benevolent nature at work, and counts on
education and hygiene to mend matters.

In Loveling's work as a whole, the notion of God disappeared and
made room for heredity, adaptation and degeneration. Loveling opts for
a pessimistic interpretation of Darwin's theories. Whereas Darwin left
some room for an optimistic view on nature[76] and most contemporary
writers stressed the teleological course of nature towards progress and
the existence of free will,[77] Loveling suggests a harsh struggle for life in
which most characters are doomed to fail. Will and endeavour are always insufficient.[78] Many characters fight for their lives in a lost struggle
against 'nature's course of things'.[79] Loveling even speaks of 'something
more powerful than nature, stronger than the skills of man: an element
of destruction of the newly born, rejoicing at destroying the harmony of
all things'.[80]

## 2. Sexual selection

As in Darwin's theories, for Loveling, the 'struggle for life' does not only
refer to a literal struggle for food, space or dominance. Survival also im-
plies a quest for the right partner with whom to share one's life and create healthy offspring. Although the struggle for power is a central part

[74] Loveling, *Revolverschot*, p. 44 (translation lv).

[75] Loveling, *Erfelijk belast*, p. 193 (translation lv).

[76] Johan Braeckman, *Darwins moordbekentenis. De ontwikkeling van het denken van Charles Darwin* (Amsterdam, 2001), p. 56.

[77] Kemperink, 'Evolution and utopianism in Dutch literature around 1900. An early polemic', in: Dassen and Kemperink, eds, *The many faces*, pp. 115-128, p. 125.

[78] Gillian Beer, *Darwin's Plots. Evolutionary narrative in Darwin, George Eliot and nineteenth-century fiction* (Cambridge, 1983, ²2000), p. 18.

[79] V. Loveling, *Erfelijk belast*, pp. 100, 103, 120 and 193; Loveling, *Revolverschot*, pp. 25 and 47.

[80] Loveling, *Dure eed*, p. 113 (translation lv).

Charles Robert Darwin (1809-1882). Photograph by Julia Margaret Cameron (1815-1879), scanned from Colin Ford, *Julia Margaret Cameron: 19th Century Photographer of Genius.*

of *An Idyll*, 'Mastership' and *A Gunshot*, Loveling also dwells on courtship plots.[81] These plots feature prominently in her work, as they had done decades before, but now they appear with a Darwinian gloss. Darwin's rather progressive and often unacknowledged contribution with regard to courting is his emphasis on the importance of *female choice* of a sexual partner in many species. By emphasizing women's ability to direct the course of history, he contravened the expectations of many of his Victorian male contemporaries regarding female agency.[82] Novelists such as George Eliot, Charlotte Perkins Gilman and Olive Schreiner also emphasized this aspect of Darwinian theory in their feminist rewritings of traditional courtship plots.[83]

However, although Darwin finds that throughout most of the animal kingdom it is the female who exerts a choice, this choice is fairly limited. The female partner can only accept or refuse a male who presents himself to her.[84] This aspect of courtship is prominent in Loveling's work, where male partners displaying their charms to the female protagonists are accepted or dismissed. Reine, Aurelie, Marie and Berenice reject their admirers without having any viable alternatives. Some of the characters in Loveling's work are thus exceptions to Kemperink's findings that many female characters in fin-de-siècle narratives are forced to accept the first man who proposes to them.[85] Nevertheless, attempts by female characters to select the man of their choice by themselves have little success and are often the cause of great distress.

---

[81] Loveling, *Erfelijk belast*, p. 209; Loveling, *Revolverschot*, pp. 9, 32, 57, 70, 120 and 138.

[82] Helena Cronin, *The ant and the peacock: Altruism and sexual selection from Darwin to today* (New York, 1991, 1994). However, Darwin interprets 'the appropriation of female sexual choice by men in modern societies as a sign of evolutionary progress', thus revealing his male bias, see: Vandermassen, Demoor and Braeckman, 'Close encounters', p. 80.

[83] Vandermassen, Demoor and Braeckman, 'Close encounters', pp. 74-78.

[84] Charles Darwin, *The descent of man, and selection in relation to sex*, Paul Barrett and R.B. Freeman, eds, vols. 21 and 22 of *The works of Charles Darwin* (London, ²1989), p. 230.

[85] Kemperink, *Het verloren paradijs*, p. 181.

According to Darwin, female agency is even further limited. In *The Descent of Man* he writes that every female organism chooses *some* male, even if he is 'the one which is the least distasteful' to her.[86] While 'the females in most or all the orders [...] have the power of rejecting any particular male',[87] they do not usually reject *all* males. This is also visible in Loveling's *A Gunshot*. Marie is not able to marry the man of her preference and meanwhile she rejects other potential husbands. The novel's dysphoric end, marked by the death of Marie's sister and her own insanity, can be interpreted as a sanction for her deliberate refusal to accept the male that is the 'least distasteful' to her. However, it can also be interpreted as a covert critique on the social restrictions and demands that confronted women.

## 3. Sexual dichotomy

Sexual selection is Darwin's effort to account for differences in physical and mental characteristics of males and females.[88] According to Darwin, men are the more active partners, battling their rivals and displaying their charms, while women are less eager and comparatively passive.[89]

In *A Gunshot* the male protagonist, Luc Hancq, incessantly compliments the ladies[90] and tries to impress them with a playful dance, 'knowing well in what advantageous light the harmonious proportions of his figure [...] looked their best'.[91] He teases his rival and flaunts his own mental and physical qualities.[92] Loveling reveals Hancq's battle with his rivals by mentioning the temporary and 'solemn cease-fire of the secret competitors'.[93] Even Otto, most of the time a weak and powerless character, suddenly feels extremely combative when he realizes that Berenice is his fulfilment in life.[94] Men who are merely obedient and good during

---

[86] Darwin, *The descent of man*, p. 230.

[87] *Ibidem*, p. 341.

[88] Smith, 'The cock of lordly plume', p. 61.

[89] Darwin, *The descent of man*, p. 230.

[90] Loveling, *Revolverschot*, p. 16.

[91] *Ibidem*, p. 32.

[92] *Ibidem*, pp. 57-58 and 70.

[93] *Ibidem*, p. 120.

[94] Loveling, *Erfelijk belast*, pp. 192 and 194.

the courting process are sometimes mocked by women.[95]

When Darwin wrote: 'Man is more courageous, pugnacious, and energetic than woman, and has a more inventive genius',[96] he clearly allowed prejudice and Victorian values to pervade his views.[97] Fully in accordance with this, old and young men in Loveling's 'Mastership' strive for dominance and do so almost mercilessly. Likewise, Edward and Martinus, in *The Burden of Heredity*, want to be acknowledged and revered as masters of the house.

Women, according to Darwin, are 'inherently more tender and maternal as well as less selfish' and 'they perceive more quickly than men but only in an intuitive and imitative fashion'.[98] In Loveling's work, most female characters are initially portrayed as caring,[99] sensitive,[100] with a natural maternal instinct,[101] and sometimes willing to surrender to their husbands-to-be.[102] Colette for example, who is visiting the ill in *The Burden of Heredity*, and Marie, who has set up an alternative medical practice in *A Gunshot*,[103] both work in their households or within the confines of the biologically determined female sphere.

---

[95] Loveling, *Revolverschot*, p. 55: 'But alas! Honesty seems to be a virtue young girls seldom take into account when figuratively weighing potential husbands, and, if there are any girls who consent to marry a man in whom nothing else is praised than kindness, it is despite instead of because of that quality. Since the first visit he paid to the daughters of his predecessor, the sisters had classified him: "A boy like a girl", Marie had said, without sparing any criticism on his good manners and small figure.' Later on however, Marie is more positive, admitting 'A man who loves his mother, will love his wife' (translation lv).

[96] Darwin, *The descent of man*, p. 579.

[97] Vandermassen, Demoor and Braeckman, 'Close encounters', p. 74.

[98] Darwin, *The descent of man*, p. 586.

[99] Loveling, 'Meesterschap', pp. 85 and 89; Loveling, *Erfelijk belast*, pp. 212, 224; Loveling, *Revolverschot*, pp. 37 and 86.

[100] Loveling, 'Meesterschap', pp. 96 and 102; Loveling, *Erfelijk belast*, pp. 71, 101, 127, 174, 184.

[101] Loveling, *Idylle*, p. 175; Loveling, 'Meesterschap', p. 124; Loveling, *Erfelijk belast*, p. 51; Loveling, *Revolverschot*, p. 22.

[102] Loveling, *Erfelijk belast*, p. 42; Loveling, *Revolverschot*, pp. 82-84.

[103] *Ibidem*, p. 23.

## Alternative gender roles

### 1. Femininities

Nevertheless, Loveling also subtly departs from those views and leaves some room for alternative gender roles. She repeatedly portrays men as caring and sensitive or willing to obey, and calls it a natural urge of women to long for mastery in the house, stating that men merely consent: 'She was the mistress of the house and her father resigned his will to hers'.[104] Her view on women is far more complex than Darwin's. Loveling refuses to define women exclusively in their traditional caring roles of wives, daughters or nurses. As she sees it, the urge to care is not an essential or innate characteristic of women.[105]

Women of higher and lower classes alike fulfil manly tasks such as steering the carriage or pulling the boat.[106] Although she calls the urge to care the 'elevated' side of women's characters,[107] she also calls girls 'cruel by nature'[108] and stresses the independent and even evil sides of women's characters. Although some women sacrifice themselves for the common good, the female protagonists in 'Mastership' and *The Burden of Heredity* often behave rudely and egoistically, the maid in *The Burden of Heredity* can be brutal and careless[109] and one of the sisters in *A Gunshot* is merely indifferent to the needy and infirm.[110] Loveling also uses many of these women as focalizers, so that an identification with the reader can take place.

It is not only male sexual aggression and jealousy that feature prominently in Loveling's work. As is now generally accepted in evolutionary psychology, women also compete with each other in the process of sexual selection. The rivalry between Reine and Veria in *A Solemn Oath*, between Marie and her sister in *A Gunshot*, and between Colette and niece Berenice in *The Burden of Heredity* exemplify this view.

In *A Gunshot*, the hereditary hatred Marie harbours for her sister

---

[104] Loveling, *Idylle*, p. 14.

[105] Loveling, 'Kwellende gedachte', pp. 251 and 255.

[106] Loveling, *Idylle*, pp. 51, 57 and 93.

[107] Loveling, *Revolverschot*, p. 23.

[108] *Ibidem*, p. 17.

[109] Loveling, *Erfelijk belast*, p. 8.

[110] Loveling, *Revolverschot*, p. 38.

develops itself as a beast inside her and almost transforms her into an animal herself: 'The expression on her face became that of a predator clutching its prey. It seemed as if her bare teeth would bite, as if she would tear apart the sheet in a sudden burst of madness.'[111] Her sister Georgine also experiences this 'hating-sharp-mad feeling of the age-old human beings'.[112] She intends to kill her future husband and 'saw, full of cruel lust, quick as a bolt of lightning, the mortal fear appear in his protruding eyes, on his pale, winched face.'[113] As a result of the cunning plan, the natural course of life is influenced. The most healthy and vigorous people, Luc Hancq and Georgine, who were soon to be married, are murdered or die. The physically most feeble persons such as Marie, survive, but live on in utter misery.

Women in the fictional worlds of Loveling's novels do not merely possess sensibility, they are also rational beings.[114] She stresses women's fascination with science[115] and claims that women can attain the same intellectual standards as men.[116] This is also clear when Otto wonders about his beloved Berenice: 'Didn't he develop her mind and heart, didn't he elevate her to his equal in reason, intellectual eagerness and feeling?'[117] Although it is men who are portrayed as teachers, Loveling clearly judges the lack of education as the reason for women's possible ignorance.

Women possess poise and self-control as well as feelings,[118] and they even succeed in discarding their emotions altogether.[119] Men and women are equally vulnerable to hereditary madness and hysterical fits. When father and daughter in 'The Haunting Thought' hear that their son-in-

---

[111] Loveling, *Revolverschot*, p. 185.

[112] *Ibidem*, p. 130.

[113] *Ibidem*, p. 144.

[114] Loveling, *Dure eed*, p. 165; Loveling, *Idylle*, p. 144; Loveling, *Erfelijk belast*, p. 131.

[115] Loveling, *Dure eed*, p. 15; Loveling, *Idylle*, pp. 38-39; Loveling, *Erfelijk belast*, p. 139.

[116] *Ibidem*, pp. 43, 69, 137 and 192; Loveling, *Revolverschot*, p. 179.

[117] Loveling, *Erfelijk belast*, p. 192.

[118] *Ibidem*, pp. 3-4, 21 and 159.

[119] Loveling, *Erfelijk belast*, pp. 76 and 84; Loveling, *Revolverschot*, pp. 146, 164, 173, 177 and 180.

law and husband-to-be has died, the father tears out his hair in utter misery while the daughter 'stands motionless as a statue, realizing that the worst has eventually happened'.[120] Loveling seems to suggest similarity and harmony between the sexes,[121] rather than defining sexual difference in terms of biological difference and complementarity.

## 2. Masculinities
In addition, Loveling provides a rather complex image of the male protagonists. What is striking is Loveling's emphasis on men's abilities to care. Not only women are cast in traditional sacrificial roles, men's emotional attachment to their children is equally revealed. In her novels care is presented as developing through a complex learning process instead of being an innate and feminine ability.

The narrator in 'The Haunting Thought' expects the most tender feelings from a father's heart,[122] and Guido nurses his father during the last days of his life.[123] The youngest brother in 'Mastership' prefers taking care of his grandchildren and preparing food to guarding cattle;[124] the older brother sees caretaking as a burden, but shows himself equally fit for the task.[125] August, in *The Burden of Heredity*, puts aside his personal aspirations to take care of his disabled mother, and Otto acts as a mother to the orphan Berenice. This is explicitly mentioned several times in the novel, as when he 'looks at her, with the loving expression of a mother, nursing her child'.[126]

Many of the male characters are moved to tears in Loveling's works[127] and some men have a hypersensitive inclination.[128] When Guido suggests to Aurelie that they write a novel together, he says: 'I set the tone

---

[120] Loveling, 'Kwellende gedachte', p. 265.

[121] Loveling, *Idylle*, pp. 45 and 158.

[122] Loveling, 'Kwellende gedachte', p. 236.

[123] Loveling, *Idylle*, p. 139.

[124] Loveling, 'Meesterschap', pp. 120 and 126.

[125] *Ibidem*, pp. 123 and 136.

[126] *Ibidem*, pp. 158, 188 and 204.

[127] Loveling, 'Meesterschap', pp. 88, 99 and 102; Loveling, *Erfelijk belast*, pp. 149 and 207; Loveling, *Revolverschot*, p. 22.

[128] Loveling, *Erfelijk belast*, p. 49.

and then you answer'; he will be 'passionate, you cool and insensitive'.[129] Even courting peacocks, the classical illustration of male behaviour in the process of sexual selection, are said to be symbols of 'purity' and 'kindness'.[130]

Although Loveling thus denies the existence of innate male and female characteristics, men's subjectivities are also questioned in these novels. She emphasizes the fragmentation and multiplicity haunting these characters, thus giving the lie to stable masculinity.[131] Guido lacks independence and endurance to be the right partner, August's willingness to please is considered degrading and Otto's maternal role towards Berenice is sometimes perceived as humiliating.[132] Although the protagonists in both *An Idyll* and *The Burden of Heredity* are deeply in love, their fear of producing weak offspring becomes an insurmountable obstacle for marriage. In Loveling's work, traditional, normative masculinity is fragmented and plagued by insecurities and varieties.

Loveling presents alternative masculinities, but does not give them a straightforward support. As in the Gothic stories analysed by Cyndy Hendershot, the gap between the actual male subject and hegemonic masculinity is revealed, but still leads to a deadlock.[133] Loveling presents endings in which both women's and men's self-realization is hampered and does not yet succeed in 'writing beyond the ending'.[134] Male and female characters either marry or die, but plot structures other than euphoric or dysphoric do not yet appear.

Through this tentative stance against essentialism, however, Loveling subverts dominant notions and questions both individual and societal stability. She draws portraits that are more complex than a Darwinian view on gender differences would suggest. Loveling leaves a considerable space for doubt and presents an alternative view of men's social roles.

---

[129] Loveling, *Idylle*, p. 73.

[130] Loveling, *Revolverschot*, p. 53.

[131] Cyndy Hendershot, *The animal within. Masculinity and the gothic* (Michigan, 1998), p. 1.

[132] Loveling, *Idylle*, p. 83; Loveling, *Erfelijk belast*, pp. 140 and 158.

[133] Hendershot, *The animal within*, p. 4.

[134] Rachel Blau du Plessis, *Writing beyond the ending: Narrative strategies of twentieth-century women writers* (Bloomington, 1987).

She presents men as equally able to care and does not regard the struggle between autonomy and sacrifice as the exclusive trait of women.

## Coda

Supported by the feminist views she conveys in her non-fictional articles,[135] Loveling can be regarded as subtly criticizing the principle of separate male and female spheres, by stressing the variation among men and women and their similar abilities. Although she is unable to imagine affirmative alternatives, and although vulnerable men are sometimes mocked, women and men are not slotted into rigid gender roles. Her personal choice to live the life of an independent woman, mediating culture through translations, reviews, and last of all prose, is reflected in these untraditional depictions of masculine and feminine subjectivities. Loveling transmits culture by a wide variety of means, and lets her work bear the stamp of her personality.

---

[135] V. Loveling, 'Boekbeoordelingen. Het Doel van Middelbaar Onderwijs voor meisjes', pp. 385-387; V. Loveling, 'Moederlijk gezag', pp. 93-94; V. Loveling, 'The Conferring of Degrees', pp. 313-320.

# Laura Marholm (1854–1928): Nordic Cultural Transmission with a Heterosexual Vengeance

EBBA WITT-BRATTSTRÖM

In 1895 the German-Baltic, Danish-speaking critic and translator Laura Marholm initiated a new era in the European discussion on gender issues. By the means of a feminist, though essentialist, analysis of Nordic writing, male and female, she introduced the idea of fiction as apprenticeship in cultural representations of gender. Her first book, *Wir Frauen und unsere Dichter* (Women's authors), studies constructions of masculinity in Henrik Ibsen, Bjørnstjerne Bjørnson och August Strindberg. Also published in 1895, *Das Buch der Frauen. Zeitpsychologische Porträts* (Six Modern Women. Psychological Sketches) introduces three Scandinavian 'modern women' types: Anne Charlotte Edgren Leffler, Amalie Skram, and, the Russian professor in mathematics, Sonja Kovalevsky, who started to write fiction during her long stay in Sweden. In addition, Marholm's second international bestseller, *Zur Psychologie der Frau I* (Studies in the Psychology of Woman, 1897), presents Camilla Collett, Clara Bergsøe, Hilma (Angered) Strandberg and Stella Kleve. In two literary texts-à-clef from 1895, Victoria Benedictsson (Ernst Ahlgren) is brutally portrayed as the prominent female figure of the Modern Breakthrough (*Karla Bühring* and *Zwei Frauenerlebnisse*, Two Women Experiences).

Laura Marholm's creation in 1895 of what in the 1970s was to become the two pillars of feminist literary studies, 'Images-of-Woman-Criticism' and 'Gynocritics' (Elaine Showalter's terms), was thus to a large part based on Nordic literature. However, her contribution takes its starting point in a biased version of the Modern Breakthrough, which makes it similar to contemporary male authors' blackening of their female colleagues as 'tendentious'. The difference is that Marholm intends to use her interpretation to accomplish a change-over from 'Woman question' to 'Gender question'.

Laura Marholm 1889. From: Ingvar Holm, *Åttitalsromantik.*

Marholm's Swedish husband and intellectual partner, Ola Hansson (1860–1925), holds a unique position in her intellectual project and cultural transmission. Their alliance as a 'literary gangster duo' (Georg

Brandes' description) generated a decadent manifesto literature with gender as an analytic category. Decadence à la Marholm is a search engine, a tool for exploring for the degeneration of the sexes, as well as a provocatively polemic style, tending towards a new definition of 'femininity'. In her New Woman Fiction, Marholm tries to construct a passionately heterosexual New Woman, the contrary of a degenerate Scandinavian emancipation.

My article develops these themes, as well as the spectacular 'making' of Strindberg as 'der Dichter des Weiberhasses' (A misogynous writer). It intends to sum up the importance of Laura Marholm as a cultural transmitter at the turn of the century 1900.

With an essentialist feminist analysis of Nordic female and male authors, Laura Marholm opened a new era in the European gender issue in 1895. This was the year when *Wir Frauen and unsere Dichter* was published, a book that examines images of women and constructions of masculinity in Henrik Ibsen (1828-1906), Bjørnstjerne Bjørnson (1832-1910), and August Strindberg (1849-1912), among others. The same year *Six Modern Women. Psychological Sketches* was published and translated into eight languages: Swedish, Norwegian, English, Dutch, Russian, Polish, Czechoslovakian, and Italian. Six modern female types are presented here as different aspects of the 'terra incognita' of the female mind, three of whom are from the Nordic countries: Swedish Anne Charlotte Edgren Leffler (1849 –1892), Norwegian Amalie Skram (1846–1905), and Russian Sonja Kovalevsky (1850–1891). The first female professor of mathematics, Kovalevsky came to Stockholm in 1883, and stayed to her death in 1891. Marholm's *Studies in the Psychology of Woman*, a non-fiction work, published in 1897, includes several Scandinavian women: Norwegian Camilla Collett (1813–1895), Danish Clara Bergsøe (1837–1905), Swedish Hilma (Angered) Strandberg (1855–1927) and Stella Kleve – a pseudonym for Mathilda Kruse, later Malling (1864–1942).

Nordic authors are thus central to Laura Marholm's introduction of what came to be known, 70 years later, as the two strands of feminist literary criticism – 'Images-of-Woman-Criticism' and 'Gynocritics': the analysis of recurrent themes and experiences in works by women, 'a literature of their own' in Elaine Showalter's words.[1] However, when

---

[1] Elaine Showalter, 'Towards a feminist poetics,' in: E. Showalter, ed, *The New Femi-*

Marholm determines what is new in women's literature of the 1890s ('the beginning of a series of personal confessions at first hand /---/ an entirely new department in women's literature'),[2] she does it against the background of a biased rewriting of the significance of the modern breakthrough for the gender issue – a tendentiousness, in fact, that resembles contemporary male authors' derogation of female authors as 'tendentious writers.'[3] 'Hitherto,' Marholm claims, 'all books, even the best ones, written by women, are imitations of men's books, with the addition of a single highpitched, feminine note, and are therefore nothing better than communications received at second hand.'[4]

> We are confronted by a strange sight in Scandinavian literature. We find man's laxity and woman's prudity existing side by side. Bjørnson, Ibsen, Garborg, Strindberg, were contemporaries of Fru Edgren, and their renown was at its height. The eighties were the great period of Scandinavian romance, and this romance turned solely upon the problem of man and woman. The productive enthusiasm of those days drove a multitude of women into the fields of literature, including those whom we have mentioned, who died early, and some lesser ones, who still continue to lead a useless, literary existence. But their writings are strangely poor compared with those of the men, even though there were numbered amongst them an Edgren Leffler, an Ahlgren, and a Kovalevsky.[5]

What is deficient in these female authors, in Laura Marholm's view, is that none of them have experienced love and therefore they cannot produce a 'hymn to love.' The only one of them who had sought love (in her ill-matched relationship with Georg Brandes (1842–1927)), became an emblematic figure for the thesis-prone 1880s: Marholm's older friend, Victoria Benedictsson (1850–1888), with the pseudonym Ernst Ahl-

---

nist Criticism. Essays on women, literature and theory (London, 1986), p. 131f.

[2] Laura Marholm, Six modern women. Psychological Sketches, transl. Hermione Ramsden (Boston, 1896), pp. 71–72.

[3] David Gedin, Fältets herrar. Framväxten av en modern författarroll. Artonhundraåttitalet (Stockholm, 2004), pp. 173–214.

[4] Marholm, Six Modern Women, p. 71.

[5] Ibidem, pp. 207–208.

gren. Bendictsson appears as a 'key' figure in two works of fiction also
published in 1895 – the drama *Karla Bühring* and the short story 'The
Unspoken' in *Zwei Frauenerlebnisse*. In both works Benedictsson is brutally portrayed as a rejected woman seeking her own destruction.

Beside Benedictsson, Ola Hansson, Marholm's Swedish husband/
writer, played a special role in her activity as a cultural transmitter. She
was his main translator. Their alliance at a decisive moment in modernism produced a new variant of decadent manifesto literature with
gender as an analytic category.[6] Hansson is the greater fiction writer of
the two, though Marholm tried her hand at 'New Woman Fiction'. She
is, however, primarily known as a critic. The 'Author Company Hansson & Marholm' established themselves in Germany by stealing some of
Georg Brandes' German cultural capital. Through his wife's translation,
Hansson was the first to introduce Nietzsche as a great philosopher in
his own country – before Brandes, who was the earlier Nietzsche expert.
Brandes never forgave his old protégées, Hansson and Marholm, 'a literary gangster duo.'[7]

*Woman's Disclosure of her own Self*

> But at last the time has come when woman is so keenly alive to her
> own nature that she reveals it when she speaks, even though it be in
> riddles.[8]

With its ideological, polemic style and incisive, essentialist theme, Laura Marholm's *Six Modern Women* stirred feelings and sparked debates
about male and female aspects of modernity. As the Marholm scholar
Susan Brantly has shown, the Nordic and European press debate around
Marholm's book was intense and ambivalent: 'a dangerous book' (*Die
Frauenbewegung*), 'an absurd book' (*The Bookman*), 'pathological eroto-
mania' (*Nya Dagligt Allehanda*), an 'honest and powerful book' (*Der

---

[6] Ebba Witt-Brattström, *Dekadensens kön. Ola Hansson och Laura Marholm* (Stockholm, 2007).

[7] Pil Dahlerup, *Det moderne gennembruds kvinder*, (dissertation) (Köpenhamn, 1983), p. 90.

[8] Marholm, *Six Modern Women*, p. 71.

*Übermensch in der modernen Literatur*), 'bad literature' (*Post- och Inrikes Tidningar*).[9]

For centuries fiction, especially the novel, has been the genre in which primarily women have discussed gender relations and stimulated interest in women's questions. But the alternative gender constructions created in literary texts could easily be dismissed as fictional and imaginary. Through Marholm's polemical style, literary images of Woman (and Man) became political weapons in current debates. In addition, the overriding theme of her first two books is literature as the core curriculum of gender studies. The idea that literature is a cognitive medium particularly for gender relations may have been inspired by Camilla Collett, whom Marholm gives credit as a pioneer in the first chapter of her *Studies in the Psychology of Woman*. Collett's famous collection of essays, *Fra de Stumme Lejr*, published in 1877, includes what may be seen as a draft of Marholm's poetics which she was to develop in *Wir Frauen und unsere Dichter*, and also in *Six Modern Women*. Collett writes: 'People used to talk about the role that the novel played in women's lives. It is time to reverse the issue. Let us now open our eyes to the role women's lives play in the novel.'[10]

When Marholm takes over from Collett she characterizes contemporary women's literature as confession. 'Woman is the most subjective of all creatures; she can only write about her own feelings, and her expression of them is her most valuable contribution to literature,' she writes in *Six Modern Women*. This is not to be understood as the old patriarchal strategy reading women's literature biographically (even though Marholm is guilty of this as well). Her launching point is primarily Nietzsche's conception of power as an intoxicating feeling of sovereignty, 'the recovery of a magical universe where everything converges in the self.'[11] It is this magical universe of the self that finds its expression in Marholm's idea of woman's 'truth' and the power of the subjective testimony.

---

[9] Brantly, *The Life and Writings of Laura Marholm*, pp. 138-140.

[10] Camilla Collett, *Fra de stummes lejr. Samlede Verker. Mindeutgave. Andet Bind*, p. 380.

[11] Ebba Witt-Brattström, *Ediths jag. Edith Södergran och modernismens födelse* (Stockholm, 1997), pp. 168-204.

Laura Marholm had learned from Nietzsche's paradoxical technique of argumentation, and from the ambivalent style of decadence which does not shy away from depicting base human characteristics (perversions, affects, morbidities). She leaves no reader unaffected. The feminist critic Lotten Dahlgren complains that Marholm does not avoid 'various pathological processes in the female body, described with expressions far more realistic and undisguised than those used in medical works. All this to illustrate the physically and psychologically decadent creature into which today's culture has turned woman.'[12]

Laura Marholm's texts are self-assertive, full of contradictions and associative thrusts. They are well worth reading but often shocking to today's politically correct feminists. What is particularly hard to digest is that, in a historical perspective, feminist cultural theory is born with Marholm's provocative slogan: 'A woman's life begins and ends in man. It is he who makes a woman of her.'[13] And since her book *Wir Frauen und unsere Dichter* did not become an international bestseller, Marholm's idea of complementarity has gone unnoticed; when the New Woman meets man after her 'spiritual and physical awakening,' she becomes his 'Ein und Alles, sein Mittelpunkt, sein Genie und sein Inhalt – die durchseelte, verinnerlichte Geschlechtlichkeit.'[14] The basis is the heterosexual, Christian message, the marriage formula that the two shall be one.

It was not Ellen Key (1849–1926) (whose *Missbrukad kvinnokraft*, Misused Female Powers, was published the year after, in 1896) but Laura Marholm – as an influential intellectual around the turn of the twentieth century – who first prescribed as the cure for the evils of the times an essentialist feminist belief in motherliness, and the assertion of woman's heterosexual drive.[15] Marholm appropriates the plural form of the female gender with rhetorical skill: in *Six Modern Women* a 'we, the women' speak. It is a vampire technique intended to make the reader accept her message. 'Whether Laura Marholm is read with disgust or

---

[12] Lotten Dahlgren, ed, *Dagny* (1898), p.139.

[13] Marholm, *Six modern women*, p. 191.

[14] *Wir Frauen und unsere Dichter*, p. 87. Cf. '…I have come to the conclusion that it is the woman who either develops the man's character or ruins it.' Marholm, *Six Modern Women*, p. 187.

[15] Key felt compelled to repudiate the criticism saying that her 'opinions about the woman question [had] been tuned before Laura Marholm.'

delight, with indignation or sympathy, her phrases scorch our memory, willingly or not, and remain there like a stain, which is hard to remove,' Dahlgren writes in *Dagny*.[16] In plain language, Laura Marholm is a decadent writer.

Decadence is here to be understood as an ideologically contradictory discourse: on the one hand a nostalgic dream of stable values, on the other hand an exaggeratedly menacing picture of the decline of civilization, the degeneration of man, and the triumph of sexual perversities. Difference feminism of this period is the reverse side of decadence and shares the assumption that woman is 'entartet,' degenerated, as a consequence of the women's movement's demand that she shall compete with man in the labor-market. Instead, woman must realize that she needs man: 'It is he who creates in her a new kind of self respect by making her a mother: it is he who gives her the children whom she loves, and to him she owes their affection.'[17]

The over-determined idealization of man's life-sustaining function for woman sometimes turns into an unflattering de-individualization. Through a reversed sexism man is seen primarily as an instrument in woman's coming into being: 'for it does not much matter to a woman whom she loves, as long as she loves someone', as Laura Marholm claims.[18]

The organized women's liberation did not include any convincing visions of heterosexual love, and Marholm filled a void in the discourse. Attempting a cultural paradigm shift, which was meant to be led by her and Ola Hansson, Laura Marholm in her fiction created female characters who found self-fulfillment in a heterosexual, companionate marriage, in contrast to the Scandinavian, 'degenerate' feminist type. In the drama *Karla Bühring*, as well as in the short story 'The Unspoken' in *Zwei Frauenerlebnisse*, Marholm's autobiographically inspired and 'sound' female characters – Lilly Bloom and Lonny Borg – are contrasted to the suicidal Benedictsson-types – Karla Bühring and Louise Wikman.

Marholm is an exponent of the function of degeneration theory in decadence as she establishes a normative pole of wholesomeness against which the sick culture is measured. The purpose is to create a new, 'natu-

---

[16] Dahlgren, *Dagny*, p. 142.

[17] Marholm, *Six Modern Women*, p. 191.

[18] *Ibidem*, p. 191.

ral' female type – and body.[19] But, as Charles Bernheimer points out, the claustrophobic and self-generating decadence paradigm makes all constructed binary pairs collapse, whereupon the very norm – in Marholm the wholesome woman's 'natural femininity' – becomes one of the abnormalities described.[20] This is noticeable not least in Marholm's last fiction fragment, from 1900, when the Benedictsson-character invades the Marholm-character's subconscious, like an archaic, vengeful mother figure.[21]

## The Difference-Feminism Troika

During the 1890s, Marholm's decadence functioned like a tool for exploring the degeneracy of the times and of the sexes; it is also, simultaneously, a gender-provocative, over-determined style that gropes for a new definition of 'female gender'. In other words, decadence à la Marholm involves not only man's fall (as a norm for mankind), but also the beginning of the New Woman's individuality in relation to this 'fallen' man. This is where we see a utopian element, a visionary, 'different place' than 'the prison of woman' (to use an expression that Collett coined, in genuine Breakthrough manner).

Even in modernity Eros, love, and motherhood remain the arena where woman has the privileged right of interpretation. This is where Marholm makes a contribution: one worth considering, if not perhaps worthy of imitation. Ellen Key (known to her personally) and Lou Andreas-Salomé (1861–1937), whom she had met, form, together with Laura Marholm a difference-feminism troika around the turn of the century 1900.[22] With the intention to use the idealization of mother-

---

[19] See Kirsi Tuohela, 'Feeling sick: on change and gender in the cultural history of illness', in: Anu Lahtinen and Kirsi Vainio Koohonen, eds, *History and Change*, , pp. 46-556.

[20] Charles Bernheimer, *Decadent Subjects, The Idea of Decadence in Art, Literature, Philosophy, and Culture of the Fin de Siècle in Europe*, Kline, T.J. & Schor, N., eds (Baltimore, 2002), p. 162ff.

[21] 'Im Bann', *Der Weg nach Altötting und andere Novellen*, 1900, 'Die Hände der Angst', *Haus und Welt* 28, 7 April, 1900. See Witt-Brattström, *Dekadensens kön*, pp. 322-337.

[22] *Ibidem*, pp. 338-358.

hood as a female political strategy – a goal which does not appear very gender-politically correct today – these women sought to 'manipulate' at a symbolic level. However, to constitute the feminine-as-such, without ending up in the department for masculine projections, was a risky project. Through the re-idealization of woman's maternity, the female gender would be on a par with – that is equal with, rather than subordinate to – the male gender. This reassessment tends to exalt woman as evolutionary primary (with the argument that the relation mother-child historically precedes the relation man-woman). It is possible to interpret the ideological program of difference feminism around 1900 as a feminist vision reacting to modernity's exclusion of the female: in brief, as a woman-defined urge for a more humane 'mother-society,' instead of the emerging technological 'brother-society.'[23] Woman must follow 'her own wild path, the path of rebellion against all that is evil in society, as a consequence of man's one-sided rule,' as Key taught.[24]

Facing the threat of the extinction of female historical experiences, Marholm, Key and Andreas-Salomé invented a woman-defined, anti-patriarchal discourse centered around gender differences. Their brand of difference feminism may be labeled strategic essentialism, since it was not based on the simple, causal relation between biological sex and sexual identity that characterizes biologic essentialism. The trio may rather be seen as evolutionists who, like Darwin and Spencer, believe that mankind can change its genetic makeup through deliberate action. Laura Marholm writes: 'A great deal of what we call "woman's nature" is neither natural nor womanly. It is only a reflex. It is very difficult to uncover the imminent, basic characteristics, in woman's nature . . . '[25] Through the active affirmation of her (maternal) femininity, acquired through centuries of a patriarchal division of labor, the New Woman would be able to transfer valuable qualities to the rising generation.[26] The opposite, however, the risk that women lose their 'peculiarities,' that is their distinctive features, seemed possible as well – even dangerously close in an age of gendered decadence and equality feminism.

---

[23] Juliet Flower MacCanell, The *Regime of the Brother. After Patriarchy* (London, 1991), pp. 11-40.

[24] Ellen Key, *Missbrukad kvinnokraft* (Stockholm, 1896), p. 55.

[25] Laura Marholm, *Zur Psychologie der Frau II* (Berlin, 1903), p. 203.

[26] See Ellen Key, *Lifslinjer I* (Stockholm, 1903), p. 84.

The notion that femininity as a combination of acquired characteristics would become extinct in a world where only masculinity was valued, explains Ellen Key's idea that there is 'a natural range for woman's labor.' Similarly, this notion may explain Laura Marholm's advocating 'women's productive work' in a health sector that was to solve 'the social issue' by mitigating the effect of capitalism's ruthless exploitation (the project was to be financed by a special tax for wealthy men). With the unmarried mother as a symbol of what Key would later term 'social motherhood,' women would be able to practice all professions – from doctors and administrative directors to nurses and teachers – in a sister-state within the state; all this in order for the New Woman's productive work to be 'rooted in the fulfillment of her mother vocation, in the setting free of her motherly feeling, if not in the flesh, then in the mind and soul.'[27]

The starting-point for Laura Marholm's poetics and cultural criticism was to use woman instead of man as a standard. As Rita Felski points out, it is possible to understand historical feminism as an expression of 'symbolic politics': a 'struggle for social change, with analytical and theoretical claims that were inseparable from specific metaphors and symbols' signifying evolution and revolution. She suggests a double symbolic and political interpretation of difference feminism as an 'intervention.'[28] The same term is used by Luce Irigaray, as she argues for an intervention into the patriarchal social order which, she holds, is based on a 'metaphoric' matricide.[29] Intervention in Irigaray's terms is to inscribe a feminine historical genealogy, a matrilineal succession, at a symbolic level, in order to give daughters a field of action that the unisexual society denies them.

Laura Marholm is perhaps the first to use woman's history as an ideological instrument in political essays. In *Studies in the Psychology of Woman* she foregrounds women's 'psychophysical developmental history' (including, for instance, a good analysis of the witch trials) in order to correct a patriarchal history writing that has excluded women's experiences. In *Die Frauen in der socialen Bewegung* (Women in the Social Movement, 1900) Marholm also tries to create a symbolic space for a

---

[27] *Studies in the Psychology of Woman,* transl. Georgia A. Etchison (New York, 1906), p. 341.

[28] Rita Felski, *The Gender of Modernity* (Cambridge, Mass, 1995), pp. 145-173.

[29] Margaret Whitford, *Luce Irigaray* (London, 1991), pp. 75-97.

female historical subject (starting with St Birgitta's 14th century) through a re-interpretation of history, focusing on women's difference.

In feminist historiography it is Ellen Key rather than Laura Marholm who has survived, despite the fact that they represented the same feminist politics around the turn of the twentieth century. One reason is probably that Key, in contrast to Marholm, was manifestly unpolemical against men. Another reason why Marholm is forgotten today is that she consistently used the stylistic matrix of decadence which quickly became outdated. People grew tired of extravagant horror shows, the gender-coded exaggerations, and the nervous style of her cultural analyses.

However, Laura Marholm's combination as translator, critic and author is interesting to this day. And it was through her early meeting with, and mediation of, several important Nordic authors to a German-speaking audience that she turned into the European difference feminist à la mode in the 1890s.

## Laura Marholm, née Mohr[30]

In 1854 the woman later to use the penname Laura Marholm, was born as Laura Katarina Mohr into the German-speaking gentry in Riga, at that time the capital of Livonia, a Russian province. Her mother came from a German merchant family who had emigrated from Göttingen, and her father was a Danish sea captain, and later a customs officer, in Riga. Laura was an only child and was given a good education at a 'höhere Töchterschule' and was taught the profession of a teacher. As an adult she lectured in Baltic history to educated ladies. Under the pseudonym Leonhard Marholm this young lady was a theatre reviewer in *Nordische Rundschau*, and wrote articles and author biographies in *Baltische Monatsschrift* and in the Riga newspaper *Zeitung für Stadt und Land*. All this, according to her alter ego, Mohrenfratz, with the purpose of creating a future for herself:

> Mohrenfratz blushed. She was always terribly embarrassed when her work was spoken of. She did not, after all, write out of vanity, not even out of inclination – she wrote only for self-preservation. Because life was all too *confined* in this town, in this country, under her

---

[30] Biographical details are from Brantly, *The Life and Writings of Laura Marholm*.

parents' wings. She wanted to get away, expand, look around, live! And she owned no other key to the world out there, than her powers of perception and her verbal skills.[31]

Laura Marholm became Latvia's first national playwright. Only 24 years old, she wrote her first play, a Schiller drama in blank verse about Johan Reinhold Patkul, the liberation hero of the Livonian aristocracy, a play which was very successful. The first part is entitled *Gertrud Lindenstern* and the second *Johan Reinhold Patkul* (1880). Her third play, *Frau Marianne*, was performed in Riga in 1882. This play could have become Laura Mohr's hit and given her access to the European market, but when a cut-down version of it was staged at the Berliner Residenztheater, it was cried down. Marholm scholar Susan Brantly writes that in light of Ibsen's drama, *Frau Marianne* looked like a romantic imitation. She suggests that her discovery of Ibsen was the main reason why Marholm stopped writing plays and contented herself with being a critic and translator.[32]

In 1883 Marholm read Ibsen, and after that she was focused on one thing: to leave the Baltic region where the only standard was 'what people would think?' as she complained to Georg Brandes in June, 1885.[33] It is also with her article on Ibsen's *A Doll's House* as a topical play that she 1884 began her career as a divulgor of Nordic literature in *Nordische Rundschau*.[34] Eleven years later, in *Wir Frauen und unsere Dichter*, she scolded Ibsen for being a 'cerebral poet' instead of an 'erotic' one, and thereby responsible for the emancipation ideal of the Modern Breakthrough. However, at the same time Marholm quotes an anonymous woman who bears a suspicious likeness to Miss Mohr in Riga:

---

[31] 'Die Schiefe Nase', *Frankfurter Zeitung*, 30 January, 3, 6 February, 1901.

[32] Brantly, *The Life and Writings of Laura Marholm*, p. 29.

[33] *Ibidem*, p. 24.

[34] 1: 1844. Barbara Gentikow, *Skandinavien als präkapitalistische Idylle. Rezeption gesellschaftskritischer Literatur in deutschen Zeitschriften 1870 bis 1914* (Neumünster, 1978), p. 120, footnote 297. She also writes about Ibsen in German: 'Henrik Ibsens neueste Dramen', *Die Gegenwart* (31:1887), 'Die Frauen in der skandinavischen Dicthtung. Der Noratypus', *Freie Bühne*, 12 March, 1890, and in *Wir Frauen und unsere Dichter* (1895).

I was lying on the floor and wallowed in feelings that found expression in thoughts and words. People and conditions in his social
dramas were precisely my circles, my conditions, my own personal
surroundings. I saw everything that confined and oppressed me with
greater clarity than ever. And I realized that I had to get away. I could
not find peace to stay. I had to get away at once! I had no connections
but went into an unknown world, forced to rely solely on my only as-
set: my little talent. Without Ibsen I would never have broken away.
For years I was alone in a foreign country, among strangers, indifferent people – but I did belong to myself. I was free from the prejudices
and whims of other people. I was free to think and to read what I
chose. I was my own person! I earned my own living and felt how my
spiritual and mental self grew into freedom.[35]

It is true that Laura Marholm, along with the ideological shift of the
time from Ibsen to Nietzsche, dissociated herself from Ibsen, her earlier
idol. But she had once, like many a middle-class young lady in Europe,
obtained a new identity as a misunderstood and sensually unliberated
Ibsen heroine, with 'a spirit of rebellion and doubt,' as Ellen Key wrote
in a complimentary speech to Ibsen in Stockholm in April 1898. Ibsen
showed how 'woman is a personality in all areas, who gives herself away,
and not a creature who throws herself away,' according to Key.[36] This is
also Marholm's understanding of woman in all her writings.

The other Nordic writer whom the young Laura Mohr wrote about
was Georg Brandes.[37] He encouraged her to come to Copenhagen to at-
tend his lectures. She arrived there late in October 1885, with such heavy
luggage that the customs officer exclaimed: 'Miss comes to Copenhagen
to get married?'[38] In April 1884 Laura Mohr had joined Brande's court,
his circle of literary ladies, with a fan letter. Very soon she made herself useful by translating and introducing Brandes to a Russian audience
in St. Petersburger Zeitung. The third Nordic author she wrote about
was Bjørnstjerne Bjørnson, in St. Petersburger Zeitung, October 23/24

---

[35] Marholm, Wir Frauen und unsere Dichter, p. 14.

[36] Brigitte Mral, Talande kvinnor, pp. 207-209.

[37] 'Georg Brandes und die moderne literarische Kritik', Rigasche Zeitung, 1 June,
1885.

[38] 'St. Anneplatz', Der Tag, 13 March, 1903.

1886.[39] The fourth was August Strindberg. In a review in *Die Gegenwart* titled 'Ein Dichter des Weiberhasses' (A misogynist writer, 33:1888) Laura Marholm wrote about the first stageing of *Fadren* in Copenhagen. Strindberg threatened to bring Miss Mohr to trial but soon realized that he could use her to promote him as the foremost enemy of the women's movement in Europe. It was after this traumatic event - when Strindberg exposed the signature Leonhard Marholm as an unmarried lady – that the signature Laura Marholm was born.

Even greater changes were at hand: on May 24, 1888, she introduced a 'Swedish love poet' in the Vienna paper *Neue Freie Presse*: Ola Hansson and his decadent scandalous book, *Sensitiva amorosa* (1897). On midsummer's eve, 1888, the couple met in the home of Brandes and fell in love. On September 27, 1889, they were married in Copenhagen, and on February 7, 1890, the writer-, critic-, and translator company, Hansson & Marholm, began their peregrinations in Europe, living at more than twenty addresses (in St. Vévier, Berlin/Friedrichshagen, Schliersee, Munich, Paris/Meudon, Buydukdere). Their life in exile would last until their deaths in 1925 (Ola Hansson) and 1928 (Laura Marholm).[40]

Marholm's greatest service to an author was done for her husband, whom she gave a status as a German writer. The introductory article about *Sensitiva amorosa* in *Neue Freie Presse* in 1888 was followed by her translation of a couple of the short stories it contained. In December the same year she wrote about Hansson in *St. Petersburger Zeitung*,[41] and the year after yet again in *Neue Freie Presse*.[42] The totality of Ola Hansson's essays and criticism, published during his lifetime, passed through his

---

[39] She also writes about Bjørnson in *Die Gegenwart* 33:1888, *Freie Bühne* 1:1890, *Nord und Süd* 63:1892, *Finsk tidskrift* 2: 1892. Other male, Nordic writers were Alexander Kielland (*Die Gegenwart* 31:1887), Jonas Lie (*Unsere Zeit* 1:1888), Karl A. Tavaststjerna (*Wiener Rundschau* 4:1898) Henrik Pontoppidan (*Die Zeit* 1 June, 1901).

[40] About Ola Hansson as a cultural transmitter, see Arne Widell, *Ola Hansson i Tyskland. En studie i hans liv och diktning åren 1890–1893*, dissertation (Uppsala, 1979); Inger Månesköld-Öberg, *Att spegla tiden – eller forma den. Ola Hanssons introduktion av nordisk litteratur i Tyskland 1889–1895*, dissertation (Göteborg, 1984).

[41] Laura Marholm, 'Zwangsvorstellungen in der Dichtung', 15/16 December, 1888.

[42] Laura Marholm, 'Ein schwedischer Liebesdichter', 1 February, 1889.

wife's pen, as Brantly remarks, being published in German (and French) papers, while his fiction was translated either by her or by the Austrian Marie Herzfeld.

In 1890, through his 'German' debut with *Parias*, Marholm's husband was established as the foremost modern writer in German-speaking literature. He was exceptionally successful over the next few years. When Laura Marholm subsequently published *Wir Frauen und unsere Dichter,* and *Six Modern Women* met with success, it was Ola Hansson's turn to translate her into Swedish. Being each other's translators, they influenced each other's stylistic idiom – and, significantly, Marholm was the better translator, which made her prospect of getting an audience in Sweden less promising. In addition, Laura Marholm possessed a greater cultural capital to invest in her husband's German career than he had to help launching her career in Sweden. In 1890 she wrote regularly in several large daily papers, such as *Frankfurter Zeitung*, the Berlin paper *Vossische Zeitung*, and the Vienna paper *Neue Freie Presse*. When she was invited to write in the weekly magazine *Deutschland*, which merged with *Das Magazin für Literatur* in 1891 (whose Scandinavian editor Ola Hansson became), her first contribution was poems from her husband's lyrical Nietzsche paraphrase, *Young Ofeg's Ditties,* and an article of his on Strindberg. 'I translated it before the ink dried,' she wrote in the accompanying letter.[43]

## The Making of a Strindberg

Laura Marholm's second successful effort to promote a particular author was her criticism of August Strindberg. His work had been translated into German during the 1880s, but he had not been labeled 'modern,' as Ola Hansson, which made his success in the beginning of the 1890s. Strindberg achieved this reputation as soon as Marholm launched him as a 'Misogynist Writer,' in addition to her review of *Fadren* in *Die Gegenwart* in 1888, an analysis of the 'Laura-type' in *Freie Bühne* in 1890, a large Strindberg portrait in *Nord und Süd* in 1893, a chapter in *En bok om Strindberg* (A book on Strindberg) in 1894, and, finally, in *Wir Frauen und unsere Dichter.* [44] Laura Marholm became, more or less

---

[43] Brantly, *The Life and Writings of Laura Marholm*, p. 89.

[44] The analysis of Laura in 'Fadren', *Freie Bühne*, 30 April, 1890, *Samtiden* (1:1890),

against her will, August Strindberg's best promotor. According to her Strindberg is a crass materialist who refuses to acknowledge 'the mystic element in sexual relations, that is, love,' which is why he consistently shows 'how the union between two cultured people without love leads to rapid degeneration.' Apart from some racist markers typical of its time (for instance that Strindberg, because of his 'Laponian blood,' is really a Mongol and therefore Russian in his misogyny!), Marholm's Strindberg criticism is an example of her 'images-of-women-criticism' at its best: sharply analytical and gender-dialogical.

Laura Marholm's series about Ibsen's Nora-type, Bjørnson's Svava-type, and Strindberg's Laura-type, in *Freie Bühne* (and the Norwegian periodical *Samtiden*), 1890, received a great deal of attention and gave rise to a debate in which even Friedrich Engels participated.[45] About her namesake in *Fadren* Marholm writes that she was the 'Medusa who neither loves nor fears man.' At that time Marholm did not know that she herself would fall victim to Strindberg's Medusa-fear. This was an ironic reward for the image of Strindberg that she carved - whom we believe has not been subject to such penetrating feminist analyses until our own day. Marholm was in fact the first to point out that Strindberg is the great masculinist in Swedish literature, and the foremost constructor of male consciousness. By directing attention to the cracks in the armor – the exaggerations, the repetitions, the strong affective charges – Marholm shows the significance of woman as man's Other. As early as 1888, in her first Strindberg article in *Gegenwart*, she is on the track of his misogyny and its function in his writings. She maintains that the new literary terrain Strindberg staked out is the war between the sexes:

And for every single misdeed the whole sex is brought to trial. Woman is not only unnatural; she is stupid, lazy, man's blood-sucker, false – and she is, above all, what cannot be forgiven – indispensible.[46]

In all her studies of Strindberg she heaps ambivalent praise on Strindberg. On the one hand he has given the struggle between the sexes 'a

---

pp. 353–396.

[45] In *Berliner Volksblatt*, 5 October, 1890. Brantly, *The Life and Writings of Laura Marholm*, p. 99f.

[46] Holger Drachmann, *En bok om Strindberg*, (Karlstad, 1894), p. 200ff.

language, a dialectics, an artistic shape,' on the other hand he is 'an inquisitional magistrate' who misses the 'richly fertile ground *below* consciousness.'[47] However, there has 'never been a writer who has offered suggestions with such brutal authority' and therefore given shape to 'the dark instincts of the hatred between the sexes.' On top of that, no writer has ever been so personal, which makes 'the riddle of his self' a perfect psychological raw material. In Strindberg's texts it becomes apparent that woman as a sphinx in man's unconscious is really 'man as a sphinx to himself', Marholm claims.

The couple Hansson-Marholm knew August Strindberg and invited him to join in on their exalted position as trendy intellectuals in Friedrichshagen, outside Berlin, in October 1892. Laura Marholm translated a couple of short stories from *Giftas* (*Married*), and *Fordringsägare* (*Creditors*) for free (the play was to be Strindberg's first success with seventy-one performances at the Residenztheater in Berlin around new-year 1893). Instead of thanking her, the paranoid Strindberg fled after only one month from 'Mrs. Bluebeard,' 'Mrs. Ola,' 'Mrs. Mara.'[48] A contributing cause to Ola Hansson and Laura Marholm's packing up their small family (a son had been born on September 8, 1890), and their moving to Schliersee in Bavaria was Strindberg's slanderous campaign against them.

Still, Strindberg had a point when he reproached Marholm for proclaiming 'the inferiority of the other lady writers,' so that she herself would appear as the great exception. When her female colleagues were dead, 'no longer able to spurt ink' she 'washes the corpses clean and exhibits them in the papers.'[49] Strindberg here refers primarily to Marholm's series 'Eine von ihnen,' alluding to Benedictsson's fate, which was published in three parts in *Das Magazin für Literatur*, while he shared a house with Hansson-Marholm in Friedrichshagen. Perhaps he knew that she was also writing about the recently deceased Anne Charlotte Edgren Leffler and Sonja Kovalevsky – as case studies of failed women's lives (for *Six Modern Women*).

---

[47] *Ibidem.* The essay is based on the Strindberg chapter in *Wir Frauen und unsere Dichter*, pp. 23-50.

[48] Adolf Paul, *Strindberg – minnen och brev* (Stockholm, 1915), p. 84f.

[49] *Ibidem*, p. 42.

*The New Woman and the Female Poetics of Decadence*

Laura Marholm's 'images-of women-criticism' in *Wir Frauen und un-sere Dichter* ends with the recommendation that women should not read male authors in order to understand themselves better. In most modern male literature women are portrayed as 'scum, vampires, wenches, hor-rid, sickly, disruptive creatures.' 'Everything that man has written about woman is a fiction based on their understanding of Woman.'[50] Primarily because of Strindberg, woman has become 'a parasite that man wants to rid himself of when she starts ageing.' Thus the modern woman needs a different role model, one that does not reduce her to a subordinate func-tion in man's egocentric imagination.

In *Six Modern Women* Marholm argues that it is in the most recent women's literature, that women can find resistance strategies against definitions of her as the Second sex. *Six Modern Women* was intended as a sequel to *Wir Frauen und unserer Dichter*. Both books consist on articles and reviews previously published in German-speaking papers. The first women writers to be treated by Marholm are French-Russian Marie Bashkirtseff's (1858-1884) posthumous diary in *Neue Freie Presse* in March, 1889,[51] and Victoria Benedictsson in 'Eine von ihnen' referred to above, in *Das Magazin für Litteratur*, 1892. The third writer was the English New-Woman writer under the pen-name George Egerton (Mary Chavelita Dunne Bright (1859-1945), in *Frankfurter Zeitung*, 1894.[52] It is in her analysis of Egerton's writings that Marholm offers the definition of New Woman fiction that is quoted to this day, and which she uses as a standard for Nordic writers.[53] It is also in this chapter that Marholm ex-hibits her stylistic repertoire and argues for an aesthetic feminism based on woman's essential difference from man.

[Men] have all overlooked the eternal wildness, the untamed primi-tive savage temperament that lurks in the mildest, best woman. Deep

---

[50] Laura Marholm, *Wir Frauen und unsere Dichter* (Wien, 1895), pp. 107-136.

[51] Laura Marholm, 'Das Tagebuch einer Künstlerin', *Neue Freie Presse*, 12 March, 1889.

[52] Laura Marholm, 'Nervöse Grundtöne. Ein Buch für Frauen', *Frankfurter Zeitung*, 22 April, 1894.

[53] Ann Ardis, *New Women, New Novels* (London, 1990), pp. 43-45.

in through ages of convention this primeval trait burns, an untam-
able quantity that may be concealed, but is never eradicated by culture, – the keynote of woman's witchcraft and woman's strength.[54]

According to Marholm, Egerton opens 'a new phase in woman' s nature'[55] with her first work, *Key Notes*, in 1893, a phase in which woman
no longer imitates man but instead perceives 'that he is quite different
from themselves, that he is the contrast to themselves.'[56] Egerton wrote
Galatea's history before Pygmalion. Undoubtedly George Egerton's focus
on the New Woman's self-confidence is also Marholm's stylistic ideal. The
Egerton chapter is her literary-political manifesto, an 'écriture féminine'
of a kind that looks at gender through the prism of the aesthetic rather
than the other way around: [57] 'Now that woman is conscious of her individuality as a woman, she needs an artistic mode of expression; she
flings aside the old forms, and seeks for new.'[58]
    Writing about women was a new territory for Laura Marholm who,
not least through her combat with Strindberg's projections, must have
realized the necessity to create a contrary discourse, a woman's speech.
Marholm wanted to become a 'Laura' who spoke back and thus created
a space for a gendered dialogue within modernity. Through her aesthetic
feminism Marholm intends to transform Strindberg's 'female beast' into
a wildly vibrating woman of the future, 'a new race of women'[59]. 'There
can be no doubt that there is a kind of genius peculiar to women, and
it is when a woman is a genius that she is most unlike man, and most
womanly; it is then that she creates through the instrumentality of her
womanly nature and refined senses.'[60]

---

[54] Marholm, *Six Modern Women*, p. 66.

[55] *Ibidem*, p. 81.

[56] *Ibidem*, p. 82.

[57] See Isobel Armstrong, *The Radical Aesthetic* (Oxford, 2000), pp. 13, 20. Armstrong, however, applies this question to the second-wave feminist theories of
Luce Irigaray, Julia Kristeva, and Hélène Cixous, who, deeply influenced by psy-
choanalysis, realized that the structural movement of thought and feeling is what
constitutes the aesthetic.

[58] Marholm, *Six Modern Women*, p. 79.

[59] *Ibidem*, p. 83.

[60] *Ibidem*, p. 126.

Provided that woman write without a 'tendency' – preferably auto-biographically about her own female experiences – fiction is the New Woman's natural territory. According to *Six Modern Women* it is only in the most recent women's literature that the New Woman speaks out: 'Another characteristic is beginning to make itself felt, which was bound to come at last. And that is an intense and morbid consciousness of the ego in women. This consciousness was unknown to our mothers and grandmothers.'[61]

*Six Modern Women* reached the German bookstores just before Christmas 1894, in an exquisite gift edition with photo portraits. Six current women types are scrutinized through an essentialist lens in separate chapters: Marie Bashkirtseff ('A Young Girl's Tragedy'), Anne Charlotte Edgren Leffler ('The Woman's Rights Woman'), Eleonora Duse (1858–1924) ('The Modern Woman on the Stage'), George Egerton ('Neurotic Keynotes'), Amalie Skram ('The Woman Naturalist'), Sonja Kovalevsky ('The Learned Woman'). In this Internationale of women as upholders of culture Marholm is not looking for their professionalism or fame, but their 'keynote,' and she asks herself how these six modern women manage the life experience of being a woman, after the woman question has created an 'internal division' affecting women's sense and nature?[62]

The question about woman's true nature proved to be a matter of life and death. Three of Marholm's typical women had ended up dead (Bashkirtseff, Kovalevsky and Edgren Leffler), according to Marholm because of their inclination for modernity's 'urge for hybrid sterility' instead of motherly, heterosexual femininity. The fact that both Kovalevsky and Bashkirtseff were 'superior natures, innate children of nature, possessing freedom's proud, unbounded power and charm' did not help.[63] When they, being women, tried to compete with men, they still became, in Key's words, examples of 'misused female powers.'[64] Marholm insists on having woman's self-fulfillment rest on the necessity to being loved by a man, which tends to lock the New Woman into a Sleeping-Beauty stereotype: 'Not motherhood, but the lover's kiss, awakens the Sleeping

---

[61] *Ibidem*, p. 79.

[62] From the preface of the German edition. Laura Marholm, *Das Buch der Frauen. Zeitpsychologische Portraits* (Paris/Leipzig, 1895), p. 3f.

[63] *Ibidem*.

[64] Key, *Missbrukad kvinnokraft*.

Beauty.'[65] Marholm's often seductively reassuring text – for women readers – takes on a manipulative and conservative trait through its heterosexual tendency.

The two Scandinavian women in the book exemplify two poles of the female scale: the successful (Amalie Skram) and the failed (Anne Charlotte Edgren Leffler). According to Marholm, Amalie Skram became the greatest 'natural' naturalist when she stopped being 'a thinking, working, neutral organism'[66] and let her husband's, Erik Skram's 'superior culture' liberate 'her fresh, wild, primitive nature from the parasites of social problems.'[67] Anne Charlotte Edgren Leffler, on the other hand, had a longer road to travel before she found favor with Marholm – with the novel *En sommarsaga*, published during her last years. Here is to be found, according to the severe critic, 'a hasty, uneven beat of the pulse, something of the fever of awakened passion',[68] which saves Swedish literature from the philistinism that characterizes Anna-Maria Lenngren (1754–1817), Fredrika Bremer (1801–1865) and Emilie Flygare–Carlén (1807–1892), in Marholm's view. The chapter ends with Edgren Leffler's marriage to the mathematician and Count of Cajanello in Naples, in 1890, her maternity at the age of forty-three, and sudden, tragic death (in appendicitis). Whenever femininity equals experienced heterosexual eroticism, Edgren Leffler conforms to Marholm's concept:

> The unfruitful became fruitful; the emaciated became beautiful; the woman's rights woman sang a hymn to the mystery of love; and the last short years of happiness, too soon interrupted by death, were a contradiction to the long insipid period of literary production.[69]

It should be noted that Laura Marholm, who was a well-known and skilled theatre critic, writes a competent and largely positive survey of Anne Charlotte Edgren Leffler's plays, that were known also in Europe. An exception is her successful play *True Women* (1893) is an exception. With this work, Edgren Leffler became 'the ordinary platform woman,'

---

[65] Marholm, *Six modern women*, p. 41.

[66] *Ibidem*, p. 135.

[67] *Ibidem*, p. 141.

[68] *Ibidem*, p. 211.

[69] *Ibidem*, p. 213.

according to Marholm, and is made to represent the triumph of medi-
ocrity over female individuality, and of woman's critique of man' which
'has inspired man to write a misogynist Song of Songs.'[70] With this mer-
ciless verdict Marholm condones the view of the female Breakthrough
as banal, mediocre, and moralizing, a view that has come to dominate
literary history and has, to this day, withheld great Swedish playwrights
from the audience, playwrights such as Edgren Leffler, Alfhild Agrell,
Victoria Benedictsson, and others.

However, in *Six Modern Women* the disgraceful portrayal of Edgren
Leffler as a representative for the 1880s was meant to facilitate Marholm's
launching of the George Egerton program and, in addition, of her own
New Woman fiction. Marholm's fiction, with its focus on the significance of motherhood for woman, is more closely related to Egerton than
Edgren Leffler and to women authors of the Modern Breakthrough. The
omniscient narrator of realism is replaced by an inner narrator, often
'we women,' inviting the reader to identification. Similarly to Egerton,
Marholm tried to develop what was to become the modern, psychologically dense short story, with its focus on the intense moment of a
decisive meeting, a self-realization, and a love-affair. According to Gerd
Bjørhovde, New Woman fiction is characterized by rudimentary plots
and vague endings open to interpretation, and thus by a certain disharmony and ambivalence.[71] This applies to Marholm's fiction as well.
Her alter egos Lonny and Lilly in 'What was that?' in *Zwei Frauenerlebnisse*, and in *Lilly som ungmö, maka och mor* (Lily as maiden, wife, and
mother), are attempts to portray the psychologically, intellectually and
sexually self-confident New Woman, at home in metropolitan as well
as in provincial communities – looking for a New Man (with traits of
Ola Hansson). The idealization of the New Man's capacity to appreciate
the New Woman's complexity has its rifts, which is evident not least in
Marholm's second best-seller.

In *Studies in the Psychology of Woman* there is, as Susan Brantly remarks, 'a change in woman's raison d'être from her love for a husband
to carrying a child.'[72] The book is a manifesto of difference feminism, an

---

[70] *Ibidem*, p. 209.

[71] See Gerd Bjørhovde, *Rebellious Structures. Women Writers and the Crisis of the
Novel 1880–1900* (Oslo, 1987).

[72] Brantly, *The life and writings of Laura Marholm*, p. 184.

attempt to write the history of the sexes' culture and degeneration, and a magnificent showpiece of decadence theory. With this work Marholm sought to match the great social critics of her day: Max Nordau, Cesare Lombroso, Richard Krafft-Ebing and Havelock Ellis. In the very opening Marholm states that gender is the fateful question of the times, and that the relations between men and women are as unfamiliar as America before its discovery. Humanity appears shattered through unsatisfied women and indifferent men. As a consequence of these conditions woman loses respect for man and turns feminist out of desperation. To Marholm, woman's emancipation is synonymous with her despair over herself as a woman.

In *Studies in the Psychology of Woman* we read that it was 'Camilla Collet, one of the oldest 'Woman's Rights' women in Europe" who, with her novel '*The Magistrate's Daughter*', [---] the first bugle-call from the 'camp of the dumb', had given Ibsen the impetus to that great literature on the position of woman' which made him famous.[73] Collet herself, 'like a lost spirit,' was made to wander 'from one acquaintance to another, unsocial, solitary, perplexed; seeking; [---] embittered, lonely, revolving in a circle about her own shrunken ego; tenacious, careworn, a strange contradiction of all the richness of her experience.'[74] It is in response to Collett's summons that Marholm, in the book's opening allegory, appears as the interpreter of all dissatisfied contemporary women who, with 'the distressed cry of unhappy woman,'[75] look for their task but sometimes 'die on the Way'.[76] One of them is her husband's former companion in the writers' constellation 'Unga Skåne', Mathilda Kruse (1864–1942, with Malling as her married name).[77] Under the pseudonym Stella Kleve she was promising when she daringly described 'the psychology of feminine artfulness and the erotic side of young maidens,' in works such as 'Pyrrhus Conquests' in the 1880s.[78] However, she was 'simply trampled and thundered down by the apostles of morality, by

---

[73] Laura Marholm, *Studies in the Psychology of Woman*, transl. Georgia A. Etchison (New York, 1906), p. 24.

[74] *Ibidem*, p. 25.

[75] *Ibidem*, p. 27.

[76] *Ibidem*, p. 158.

[77] See Witt-Brattström, *Dekadensens kön*, pp.137-163.

[78] *Ibidem*, p. 228.

woman's rights advocates with and without petticoats, and by the intellectuals in her homeland; and no one came to her aid.'[79]

It is striking that Marholm, despite her heterosexual love ideal dwells on the resistance that women encounter, be it negative criticism or unhappy life conditions, which lends the narrative a sad key. For instance, the book's female ideal, the Swedish writer Hilma Angered Strandberg who was broken down as an emigrant in the USA, is not the least relieved by being happily married.[80] It is due to the spirit of the age that even a sterling woman perishes, a woman with the qualities of a Selma Lagerlöf (1858–1940), 'whose Vermlandic heart would like to thaw and melt, but finds no material – no substance to fasten upon and make itself live thereby' – read no motherhood.[81] This is all that Marholm has to say about Lagerlöf. About Victoria Benedictsson, however, she has a great deal to say, as she is made to illustrate the precariousness of constructing the New Woman at the expense of the 'old' one. The disharmony that characterizes New Woman fiction in Bjørhovde's view, in Marholm's work causes the daughter's unresolved conflict with her archaic rival (the phallic mother), lurking beneath a programmatic heterosexuality, as we now shall see.

*The Combat between the New, and the Dead Woman*

Laura Marholm's female characters Lonny and Lilly get married. Lonny's happy female life as Mrs. Lonny Borg in 'The Unspoken' in *Zwei Frauenerlebnisse* is compared to the unhappy writer Emma Louise Wikman (alias Victoria Benedictsson), who commits suicide. The naturalistic, detailed account of her Swedish colleague's taking 'the knife in her hand to mangle herself, like a bungling slaughterer a resistant animal,' upset the Nordic readers when it was published in Swedish in 1896, eight years after Benedictsson's suicide in Copenhagen as a consequence of her much publicized love-affair with Brandes, which attracted much attention. The male character that causes Wikman's death bears a resemblance to Georg Brandes, as do similar characters in the other texts-à-clèf.

---

[79] *Ibidem*, p. 232.

[80] *Ibidem*, pp. 162-179.

[81] *Ibidem*, p. 178.

The story that 'The Unspoken' is based on, 'En av dem' ('One of Them'), was serialized in three issues of *Das Magazin für Literatur*, 1892. Here the suicidal character is named Emma Lovisa Arnoldson (with the pen-name 'Onkel Karl', alluding to Benedictsson's male pen-name), and it is this story that made Strindberg call Laura Marholm 'die Leichenfrau', at the time when they shared house in Friedrichshagen. It is implied that Mrs. Mara was a parasite on the fate of Victoria Benedictsson - in order for Marholm herself to appear as a successful female writer, loved by her husband. 'Onkel Karl' is described as 'a neuter, a monstrosity without a keen scent, without psychological kinship', and her writing as 'female botch-up'. Laura Marholm who had associated with Victoria Benedictsson during a stay in Paris in 1887, knew that a contributing cause to her suicide was Brandes' disparagement of her novel *Fru Marianne* as a 'lady's novel'.[82] In other words: *Fru Marianne*'s female experiences were uninteresting in the modernity's brother-society.

The younger writer's obsession with her older colleague is interesting from a literary-political perspective and uncanny from a female psychological perspective. Besides being the model of characters in 'One of them' and in 'The Unspoken', Victoria Benedictsson is also the model of the world-famous violinist in *Karla Bühring* – 'Ein Frauendrama' (A Woman drama, 1895). The story takes place at a seaside resort. Karla Bühring loves the Aryan Otto von Wetterberg but is willingly seduced by the Jewish Dr. Siegfried Collander (Brandes was of Jewish extraction), whereupon she shoots herself out of self-contempt. Karla's Baltic-German friend, Lilly Bloom, also figuring in the play, is secretly in love with von Wetterberg. But for this Nordic man, with unmistakable traits of Hansson (a blond mustache and a self-esteem unfashionable in a Plebeian age), to notice the plain Lilly, the self-assertive Karla has to die. With such a triangle of desire it is no surprise that Victoria Benedictsson (whom Ola Hansson knew well during the 1880s) is the great Scandinavian predecessor that has to be removed time and again in Marholm's writings. In these three texts-à-clèf the focus – in accordance with Marholm's New Woman perspective – is on the female body's sensual experiences and, to a greater extent than in the genre as a whole – on manic depression and self-hatred. Both themes point to Marholm's psy-

---

[82] Ebba Witt-Brattström, ed, *Ord på liv och död I-II, Kortprosa, dramatik, dagbok* (Stockholm, 2008), p. 834.

chological breakdown which culminated in her confinement for 'severe paranoid psychosis' in April to September 1905 at the Kreisirrenanstalt in Munich.[83] Thereafter she laid down her pen.

In Marholm's writings Benedictsson figures as the specter of the fettered female sex – a symbol of oppression which the New Woman wants to reject but which instead invades her unconscious. Benedictsson's posthumous prose narrative, 'Out of the Darkness', where the depressive Nina gives evidence of her failed woman's life, is to Marholm her colleague's symbolic legacy: woman as modernity's pariah. 'In a woman everything is shame, for she is nothing in herself, only part of her sex,' says Nina, before she confesses her unrequited love: 'But I felt one day, that I was a woman, because I fell in love.'[84] We recognize the main principle of Marholm's difference feminism. In 'The Unspoken' Lonny claims that there was 'a formula which could save Emma Wikman,' – that instead of adapting to men as a degenerate half-woman, she should have taken her womanly nature seriously. The dead Emma Wikman haunts Lonny like a specter with black, reproachful eyes, and says: 'Why did you not tell me what you saw through and I did not? Why did you not speak to me, woman to woman? Why did you let me perish?'[85]

When Victoria Benedictsson's alter ego commits her blood-stained suicide in 'Det osagda,' it appears through the intense narration as a symbolic action that de facto undermines the message of the heterosexual ideal, the natural alliance between the sexes that Marholm wanted to convey through her Nordic cultural transmission. Thus a natural, proud woman figure that can attract man with her 'womanly nature', is shown to be an illusion All that is left is the self-hatred and shame of the superfluous female gender in modernity's unisexual society. Expressed differently: the female poetics of decadence, 'woman's disclosure of her own self,' for all its zealous truth-seeking, seems to lead unfailingly to a melancholy that inscribes its heterosexual vengeance on the body of woman:

Only a very little blood crept out, and it was taking far too long for her. She reached for the hand mirror, adjusted the lamp and bent her

---

[83] Witt-Brattström, *Dekadensens kön*, pp. 359-364.

[84] Witt-Brattström, *Ord på liv och död I*, p. 95.

[85] Laura Marholm, *Zwei Frauenerlebnisse, Novellen* (Berlin, 1895), p. 209.

neck to the side. So! But once again it did not cut. At that point an inexpressible rage swelled within her, a brutal need for self-destruction, a base desire for the vile, the loathsome – and, like a momentary flash of lightning, the whole, loathsome insipidity of her life passed before her, she leapt out of the bed, stood up straight, pulled the knife across the carotid artery in her neck behind her ear, once, and so again, cutting, cutting, cutting… She collapsed, writhing on the mat beside the bed, then stretched out and remained lying there, her limbs long, rigid and outstretched.[86]

---

[86] Translation by Claire Hogarth, from Lisbeth Larsson, 'About Her Dead Body', in: Ebba Witt-Brattström, ed, *The New Woman and the Aesthetic Opening. Unlocking Gender in Twentieth-Century Texts* (Stockholm, 2004), p. 45.

# Margaretha Meyboom (1856–1927) – 'Cultural Transmitter', Feminist or Socialist?

> Jag känner mig tacksam mot hennes fosterland, som har skänkt mig denna trogna banbryterska, denna oöverträffliga hjälparinna, denna goda och tåliga vän.[1]

Scandinavian literature was considered as something new and 'refreshing' in many literary circles in Europe around 1900. This period in literary is history called the 'Modern Breakthrough', a movement which criticized the social structure. Modern ideas such as feminism and equality flowed into Europe from the North.[2] Of course, translators – or cultural transmitters – played an important role in this process.

One of the many translators in the Netherlands at that time, was Margaretha Meyboom. She is the centre point of this article. Her life and work will be thoroughly scrutinized, and after that the following question will be discussed: Was Margaretha Meyboom mainly a 'cultural transmitter', a feminist or a socialist? At this point there will also be a closer examination of the term 'cultural transmitter'.[3]

---

[1] 'I feel grateful towards her fatherland which has given me this faithful pioneer, this unsurpassable helper, this good and patient friend.' Selma Lagerlöf about her translator Margaretha Meyboom in: Claudine S. Bienfait, ed, *In herinnering aan Margaretha Meyboom. Door haar vrienden* (s. l., [1930]), p. 58.

[2] Sven H. Rossel, ed, *A History of Danish literature* (=Vol. 1 of A History of Scandinavian literature) (Nebraska, 1992), pp. 261-316.
Petra Broomans, 'Hur skapas en litteraturhistorisk bild? Den nordiska litteraturens fräschhet i Nederländerna och Flandern?', in: Per Dahl and Torill Steinfeld, eds, *Videnskab og national opdragelse. Studier i nordisk litteraturhistorieskrivning* 2 (København, 2001a), p. 494.

[3] This article on Meyboom forms part of PhD-research that is currently being conducted at the Institute for Scandinavian Studies at the University of Groningen. This research is investigating the work and networks of female cultural transmit-

*Main stages of Margaretha Meyboom's life*

Margaretha Meyboom was born into a preacher's family in Amsterdam in 1856. From her father Louis Susan Pedro Meyboom (1817–1874), a liberal priest of the Dutch reformed church, Meyboom inherited her social ideas and also her interest for Scandinavian literature. On the one hand Louis Meyboom was a pioneer of modern theology, on the other hand was he very interested in old, heathen religions. His work included a piece titled *De godsdienst der oude Noormannen*[4]. He read to his children from this book, which might have laid the foundation for Margaretha's literary interest. With help of from her father's books and a Danish grammar book, she taught herself Danish at the age of 17 in order to read his other Scandinavian books. A priest of the Norwegian sailor's church helped to teach her the right pronunciation. Soon Meyboom started to translate stories from these books and send them to newspapers such as *Nieuws van den Dag*, where they were published. Her translating career had begun.[5]

In 1881 the Meyboom family moved to The Hague, where Margaretha became involved in social work. After a while of private tutoring at their home, Meyboom developed the need for further education and meaningful occupation. She accepted a teacher's position at a Sunday school, where she taught people how to read.

During her first stay in Denmark in 1890 she perfected her Danish. Around this time she also acquired sufficient knowledge of Norwegian and Swedish to enable her to begin translating literature in 1891. Soon after her return to Holland she moved to Groningen to support her widower brother. There she continued with her translating and social work.

---

ters of Scandinavian literature around 1900 in the Dutch/Flemish region on the one hand, and the Austrian/German speaking region on the other hand. Ester Jiresch, *Die Rolle von Netzwerken in der Arbeit von weiblichen Vermittlern skandinavischer Literatur und Kultur und das von ihnen vermittelte Bild in Europa um 1900. Eine vergleichende Studie des niederländischen/flämischen und deutschen/österreichischen Sprachraums* (Groningen, in progress).

[4] Louis S. P. Meyboom, *De godsdienst der oude Noormannen* (Haarlem, 1868).

[5] Hendrik G. Cannegieter, 'Karakterschets. Margaretha Meyboom', *Morks-Magazijn* 27 (1925), pp. 3-4. Cannegieter did not give further information on which books Meyboom actually read and translated.

In 1903 she moved again to Rijswijk (North Holland), where she carried out her biggest social enterprise and stayed there for more than 20 years. More information on this enterprise will follow later on. Meyboom spent her last three years in Voorburg (North Holland) until her death in 1927.[6]

## Work in the literary field

### 1. Translations

Starting in 1891, Meyboom translated more than 50 pieces by Scandinavian authors in her life. Besides the two Swedes Selma Lagerlöf (1858–1940) and Tor Hedberg (1862–1931) she mainly translated Danish and Norwegian authors. Amongst them you can find Bjørnstjerne Bjørnson (1832–1910), Henrik Ibsen(1828–1906), Knut Hamsun(1860–1952), Alexander Kielland (1849–1906), Carl Ewald (1856–1908), Adda Ravnkilde (1862–1883), Arne Garborg (1851–1924).[7]

Her favorites were Lagerlöf and Bjørnson, of whom she translated almost the whole oeuvre. Meyboom continued exchanging letters with Lagerlöf for decades. The content of this correspondence was first and foremost related to business. Meyboom, intrigued by Lagerlöf's work and personality, tried to establish a more personal relationship with the author. But the Swede kept her distance and declined several invitations by Meyboom to visit the Netherlands to give speeches there. They only met once in person in 1894 at the 50 years anniversary of the Copenhagen Womens Library.[8]

In Amsterdam Meyboom used Herman Johan Wilhelm Becht

---

[6] Lizet Duyvendak, 'Meijboom, Margaretha Anna Sophia', in: *Biographisch woordenboek van Nederland 5* (Den Haag, 2001), pp. 332-334.

[7] For a detailed overview of Meyboom's translations see Sent Marks, *Margaretha Meyboom (1856-1927). En eldsjäl för den nordiska litteraturen i Nederländerna. En inventering av Meybooms litterära aktiviteter* (Groningen, 2000) (unpublished masterthesis).

[8] Margaretha Meyboom, *Selma Lagerlöf* (=*Skandinavische Bibliotheek*, H. Logeman, ed, volume missing) (Leiden, 1919), p. 63; Stine de Vrieze, 'Selma Lagerlöf och Margaretha Meyboom', in: Lagerlöfsällskapet (Bengt Ek et. al., eds), *Lagerlöfstudier 6* (Lund, 1979), p. 103.

(1862–1922) to publish Lagerlöf's work.[9] She kept a strong professional
relationship with Becht and he also published several of her other translations. Another publishing house, *Wereldbibliotheek*, employed Meyboom as their regular translator for Scandinavian languages.[10]

In various contemporary articles her translations were praised a great
deal by the critics.

> Ze [Meyboom ej] voelt het verborgene, het onuitgesprokene, dat,
> wat achter de dingen ligt. Vandaar die sobere, ik zou bijna zeggen,
> ingetogen vertalingen. De woorden werden overgebracht in een an-
> dere taal, maar de kleur werd vastgehouden, de sfeer waarin het boek
> ontstaan was, ging niet verloren. Het bleef een Scandinavisch boek.
> Haar poëtische geest kon Selma Lagerlöf's figuren volgen in al hun
> grillige grootheden hun even grillige onvolkomenheid.[11]

The authors themselves were also satisfied most of the time. This information can be retrieved from personal letters that the authors wrote to
Meyboom. For example Lagerlöf, after receiving some newspaper reviews, wrote the following:

> Det var mycket roligt att se recensionerna och finna att boken [*Gösta
> Berlings saga*[12] ej] i allmänhet fått ett så gott mottagelse. Det gläder
> nog också Er, som haft det stora arbetet med öfversättningen.[13]

---

[9] *Ibidem*; Jan Schilt, *100 jaar H. J. W. Becht uitgever 1892–1992. Impressie van een
eeuw boeken maken en verkopen* (Haarlem, 1992).

[10] Duyvendak, 'Meijboom, Margaretha Anna Sophia', p. 333.

[11] 'She [Meyboom ej] feels the hidden, the unspoken, what lies beneath things. That
is why her translations are sober, I should almost say reserved. The words are
transmitted into another language, but the colour is preserved, the atmosphere
where the book has developed is not lost. It remained a Scandinavian book. Her
poetical spirit could follow Selma Lagerlöf's characters in all their quirky greatness and their even quirky unperfection.' See Claudine Bienfait, 'Margaretha
Meyboom.' in: *Leven en Werken. Maandblad voor Meisjes en Vrouwen 12* (Amsterdam 1927), p. 832. [All translations from Dutch into English have been made
by Ester Jiresch]

[12] Selma Lagerlöf, *Gösta Berlings saga* (Stockholm, 1891).

[13] 'It was very nice to see the reviews and to realise that the book [Gösta Berlings

## 2. Articles and magazines

Besides her work as a translator, Meyboom gave Danish and Norwegian lessons and wrote many articles concerning Scandinavian culture and literature and about social issues. These articles were published in well known Dutch magazines like *De Gids, De Boekzaal* and *Eigen Haard*. On several occasions Meyboom indicated very clearly why she and many of her colleagues were so enthusiastic about the Scandinavian countries, for example in this article she wrote on Scandinavian literature in the Netherlands in 1911:

> Toen we eenmaal gezien hadden hoeveel wij Hollanders van Deenen, Noren en Zweden konden leren op het gebied van sociale toestanden, vrouwenbeweging, handenarbeid en onderwijs, namen wij elke gelegenheid waar, daar met allen nadruk op te wijzen, en er allerwege belangstelling voor te wekken.[14]

Moreover Meyboom managed to launch her own magazines in 1904. These magazines dealt with Scandinavian topics exclusively. Her main goal was to spread knowledge about Scandinavian culture and intensify interest in it in the Netherlands. The Dutch people needed to become acquainted to the – in her eyes – wonderful culture of the Scandinavian countries. Meyboom's magazines can be seen as the peak of interest in the Scandinavian cultures in the Netherlands around 1900.[15]

---

saga ej] was generally well received. This must be pleasing as well for you, who had all the hard work with the translation.' Letter from Lagerlöf to Meyboom Falun, 30 May, 1899. Nederlands Letterkundig Museum in The Hague.

[14] 'When we finally realised how much we Dutch could learn from the Danes, Norwegians and Swedes on the field of social conditions, women's movement, handicraft and education, we seized every opportunity to overemphasise this, and to arouse interest everywhere.' See Margaretha Meyboom, 'Skandinavische litteratuur in Nederland', in: *De Boekzaal* 5 (Zwolle, 1911a), p. 48.

[15] Petra Broomans, 'Scandia i Nederländerna. Om Margaretha Meijboom och hennes nordiska tidskrifter', in: *Tijdschrift voor Skandinavistiek Vol 22*, Nr. 1 (Amsterdam, 2001b), pp.159-161.

The first magazine was called *Scandia*[16] (first published in 1904) and
was actually not an independent paper, but a supplement too *Lente.
Weekblad voor jonge dames*.[17] *Lente* was published from 1899 until 1904
and Meyboom was employed as an editor from 1902 until 1904. She had
already published several articles in *Lente* about Scandinavia.

*Scandia* contained articles about Scandinavian literature and culture
in Dutch and the Scandinavian languages. There was even a special issue printed with Dutch translations of literary texts, for instance stories,
parts of novels and travelogues.

In 1904 the weekly paper *Lente* stopped and so did its Scandinavian
supplement. From 1905 until 1906 Meyboom launched the successor
of *Scandia*: *Scandinavië-Nederland*.[18] With this paper she wanted to address not only a Dutch, but also a Scandinavian audience. There were
articles about Scandinavian topics in Dutch and vice versa. The magazine contained different categories including literature, languages and a
chronicle. Meyboom had many co-workers. Even some of the Scandinavian authors she was so fond of supported her, like Arne and Hulda
Garborg (1862–1934). The famous literary critic and historian Georg
Brandes (1842–1927) also belonged to her staff. In editing the paper
Meyboom was supported by Hendrik (Henri) Logeman (1862–1936), a
professor for Scandinavian languages at the University of Gent, his wife
Dina (Dien) Logeman–van der Willigen (1864–1925), a translator colleague of Meyboom and publisher Geertruida Römelingh (1850–1944)
in Groningen. The staff of the magazines remained more or less the
same. Meyboom had access to a widespread network of Dutch and international co–workers.[19]

---

[16] Margaretha Meyboom, et al., eds, *Scandia. Maandblad voor Scandinavische Taal
en Letteren* (Groningen, 1904)

[17] For further information on this paper see Marks, *Margaretha Meyboom*, pp. 43-
48.

[18] Margaretha Meyboom, ed, *Scandinavië-Nederland. Tijdschrift voor Nederlandsche en Scandinavische Taal, Letteren en Kultuur* (Amsterdam 1905–1906);
Broomans, 'Scandia i Nederländerna. Om Margaretha Meijboom och hennes
nordiska tidskrifter', p. 164.

[19] Broomans, 'Scandia i Nederländerna. Om Margaretha Meijboom och hennes
nordiska tidskrifter', pp. 159-161; Jiresch, *Die Rolle von Netzwerken*.

Unfortunately *Scandia*, and his successor *Scandinavië-Nederland*, were forced to stop after two years due to a lack of money.[20] Nevertheless this must be seen as a major attempt at transmitting a foreign country's literature and culture.

## Transmitting Scandinavian literature and culture

As already has been mentioned, Meyboom translated more than 50 pieces by Scandinavian authors and she even wrote several articles on Scandinavian literature. In these articles a clear picture emerged of these Scandinavian writers and their culture in general. Meyboom's opinion of the North and the picture she transmitted through her written work were principally very positive.

For example, she held Bjørnstjerne Bjørnson, one of her favorites, in such high regard because in her eyes he represented an ideal personality. His dedication to justice in his actions and writings was praised a great deal by the translator. In Bjørnson's stories, the ancient sagas from the North, which Meyboom felt so related to, were resurrected from the past. To Meyboom, Bjørnson was fresh and vigorous, as a writer and as a human being.[21]

Shortly after his death, Meyboom honored the Norwegian National poet in an elaborate article.[22] In it she provided an overview of his life and writings. Meyboom was of the opinion that one had to be acquainted with Bjørnson's childhood and adolescence in order to understand the special meaning of his work. Many of his memories and experiences were used in his writings. His adventurous fights against the raw, Norwegian nature, his observation of nature's beauty, his profound knowledge of the ancient sagas, his subtle psychological understanding and his touching description of characters were part of his inner life and his works. Meyboom wrote: 'En wat hem als schrijver zoo onweerstaan-

---

[20] For further information on Meyboom's magazines see Broomans' articles 'Scandia i Nederländerna. Om Margaretha Meijboom och hennes nordiska tidskrifter' and 'Hur skapas en litteraturhistorisk bild? Den nordiska litteraturens fräschhet i Nederländerna och Flandern'.

[21] Marks, *Margaretha Meyboom (1856–1927)*, p. 26.

[22] Margaretha Meyboom, *Bjørnstjerne Bjørnson* (=*Mannen en vrouwen van beteekenis in onze dagen* 41, no. 7) (Haarlem, 1911b).

baar maakt, is dat men in elk van zijn werken een menschenhart voelt kloppen, een menschenziel hoort jubelen of klagen.'[23] As person and as author, he appeared with 'de frissche kracht van een bruisend voelen'[24], never with false reservation. Meyboom used to cite numerous examples from his works, where childhood memories play a big part. On the whole the article is a dedicated glorification. One almost can feel Meyboom's great admiration and appreciation:

> Zijn vertellingen hebben een zeldzame frisschheid met hun korten, snellen dialoog, hun teerheid van stemming, hun grote dramatische kracht. Het forsch ingehoudene uit de oude sagen, de fijne buigzaamheid van de moderne schildering is er vereenigd in ongeëvenaarde harmonie.[25]

Meyboom composed a biographical monography about Lagerlöf, even when the writer was still alive.[26] There she offers a chronological overview of Lagerlöf's works and a lot of biographical information. Long citations from the originals are combined with Meyboom's personal comments and explanation of the texts. A consistently positive impression of Lagerlöf's prose prevailed, however Meyboom did not stay completely uncritical and pointed out some aspects and passages that she deemed dissonant or poorly conceived. She critisised, for example, Lagerlöf's tendency towards black and white painting. As an example she gave the character of the stepmother in *Liljecronas hem*[27]: 'Toch treft het ons, dat Selma Lagerlöf geen meesteres is in 't tekenen van diep bedorven

---

[23] 'And what makes him so irresistible as a writer, is that one can feel the beating of a human heart in every of his stories, one can hear the cheers and laments of a human soul.' *Ibidem*, 18.

[24] 'the fresh power of a booming sentiment' *Ibidem*.

[25] 'His stories own a rare freshness with their short, quick dialogues, the tenderness of their mood, their great dramatic power. The vigorous restraint of the ancient sagas, and the smooth flexibility of the modern narration are combined in unexcelled harmony.' *Ibidem*, 22.

[26] Meyboom, *Selma Lagerlöf*.

[27] Selma Lagerlöf, *Liljecronas hem* (Stockholm, 1911).

mensen. De stiefmoeder gedraagt zich als een ware draak.'[28] Meyboom
compares her to Jonas Lie (1833–1908):

> Ze doet ons denken aan Lindelin,[29] de booze vrouw, die Jonas Lie in
> zijn drama van dien naam teekende, zoo slang-achtig, zo booze geest-
> achtig, dat we den schrijver verdenken haar uit de troldenwereld te
> hebben gehaald, en ze niet in de werkelijkheid te hebben ontmoet. In
> beide figuren missen we dat mengsel van goed en kwaad, van donker
> en licht, dat zelfs in den grootsten booswicht te vinden is.[30]

Nevertheless Meyboom's book is primarily showing her deference to
and appreciation of Lagerlöf's art of storytelling. Very similar to her article about Bjørnson, Meyboom's goal was to convey this enthusiasm to
her audience. She seemed to want to take the reader's hand (talking to
him/her personally) and guide him to her beloved literature. Her way
of giving comments was very lively. Meyboom's enthusiasm gave the
impression that something very precious would be missed if one did
not delve into Lagerlöf's books. Lagerlöf's keen sense of emotions and
her profound way of depicting natural phenomena and interpersonal
relationships were especially praised by Meyboom. In her other articles
Meyboom proceeded in a similar vein. We meet the same enthusiasm
when Meyboom speaks about the literature she appreciated so highly,
although she always took the position of a competent critic.

Meyboom chose the works she translated according to her view of
life and her ideals. She primarily translated authors' social realistic prose.
Some of them belonged to the movement of the 'Modern Breakthrough'
like Ibsen, Bjørnson, Hamsun, etc. In both her enterprises [see below]
and her literary activity she tried to create a better world.[31]

---

[28] 'It hits us though, that Selma Lagerlöf is no master in drawing deeply corrupted
persons. The stepmother acts as a true dragon.' Meyboom, *Selma Lagerlöf*, p. 72.

[29] Jonas Lie, *Lindelin* (Kopenhagen, 1897)

[30] 'She makes us think about Lindelin, the mean woman, who Jonas Lie depicted
in his drama of the same title, so snake-like, so evil spirited, that we suspect the
author to have picked her from the world of trolls, not having met her in reality.
In both characters we miss the mixture of good and bad, of darkness and light,
which we find even in the greatest villain.' Meyboom, *Selma Lagerlöf*, p. 72.

[31] Marks, *Margaretha Meyboom (1856–1927)*, p. 40.

Meyboom did not just set a value for content but also for style. This can be observed in her essay[32] from 1911. This article presents the first list of Scandinavian literature translated to Dutch in the period of 1847 until 1909. Meyboom did not claim that her compilation was complete, and she only based herself on the lists of published books: 'Dit korte overzicht geeft allerminst een volledig beeld van den omvang van de in 't nederlandsch overgezette literatuur. Het is alleen gebouwd op de lijsten van in den handel gekomen boeken.'[33] She dwelled on different genres and authors and described several periods of reception. Famous names as Ludvig Holberg (1684–1754), Henrik Ibsen, Selma Lagerlöf, Ellen Key (1849–1926), August Strindberg (1849–1912), Tor Hedberg and Gustaf af Geijerstam (1858–1909), who appeared at the end of the nineteenth century, were noted to be of literary value.

A statistic from the years 1903–1909 shows that the translation and distribution of Scandinavian literature reached their peak in this period. 1906 was the top year with 32 works. The languages of origin were equally distributed. After 1907 the numbers declined noticeably. Meyboom observed that from this time on many unknown names and pseudonyms appeared amongst the writers. 'We zijn blijkbaar in den zondvloed van moderne schrijvers geraakt.'[34] She criticised the choice of translators and publishers, who in her opinion randomly accepted everything that came from the North, without paying attention to the quality of the literature. Moreover it astonished Meyboom not to find more works of Verner von Heidenstam (1859–1940), Georg Brandes or Arne Garborg, who she regarded as of literary higher standing than Ingeborg Maria Sick (1858–1951) and Jenny Blicher–Clausen (1865–1907), whose books appeared more often in the distribution lists. Meyboom expressed her concern that the Dutch audience would not get a good picture of Nordic literature: 'En 't groote publiek raakte in de war en kon zich geen heldere vorstelling maken van de letterkunde van het Noorden.'[35]

---

[32] Meyboom, 'Skandinavische litteratuur in Nederland,' pp. 45-49.

[33] 'This short overview does not in the least provide a complete picture of the amount of literature translated into Dutch. It is merely based on lists of books appeared in commerce.' *Ibidem*, p. 47.

[34] 'We have apparently been flooded by the deluge of modern writers.' Meyboom, 'Skandinavische litteratuur in Nederland,' p. 48.

[35] 'And the wider audience was confused and could not develop a clear picture of

At last Meyboom disapproved of translators with – according to her - less profound judgment and those who, due to economic reasons, would translate everything that was offered to them. Meyboom stated these reasons, as well as an increased knowledge of foreign languages, as the causes for the decline in interest in translations from Scandinavian literature.

Diedrik Grit commented in his bibliography[36] on Meyboom's article quite negatively: 'Medtager kun oversættelser i bogform. Meget mangelfuldt.'[37] This may indeed comply to scientific truth, but at this point Meyboom's personal circumstances and her possibilities of investigation should nevertheless be taken into consideration prior to an evaluation. The author herself offered the reasons for solely dealing with books. The fact that it was the first time[38] that somebody had tried to compile such an overview for the Netherlands, is inherently remarkable. Looking at her comments and conclusions, Meyboom appeared by all means to be competent and realistic. It is obvious that she was consistent with the Zeitgeist. Another thing that is striking is her self-assurance about her competence concerning Scandinavian literature. She certainly considered herself an objective expert in this area.

*The Scandinavian library*

In the late 1880s Meyboom was the co-founder of a small club which was called *Scandinavisch Leesgezelschap*, or *Scandinavian Reading Society*. This group primarily consisted of a few friends who were interested in Scandinavian literature. Together it was much easier to purchase the expensive books. Over time the society grew and was renamed *Scandinavische Bibliotheek* or *Scandinavian Library*. At the same time, Meyboom was a member of the board of the *Damesleesmuseum* in The

---

Nordic literature.' *Ibidem*, p. 49.

[36] Diederik Grit, *Dansk skønlitteratur i Nederland og Flandern 1731–1982. Bibliografi over oversættelser og studier* (Ballerup, 1986), p. 8.

[37] 'Contains only translations in book form. Very insufficient.' *Ibidem*.

[38] Lode Baekelmans referred in his overview from 1929 to Meyboom's article, which he described as excellent. He did not mention any other articles of that kind. Baekelmans, 'Skandinavische literatuur in vertalingen', in: *Dietsche Warande en Belfort* (1929), pp. 661-675.

Hague. This was a bigger library especially for well situated women. Meyboom arranged that her Scandinavian reading circle could join the *Damesleesmuseum* which provided them with a proper reading room.[39]

*Social and feminist achievements*

*1. Publications*
As mentioned before, Meyboom was very busy writing articles not only about Scandinavia, but also about social issues. In 1895 she composed a book called *Vrouwenwerk*,[40] which means 'women's work'. It contained several essays on women and their part in domestic work. In the following years Meyboom continued to write articles where she pleaded for a better division of responsibilities amongst women concerning domestic work and for the women's right to take on work of their choice. In line with the discussion around the feminist novel *Hilda van Suylenburg*,[41] Meyboom sent an *Open brief*[42] [open letter] to Anna De Savornin Lohman (1868–1930). In her brochure *De liefde in de vrouwenkwestie*[43] De Savornin Lohman expressed her belief that a knowingly unmarried and economic independent woman was not a 'real' woman. The most important thing in a woman's life should be her love to a man. There she referred amongst others to Laura Marholm's (1854–1928) book *Das Buch der Frauen*,[44] whose central thesis can be summed up with the words: 'Des Weibes Inhalt ist der Mann.'[45] In her *Open brief* Meyboom fiercely

[39] Margaretha Meyboom, 'De Scandinavische Bibliotheek', in: *Eigen haard Vol 34* (Amsterdam, 1908), pp. 822-824.

[40] Margaretha Meyboom, *Vrouwenwerk. Schetsen* (Leiden, 1895).

[41] Cecile Goekoop-de Jong van Beek en Donk, *Hilda van Suylenburg* (Amsterdam, 1897).

[42] Margaretha Meyboom, *Open brief aan Freule Anna De Savornin Lohman naar aanleiding van haar brochure "De liefde in de vrouwenkwestie"* (Amsterdam, 1899).

[43] Anna de Savornin Lohman, *De liefde in de vrouwenkwestie. Laura Marholm: Das Buch der Frauen en Mevrouw Goekoop: Hilda van Suylenburg* (Amsterdam, 1899).

[44] Laura Marholm, *Das Buch der Frauen. Zeitpsychologische Portraits* (Paris/Leipzig, 1895).

[45] 'The woman's content is the man.' *Ibidem*, p.44. See Susan Brantly, *The life and*

refused De Savornin Lohman's opinion that a working, independent woman would not be a real woman. Meyboom insisted on the right to self-determination and for individuals to shape their own lives. According to her, the love for fellow human beings, and especially for work, could make women happy as well.[46]

But Meyboom was not content with merely writing and discussing her societal ideals. She also founded and ran enterprises, which responded to her beliefs, over decades. These enterprises will be discussed in the following passages.

## 2. De Wekker

In the summer of 1898 Meyboom was working at the National Exhibition about women's work in The Hague. There she found her inspiration for her first co-operative enterprise. The co-operative movement arose in the middle of 19th century in the US and Western Europe. It contained revolutionary ideas about production and rural economics. The workers should be freed from wage labour, take over production and live together in collective households (in so called 'colonies'). The aim was to create a better society. In the Netherlands the leading man of this movement was the famous writer Frederik van Eeden (1860–1932), whom Meyboom knew personally.

Meyboom started her enterprise *de Wekker* in 1899. The name signifies 'alarm clock', but also the 'awakener'. This small enterprise produced handicrafts, small pieces of furniture and clothes for women. These clothes were simple, naturally falling dresses that offered an alternative to the tight corset. All the workers (mainly female) received fixed wages, a share in profits and a pension, which was quite progressive for this time. It is no longer possible to find out how many years *De Wekker* existed, although it probably must have ceased in 1924, after several financially difficult years during which idealists like Meyboom herself had invested some private money.

Meyboom managed to obtain assignments from the *Damesleesmu-*

---

writings of *Laura Marholm* (= Beiträge zur nordischen Philologie. Schweizerische Gesellschaft für skandinavische Studien, ed) (Basel [et al.], 1991), p. 3.

[46] Saskia Poldervaart, 'Margaretha Meijboom en Westerbro. Coöperatieve huishouding als feministisch ideaal', in: *Jaarboek voor Vrouwengeschiedenis 14* (Amsterdam, 1994), pp. 48-49.

*seum* once in a while, like a new table for the reading section.[47] This is a fabulous example of Meyboom's ability to combine her different areas of activity.

### 3. Westerbro

This enterprise turned out to be her greatest achievement in this area.

Her journey to Copenhagen not only fortified Meyboom's love for the Scandinavian language and literature, but there she also witnessed functioning examples of co-operative household associations for the first time, which impressed her significantly. Therefore she called her next project after a Copenhagen suburb: *Westerbro*. In 1903 she bought four houses in Rijswijk near The Hague together with a few friends (Meyboom's lady companion Clara Bokkes and her sisters) and started the enterprise consisting of a bakery, a studio for handicraft, market gardening and a guesthouse for paying visitors.

Meyboom and her followers intended to stand up against the injustice of society. They despised class distinction, the pursuit of profit and living off interest. Once again Meyboom's belief that women could achieve happiness not only in marriage but also in work could be put into practice.

Meyboom received further input for her colony at speeches held by Frederik van Eeden, founder of the colony *Walden*.[48]

Besides full members and probationary members (not everyone was suitable and accepted) many paying pension guests also lived in *Westerbro*. The latter actually formed the most important source of income for the colonists. Because the activities initially thought to sustain the colony, such as the bakery, growing vegetables and producing handicraft, could not yield enough profit, they had to be abandoned after a while. Being surrounded by 'wonderful idealists',[49] Meyboom felt emotionally and idealistically supported, however she lacked the necessary know-how for business.[50]

---

[47] Lizet Duyvendak, *Het Haags damesleesmuseum: 1894–1994* ('s-Gravenhage, 1994), pp. 181-182.

[48] *Ibidem*, p. 51.

[49] Wilhelmina van Itallie-van Embden, 'Margaretha Meyboom', in: *Vrouwenjaarboek Vol. 1* (Amsterdam, 1929), p. 185.

[50] Poldervaart, 'Margaretha Meijboom en Westerbro. Coöperatieve huishouding als feministisch ideaal', pp. 52-54.

Margaretha Meyboom in front of her house at Westerbro, about 1904.
From Collection Institute of Social History, Amsterdam.

Meyboom was the leader and soul of *Westerbro*. She kept herself busy with her literary work, organised weekly evenings for discussions and was always open to new ideas, sciences and arts, which could enrich their lives. Meyboom often presented work of her loved Scandinavian authors. She also invited some of those writers and philosophers to give speeches at *Westerbro*. This and curiosity about the alternative lifestyle attracted many guests to the colony.

Always being a listener to the problems of others, Meyboom managed to appease whatever disagreements emerged.[51] Throughout Claudine Bienfait's[52] memorial book we find loving, reverent remembrances of Meyboom:

> Zij schiep een sfeer van schoonheid, warmte en vertrouwen, waarvan je je niet wist los te maken, waarin je werd opgeheven en waarin je beter en grooter werd dan je was voor dit uur. (…) Zij wist in ieder mens het beste naar voren te brengen en toonde hem hierdoor zijn kracht en zijn kunnen.[53]

Meyboom kept in touch with other colonies from Van Eeden or Jacobus van Rees (1854–1928), because their ideas corresponded in many issues. The peaceful pursuit of collaborative living together and the importance of acting instead of just talking, were concerns those three shared.[54] Frederik van Eeden, who visited Meyboom a lot, attributed the prosperity of *Westerbro* first and foremost to Meyboom's leadership. He praised *Westerbro* highly, saying that it might be smaller, but was much more cultivated than his own *Walden*. Meyboom was a 'toegewijdde,

---

[51] *Ibidem*, p. 54.

[52] Claudine Bienfait (1873–1960) was a translator colleague and friend of Meyboom.

[53] 'She created an atmosphere of beauty, warmth and trust, which you could not evade, there you would be lifted up and become better and greater than you have been before this hour. (…) She knew how to bring out the best in every person and showed them their power and ability.' See C.H. Vernede, 'Herinneringen. Want slechts liefde was haar leven', in: Bienfait, *In herinnering aan Margaretha Meyboom*, p. 17.

[54] Poldervaart, 'Margaretha Meijboom en Westerbro. Coöperatieve huishouding als feministisch ideaal', p. 55.

huishoudelijk aangelegde, flinke en energieke vrouw'[55]. In her company there was no etiquette necessary and she possessed the gift of sustaining order and peace in her group.[56]

The difference between the two colony leaders was that Van Eeden approved of a more dictatorial leadership and Meyboom of a democratic one. In addition the groups consisted of different kinds of people: with Meyboom there were primarily unmarried women, even single mothers. At the other colonies women were mostly just the company of their husbands and would only be occupied with domestic tasks. Meyboom strove toward changing the conventional views on gender equality. She wanted to provide women with a better position in society by providing all members of *Westerbro* with an economically independent existence, as she already managed before with *De Wekker*. One can say that Meyboom extended the socialist co-operative ideal with a feminist dimension.[57] With her working-and-living-together community, as a manifestation of her struggle against gender and class differences, could she live her ideal life and present others with an example for an alternative way of life.[58]

In 1924 Meyboom moved with Clara Bokkes, due to her health condition, to Voorburg where she stayed until she passed away in 1927. After Meyboom's death the remaining members of *Westerbro* had to rent out the houses in order to meet their financial obligations.[59]

## Conclusion

As we have seen, Margaretha Meyboom worked at various levels to spread the knowledge of Scandinavian literature, lifestyle and ideas about society. In other words, she made a great effort to 'transmit' parts of a foreign culture to her own environment. Besides this her work was

---

[55] 'dedicated, down-to-earth, alert and energetic woman'

[56] Frederik van Eeden, 'Westerbro.' in: De Pionier. *Weekblad ter bespreking van binnenlandsche Kolonisatie,* 16 June, 1906, p. 1.

[57] Poldervaart, 'Margaretha Meijboom en Westerbro. Coöperatieve huishouding als feministisch ideaal', pp. 56-57.

[58] Saskia Poldervaart, *Tegen conventioneel fatsoen en zekerheid. Het uitdagende feminisme van de utopisch socialisten* (Amsterdam, 1993), p. 221.

[59] Duyvendak, *Het Haags damesleesmuseum: 1894-1994*, p. 185.

strongly influenced by socialism and feminism. At this point I would like to present my understanding and use of the term 'cultural transmitter'. Jaap Grave pleaded in his work on Dutch literature in Germany 1890–1914 for using the term 'transmitter' instead of 'translator' because of their variety of tasks:

> Zij [the transmitters ej] zochten actief naar literatuur in het buitenland, namen in veel gevallen contact op met de auteur en het kwam niet zelden voor dat zij de rechten van het boek kochten en op deze manier financieel nauw betrokken waren bij het slagen of mislukken van de door hen gemaakte vertaling.[60]

This certainly applies to Meyboom way of transmitting literature, but it is not yet a complete description of her actions. Here I would like to refer to Broomans, who developed a more elaborate definition of 'cultural transmitter':

> A cultural transmitter basically works within a particular language and cultural area. She/he often takes on various roles in the field of cultural transmission: translator, reviewer, critic, journalist, literary historian, scholar, teacher, librarian, bookseller, collector, literary agent, scout, publisher, editor of a journal, writer, travel writer, or counsellor. Transmitting another national literature and its cultural context to her own national literature and cultural context is the central issue in the work of a cultural transmitter. Transmission often reflects a bilateral situation. The motivation can be aesthetically, ideologically and/or politically based.[61]

---

[60] They [the transmitters ej] searched actively for literature abroad, contacted the authors in many cases and it was not uncommon that they bought the rights of a book and therefore became financially closely involved in the success or failure of their own translation. See Jaap Grave, 2001, *Zulk vertalen is een werk van liefde. Bemiddelaars van Nederlandstalige literatuur in Duitsland 1890–1914* (Nijmegen, 2001), p. 13.

[61] See Petra Broomans, 'The Concept of Ethnolinguistic Nationalism and Cultural transfer. The reception of Scandinavian Literature in Flanders and The Netherlands', in: Broomans, P. et al., eds, *The Beloved Mothertongue. Ethnolinguistic Nationalism in Small Nations. Inventories and Reflections.* Groningen Studies in

Meyboom clearly fits into this description, and therefore it is more than justified to grant her the 'title' of cultural transmitter. But even Broomans description can be broadened in the case of Meyboom because she was not only a cultural/literary transmitter, but also a sincere feminist and socialist. Amazingly enough her feminist and her Scandinavian side always went hand in hand with her social ambitions. She managed impressively well to intertwine her different interests. In her transmission work she not only translated literature but she also transmitted modern socialist and feminist ideas. Furthermore, Meyboom used to combine the action with the word. By engaging in the *Damesleesmuseum* in The Hague she encouraged women to read and broadened the supply of available literature there. She endorsed women's right to choose their own life style and their right to work in her writings, and she even provided jobs for women at her own enterprises. In those enterprises comfortable clothes for women were produced amongst others. And at Westerbro she exhibited a life style herself that offered an alternative to the conservative idea of a family household. In her opinion it was not enough to write beautiful books and talk about changing the world. It was necessary to act and to put ones ideas into practice. One can really say she lived her life by her ideals.

This leads me to the conclusion that it is not possible to put a simple label on Meyboom's personality. She united all these components and many more, like altruism, enthusiasm and integrity, in her personality. Her ability to combine them so well enabled her to achieve such an inspiring and fulfilling life's work.

---

Cultural Change (Leuven, 2008) p. 40.

# Catholicism as a Stepping Stone to Authorship:

## The Contribution of Women to the
## Flemish Catholic Periodical
## *Dietsche Warande en Belfort*

GERALDINE REYMENANTS

The literary-cultural periodical *Dietsche Warande en Belfort* was founded in 1900 by Eigen Leven (Own Life), an organization that must be situated within the Catholic Flemish Movement.[1] Before the First World War, more than 10 percent of the total contributions to the periodical were written by women, two women were members of the editorial board and Marie Elisabeth Belpaire (1853–1948) was the owner and financer of the periodical. In Flanders, this was quite an exceptional situation. The contribution of women writers to other Flemish literary and cultural periodicals – even in so-called avant garde or progressive periodicals – was much less significant and should a woman hold a position such as that of editor or owner it seldom meant they had any real power.

In this article I will outline the context in which women engaged in the Flemish Catholic literary field. I will argue that the contribution of women was influenced both by the orthodox position of *Dietsche Warande en Belfort* in the literary field and by its position-taking, namely it presented an ideology that was both Catholic and pro-Flemish. I will illustrate this by briefly analysing the contradictory reception of women's writing in *Dietsche Warande en Belfort*. Subsequently, I will elaborate on the position of Marie Elisabeth Belpaire as a cultural trans-

---

[1] The Flemish Movement arose as a linguistic and literary movement after Belgian independence in 1830. The first demands concerned the recognition of Flemish/Dutch as an official language in Belgium (in addition to French) and its use in law, the army, education, etc. From the end of the nineteenth century the Flemish Movement also advocated the emancipation of the Flemish people in the socio-economic and cultural domains.

mitter who promoted her ideological – Catholic – viewpoints on literature, and I will discuss the constraints or opportunities she faced doing
so as a woman.

*Dietsche Warande en Belfort* (*DWB*) resulted from the merging of
two existing periodicals, *Dietsche Warande* (1855–1899) and *Het Belfort* (1886–1899). Marie Elisabeth Belpaire, Hilda Ram (1858–1901)
and Louisa Duykers (1869–1952), the three women writers who would
play a significant role in *DWB*, had been responsible for the majority
of women's contributions to *Het Belfort*. Around 80 contributions, primarily by Dutch women writers, were published in the twelve 'Flemish'
volumes of *Dietsche Warande*,[2] with Belpaire and Ram the only Flemish
women who contributed.

In the search for a medium that would propagate its pro-Flemish
and Catholic principles, Eigen Leven, founded in 1898 by Belpaire and
the priest August Cuppens (1862–1924), did not come to *Het Belfort* by
chance. This periodical was related to the Davidsfonds, the most important pro-Flemish Catholic organization, and had a wide circulation
among Flemish Catholic intellectuals, especially priests and teachers.
Most of the members of Eigen Leven, not in the least Belpaire and her
friends Ram and Duykers, had also published regularly in *Het Belfort*
and thus had personal contacts with Alfons Siffer (1850–1941), its publisher. *Dietsche Warande* became involved in the deal because of its thor-
oughness and scientific character, which *Het Belfort* lacked, and because
of its roots, and therefore its influence, in Holland. As such, the future
*DWB* could rely on the symbolic capital of two established periodicals.

However, the takeover and merging of *Het Belfort* and *Dietsche
Warande* by Eigen Leven proved to be a difficult and – more impor-
tantly – a costly business. As money seemed to be the pivotal aspect of
the whole operation, Belpaire, who came from a wealthy family, decided
in July 1899 to finance the founding and operations of the future periodical. As such, Belpaire secured an important position in *DWB*. The
pioneering role of Belpaire in establishing *DWB* can partially explain the

---

[2] *Dietsche Warande* was originally founded in Amsterdam, Holland, by Jozef A.
Alberdingk Thijm. In 1886 the periodical was transferred to his younger brother
Paul, who was working at the Catholic University of Louvain in Belgium. The
first 'Flemish' issue of *Dietsche Warande* was published in November 1887 by
Leliaert and Siffer in Ghent, who also published *Het Belfort*.

Marie Elisabeth Belpaire in her study, 1934. From Collection AMVC-Letterenhuis, Antwerp.

'substantial' number of female contributions to the periodical (11 percent before the First World War). However, its position and its position-taking must also be considered.

*Orthodox positions*

As successor of *Dietsche Warande* and *Het Belfort*, *DWB* inherited symbolic capital within the Catholic literary field. As a result, *DWB* obtained a central position in the field almost immediately after its founding. As the holder of symbolic power, *DWB* defended the literary doxa, or dominant ideology,[3] namely the notion that literature had a didactical, utilitarian, ethical objective.

Notwithstanding the influence of modernism and its aesthetic innovations in the Catholic literary field, most authors and periodicals, *DWB* included, maintained their Catholic principles, which stated that

---

[3] Pierre Bourdieu defines the doxa as the taken-for-granted, naturalized assumptions and beliefs of a field, P. Bourdieu, *The field of cultural production. Essays on art and literature*, R. Johnson, ed (Cambridge, 1999), pp. 83–84.

good Catholic literature should answer the vital questions 'how?', 'why?', 'whereto?', and should provide 'a solution, better insight, joy because of the power, the beauty and the holiness of life'.[4] In other words, art in general, and literature in particular, was considered to have an ethical or moral significance and objective, as mentioned above.

This doxa basically guaranteed the conditions for and the justification of female authorship. As writing – and thus working – women, female authors found themselves in a 'marginal' social position. Their transgression of the traditional gender borders (women's 'natural' domains of action were the family and the household) was therefore only accepted if they kept in mind their 'natural vocation' (motherhood) and thus wrote literature from that standpoint, through which they collaborated in the realization of the ethical objectives of literature.

On the one hand, if women writers met these demands, they were assured of the praise of their 'orthodox' colleagues and the public and were accepted by the orthodox media involved. *DWB* thus looked specifically for women writers who agreed with their orthodox ideology. On the other hand, women writers themselves could feel more attracted to these orthodox positions precisely because they ensured appraisal. Taking a position against the literary doxa meant renouncing a safe, guaranteed position in the field. This heterodoxical practice was more the privilege of actors who could invest a substantial amount of economic, social and cultural capital. Due to external factors (lack of education, to name only one), women were not usually part of this group. Women writers thus attempted to establish a connection with *DWB* because it provided a safe haven for them.

*Catholic and pro-Flemish position-taking*

Positions in the field are closely linked to the position-taking of actors in that field. Pierre Bourdieu argues that while the intellectual or cultural field is relatively autonomous and functions in accordance with its own rules and power relations, at the same time it lies within the larger field

---

[4] Raymond Vervliet, *De literaire manifesten van het fin de siècle in de Zuidnederlandse periodieken 1878-1914*, I (Ghent, 1982), pp. 179–180, pp. 197–199; Oskar Van der Hallen, *Vijftig jaar katholieke letterkunde in Vlaanderen (1885-1937)* (Louvain, 1938), p. 9.

of class relations, or the social field by which it is influenced.[5] Given that there is no specific field of gender because, like class, it is part of the general social field, every field is gendered. Therefore gender, as a structuring social factor, is always relevant and present in the literary field – either in the objective structures of the field or in the cognitive and subjective structures of the actors in the field.[6] At one level this results, for example, in the horizontal and vertical segregation of the literary field; at a second level it means that actors in the literary field reproduce and produce or construct gender (discourse) over and over again.

I distinguish between 'bounded' and 'unbounded' programmatic periodicals in the Flemish literary field.[7] Guided in its critical practice by ideological (Catholic) and sociopolitical (pro-Flemish) principles, *DWB* can be defined as a bounded programmatic periodical. Periodicals that were guided by poetical principles can be called unbounded. In terms of their editorial practice, both categories were influenced by the dominant gender discourse but focused on different aspects of this discourse. The fact that progressive periodicals attached more importance to concepts such as 'great art/literature' and 'genius' constituted a major obstacle for women. Those concepts (especially genius) had an exclusively male connotation and external factors prevented women from acquiring the experiences that were seen as indispensable for the production of great art/literature: a lack of education and poetical schooling and exclusion from the public sphere, as a result of which women could not attain the position of *flâneur* or *bohemian*, could not visit bars and restaurants to network and had less opportunity to travel.

In conservative – Catholic – periodicals the notion of 'genius' was equally important in connection to literature, and all were convinced that this 'genius' was masculine. In the essay *Vrouweninvloed* (Women's influence), for example, Marie Elisabeth Belpaire wrote that 'women do not excel in genius, in ingenuity, we do not owe them the progression of science nor art, they did not bring the *Divina Commedia* into existence

---

[5] *Ibidem*, pp. 37–38, pp. 162–164.

[6] Toril Moi, 'Appropriating Bourdieu: Feminist theory and Pierre Bourdieu's Sociology of Culture', *New Literary History* 22 (1991), 4, pp. 1034–1037.

[7] Erica van Boven, *Een hoofdstuk apart. 'Vrouwenromans' in de literaire kritiek 1898-1930* (Amsterdam, 1992), pp. 23–27.

nor the Moses of Michelangelo nor the cathedrals'.[8] However, in *DWB* – as in other Catholic periodicals – ideological and sociopolitical principles were more important than poetical principles.

In this context it is significant that nineteenth-century Catholicism, as a consequence of the division of society into a public, masculine sphere and a private, feminine sphere, had become more and more the concern of women. It is argued that there was a 'demasculinization (or feminization) of Catholicism', as a result of which women who held on to the Catholic rules of faith, in behaviour and mentality, were often the only anchors for religious belief in the family, and the Church had to rely on them to transmit this belief to the younger generations.[9] In other words, women, as wives, mothers and educators, played an important role in the transfer of Catholic values.

In the above-mentioned essay *Vrouweninvloed*, Belpaire stressed the societal importance of women by arguing that although they did not possess genius and could not create artistic masterpieces, they could create another masterwork: man. By guiding their families, women educated their children in terms of religion, virtue and higher ideals and in

---

[8] 'dat de vrouwen niet uitmunten door genie, door vernuft, dat men hun niet den vooruitgang van wetenschap of kunst te danken heeft, dat zij noch de *Divina Commedia* noch den Mozes van Michael-Angelo, noch de kathedralen in 't leven geroepen hebben', Marie Elisabeth Belpaire, *Vrouweninvloed* (Antwerp, 1903), p. 9.

[9] Marcel Bernos, 'De l'influence salutaire ou pernicieuse de la femme dans la famille et la société', *Revue d'histoire moderne et contemporaine* 29 (1982), p. 459; Marjet Derks, 'Vrouwen, confessionalisering en biografie. Catharina Alberdingk Thijm of de eigenaardigheid van een karakter', in Annelies van Heijst and Marjet Derks eds., *Terra Incognita. Historisch onderzoek naar katholicisme en vrouwelijkheid* (Kampen, 1994), p. 112; M. De Giorgio, 'Het katholieke model', in Geneviève Fraisse and Michelle Perrot eds., *Geschiedenis van de vrouw. De negentiende eeuw* (Amsterdam, 1993), pp. 127–128. In relation to Belgium, the 'feminization of religion' is currently the subject of the research project 'Op zoek naar de goede katholiek M/V. Feministering en masculiniteit in het katholicisme in België sinds de vroegmoderne tijd, ca. 1750–1950' (In pursuit of the good Catholic M/W. Feminization and masculinity in Catholicism in Belgium in the early modern period, ca. 1750–1950), Catholic University Louvain and University Ghent.

this way guided society as a whole.[10]

Comparable ideas can be found in pro-Flemish discourse. At the end of the nineteenth century, men wanted to involve women in the Flemish Movement, precisely because of the so-called moral qualities of women and their influence within the family. The supporters of the Flemish Movement became aware of the fact that the non-participation or aloofness of women restricted the Flemish struggle. Because most women received a French education, which they transmitted to their children, the public efforts of men in the Flemish struggle remained without results.[11] It was argued that 'without the mingling of women our efforts will not be strong nor durable'.[12] Just as they transmitted Catholic values and norms to their sons and daughters, it was argued that mothers should transmit the mother tongue (Flemish) to the family and thus society.[13]

Flemish Catholics thus assigned an important position to women both in terms of their beliefs and in relation to the Flemish Movement. A periodical such as *DWB*, whose main objective was the moral uplifting and emancipation of the Flemish people, was 'infected' by this discourse and was therefore positive and open to contributions by women writers, critics and editors.

*Beautiful thoughts in bad verse*

I would like to illustrate this situation with the contradictory reception of women's writing in *DWB*. Because moral principles were primary in *DWB* and literary criteria were considered of minor importance, publications and authors that lived up to ideological or moral expectations

---

[10] Belpaire, *Vrouweninvloed.*

[11] Hendrik J. Elias, *Geschiedenis van de Vlaamse gedachte* IV, *Taalbeweging en cultuurflamingantisme. De groei van het Vlaamse bewustzijn, 1883–1914* (Antwerp, 1965), pp. 350–351. Cf. Nele Bracke, 'Vrouw', in R. De Schryver et al. eds., *Nieuwe Encyclopedie van de Vlaamse Beweging* III (Tielt, 1998), pp. 3606–3607.

[12] D. Claes, 'Het Davids-fonds en de vrouwen', *Dietsche Warande en Belfort* 2 (1901), 3, p. 290.

[13] Frans Crols, *Katholieke Vlaamsche vrouwenbeweging* (Bruges, 1913); Cyriel Verschaeve, *Aan de Vlaamsche vrouwen. Feestrede uitgesproken door E.H. Cyriel Verschaeve op de Landdagen der Christene Vlaamsche Meisjes te Oostacker, (16 September 1913) en te Gent (11 Augustus 1919.)* (Tielt, 1920).

were generally praised even if the stylistic quality of their work was un-satisfactory. This applied to women and men alike, but because women were considered to have high moral standards and to be influential on this basis, their writings especially were supposed to provide evidence of these standards and, if this were so, their work was judged suitable for publication and review in the periodical.

August Cuppens, for example, wrote to Belpaire about her poetry: 'Your language, verse and rhyme don't satisfy me, I am always angry that such beautiful thoughts are expressed so incompletely in your Flemish – that sometimes isn't even Flemish!'[14] The language and style of Duykers were also judged to be unsatisfactory: 'Her language is not rich, her words not colourful, her style not always elegant and a bit mat and grey', was Jules Persyn's judgement. Her prose was nevertheless published in *DWB*, partly because of its 'pronounced Christian ideology' and the 'true, firm beauty of soul' to which it bore witness.[15]

In *Vlaamsche Arbeid*, a more progressive Catholic periodical, found-ed partly as a reaction to the conservative (orthodox) literary policy of *DWB*, this caused frustration. Following the continued appraisal of Duykers's novels, one critic wrote:

I could cry when I think of the fact that Gezelle, Streuvels and Ver-meylen have fought all their lives for the truth of art, for the ortho-doxy of life, for the personality of the word ... and that afterwards I have to read *Lena's* ... But when I hear then that club spirit, that confessional fraternization causes certain critics to compare a writer such as Louisa Duykers to George Elliot and these dolls Lena and

---

[14] 'Ik heb geen vrede met uwe taal, verzen en rijmen, ik ben altijd kwaad dat zoo schoone gedachten zoo onvolledig aangekleed zijn in uw Vlaamsch – dat dikwijls geen Vlaamsch en is!', August Cuppens to M.E. Belpaire, vesp. Transfigurationus 1899. Lessius-Hogeschool, Archives of the Katholieke Vlaamse Hogeschool voor Vrouwen (Catholic Flemish College for Women).

[15] 'Haar taal is niet rijk, haar woord niet kleurig, haar stijl niet altijd sierlijk zelfs, en uit zijn aard wat mat en grijs'; 'klaar-uitgesproken christelijke levensbeschouwing', Jules Persyn, 'Lena, door Louisa Duykers. – Duimpjes uitgave, Victor Delille, Mal-deghem, 1906', *Dietsche Warande en Belfort* 1 (1907), 1, p. 102. 'echte, vaste ziele-schoonheid', M. Van Hoeck, 'Louisa Duykers', *Boekengids* 1 (1924), 5–6, p. 130.

Roza to Tolstoy's everlasting female characters from *War and Peace*, then I start to get desperate about our literature, or at least about … certain of our men of letters.[16]

For *DWB* the absence of a high moral purpose in the writings of women was the main reason to reject, or to simply ignore them. A striking example is Persyn's review of *Absolvo Te* by the German novelist Clara Viebig. Although Persyn praised the language, style and narrative qualities of Viebig, he concluded that it was 'a bad novel'.

Not because the writing of the novel is a positively sinful act that contradicts the commands of God or his Church, but because – and this is almost as bad – the nature, the essence of this novel is rotten to the core because it rests on a falsification of conscience, which is actually amorality.[17]

---

[16] 'Ik zou er bij weenen wanneer ik erop denk dat een Gezelle, een Streuvels, een Vermeylen heel hun bestaan hebben gestreden voor de waarheid van de kunst, voor de rechtzinnigheid van het leven, voor de persoonlijkheid van het woord … en dat ik daarna nog *Lenas* moet lezen … Maar wanneer ik dan hoor dat clubjes-geest, dat confessioneele verbroederlijking er zeker critici toe drijven eene schrijfster lijk Louisa Duykers te vergelijken met George Elliott en die twee poppen Lena en Roza met Tolstoï's eeuwige vrouwenfiguren uit *Krijg en Vrede*, dan ga ik bepaald aan 't wanhopen over onze literatuur of ten minste over … zekere onzer literators', A.d.R., 'Lena en Roza van Louisa Duijkers', *Vlaamsche Arbeid* 3 (1907–1908), 5, pp. 152–153. See the reviews by Jules Persyn, 'Lena, door Louisa Duykers', *Dietsche Warande en Belfort* 8 (1907), 1, pp. 101–103, and G. Hermans, 'Rosa, door Louisa Duykers', *Dietsche Warande en Belfort* 8 (1907), 12, pp. 538–541.

[17] 'Clara Viebig's laatste boek is een slecht boek. Niet zoozeer in dezen zin dat het schrijven van dit boek op zichzelf een positief zondige daad mag heeten, rechtstreeks ingaand tegen een der geboden van God of zijn Kerk, maar in dezen bijna even ergen zin dat de aard, het wezen zelf van dit boek door en door ongezond is, dat de opvatting van dit gegeven bepaald berust op een gewetensvervalsching, die neerkomt op a-moraliteit', Jules Persyn, 'Over letterkunde / Clara Viebig', *Dietsche Warande en Belfort* 9 (1908), 6, p. 551.

*Vlaamsche Arbeid* however, praised Viebig for her 'rare richness of language', her psychology, the 'natural, strict logical structure of actions' and concluded by stating that 'of the good there are never too many'.[18]

### The mother role: as performed by Marie Elisabeth Belpaire

To give women publishing space is one thing, but to accept women into central positions in a periodical and thus in the literary field is something completely different. As owner, financer and editor Belpaire possessed symbolic power in *DWB*. Belpaire's economic capital can partially explain this; however, it is not the main explanation for her position in the periodical.

It is precisely the role of women as mothers in/of society – on which their significance in Catholic and pro-Flemish ideology was based – that explains Belpaire's position of power in *DWB*. The periodical needed a 'mother' who could guide the hearts of men and women with gentle authority. This mother figure was found in Belpaire who was portrayed as the 'literary mother' of the young contributors. Esteemed for her 'devotion, admiration and willing helpfulness', she received the title 'Mother of the Flemish Movement', and it was said that 'her greatness lay in the fact that she is a valuable woman and understood – and still does – like no other, the art of being a true mother'.[19]

---

[18] 'zeldzame taal-rijkdom', 'vanzelf-sprekende, streng logische opbouw der handelingen', 'Van de goeden zijn er nooit te veel', A. Rossbach, 'Nieuwe Duitsche Boeken / Die vor den Toren, roman van Clara Viebig', *Vlaamsche Arbeid* 6 (1910–1911), 4, pp. 157–158.

[19] '"litteraire moeder" van de jongeren', J. Eeckhout, 'Juffrouw Maria, Elisa Belpaire', *Dietsche Warande en Belfort* 26 (1926), 1, p. 34; 'toewijding, bewondering en dienstvaardige behulpzaamheid', Jozef Muls, 'Toespraak van Prof. Dr Jozef Muls namens het Belpaire-Teichmann Fonds, de Kunstwereld en de Koninklijke Vlaamsche Academie voor Taal en Letterkunde', Annex to *Dietsche Warande en Belfort* 48 (1948), 3–4, p. 3; 'de grootheid van Mejuffer Belpaire daarin ligt dat ze *een volwaardige vrouw is en als geen andere de kunst verstond – en nog verstaat – een ware moeder te zijn*', Maria Baers, 'Spreekbeurt door Mej. Senator Baers uit naam van de Vrouwen van het land', Annex to *Dietsche Warande en Belfort* 48 (1948), 3–4, p. 7.

Belpaire accepted this motherly role gratefully because she perceived it as the ideal alibi for her own pursuit of power. Due to her possession of considerable amounts of economic, social and cultural capital, and especially due to her habitus, which was quite unusual for women, Belpaire had a clear understanding of social power relations, including gender relations. She realized that too much power in a woman's hands would not be accepted. To make her 'masculine' pursuit of power socially acceptable she stressed her sex or her symbolic mother role, for example through the strategic use of titles such as 'Mamieken' (little mother), which she used when engaged in activities related to girls' education and charity, where a mothering image was advantageous.

Within the context of *DWB*, Belpaire claimed the authority to decide on the content of and contributors to the periodical. However, she attempted to disguise her search for power by stressing her mothering, soft side. For example, she also used the title 'Moeder Overste' (mother superior), which referred to her faith, her age, her 'motherhood' and her authority. In addition, she took every opportunity to comment on her modest, soft, motherly character. She wrote to Lodewijk Scharpé, member of the editorial board of *DWB*, that he – and *DWB* in general – would benefit from giving her responsibility. She was 'a woman, independent, without responsibilities, outside and above the political parties' and as such did not rely on anyone else. She also claimed that '[t]he soft hand of a woman can bring about a lot, without offending the stiff pride of men'.[20]

However, as much as she attempted to exercise her power in this way, she was not always successful, as is illustrated by the conflicts within *DWB* – conflicts that arose from Belpaire's numerous interventions in relation to decisions made by Emiel Vliebergh, the periodical's chief editor, and Scharpé, his right-hand man. The main reason for these conflicts was the differences in their understanding of the guiding principles of the periodical. Whereas Vliebergh and Scharpé wanted to make *DWB* into a broader cultural periodical, also open to writers and readers of different beliefs (that is, non-Catholics), Belpaire insisted on the Catholic, ethical principles of the periodical, which, furthermore, should be literary first and foremost.

[20] M.E. Belpaire to L. Scharpé, 25 November 1899. KADOC, Archive Emiel Vliebergh, deposit Davidsfonds, DEV 501 II.

Celebration to honour Miss Belpaire: after the ceremony at the municipal *normaal-school* (teacher-training college), undated. From Collection AMVC-Letterenhuis, Antwerp.

Even before the first issue of *DWB* was published in January 1900, and following the refusal of Vliebergh and Scharpé to publish a story by Duykers, Belpaire's close friend and protégé, Belpaire felt the need to enforce her authority. She wrote: 'Let's understand each other well. The idea of giving our Flemish people a reliable periodical, of general interest, in touch with the foreign periodicals, was *mine*'. She understood her role in the periodical as follows: 'the leadership, the direction are due to *me*. I am the owner of *Dietsche Warande* ... and I am thus responsible for it, not only from a financial point of view, but also from an ethical point of view'.[21]

It was precisely these divergent points of view concerning the ethical grounding of *DWB* that would cause the split between Belpaire/*DWB* and Scharpé and Vliebergh. In June 1900 Belpaire opposed the publication of an article by Hendrik de Marez on Pol de Mont and Hélène Swarth because, she argued, the article was not written in a Catholic

---

[21] M.E. Belpaire to L. Scharpé, 23 November 1899. KADOC, Archive Emiel Vliebergh, deposit Davidsfonds, DEV 501 II.

spirit. Vliebergh argued that the rejection of an article about more progressive authors would give the impression that *DWB* was biased. Notwithstanding the protests by the younger members of the editorial board, Belpaire could not be convinced, and the article by De Marez was not published. This incident – and its outcome – illustrate that Belpaire's authority was no formality and that the decisive power of the chief editor and the entire editorial board was indeed very limited. After similar conflicts, where Belpaire's conservative point of view clashed with the more progressive viewpoints of Vliebergh and Scharpé, the latter resigned from the editorial board, leaving Vliebergh in a marginal position within the periodical – a position that he gradually realized was untenable. With her so-called soft hand Belpaire had managed to alienate the two pillars of *DWB*, but she had made sure that there was a successor, appointing Jules Persyn, a young, promising philologist, educated in literature – which guaranteed the literary editorial line of *DWB* – who maintained the 'Christian ideal' as the leading principle in life and in literature. By choosing him as the successor to Vliebergh, Belpaire guaranteed that her point of view would remain paramount.

## Clash of principles: Belpaire vs Vermeylen

The ideological conflicts were not confined to the editorial board of *DWB*. In 1905 Belpaire was engaged in a quite 'famous', much discussed debate with August Vermeylen, spokesman of the younger, progressive generation in Flemish literature. The starting point of the controversy was the question of whether literature should be ethical or aesthetic. Belpaire defended the first, Vermeylen the latter. In reviewing Vermeylen's *Verzamelde opstellen* (Collected essays) in *DWB*, Belpaire reproached Vermeylen, suggesting that he was opposed to Catholicism as such, that he was blind to the importance of a higher 'Truth' in art and that he relied too much on salvation arising from society itself and the 'I'. She argued that his thinking was limited and expressed the hope that he would eventually find – and follow – the one and only way of Catholicism, that is, of eternal truth.

Vermeylen, however, in reviewing Belpaire's essay 'Christen ideaal' (Christian ideal) in the periodical *Vlaanderen*, was as reproachful, arguing that she was ideologically biased in her criticisms of art and literature and consequently tended to deny the eternal basis of all art – that

is, the beauty of the human – and thus fell into a short-sighted and petty
clericalism. Vermeylen also claimed that as a result of her attempt to
interpret all great art from a Roman-Catholic perspective she sometimes
expressed contradictory arguments.

Belpaire did not take this as a direct critique on her essay 'Christen
ideaal', but as a critique of Catholicism as such, the Christian aesthetic
and the religious ideas of art and life. She repeated her views on truth, art
and beauty in the June issue of *DWB*. Vermeylen responded in July 1905
by stressing that art cannot be judged in terms of the beliefs expressed in
it. The debate carried on for a while, in public and in private, but ended
when it became clear that they would never reach a consensus.

This debate is interesting for two reasons. Firstly, it is an illustration
of the struggle within the Flemish literary field prior to the First World
War, between young or progressive heterodoxical position-taking (*l'art
pour l'art*) and old or conservative orthodox position-taking (*art engagé*).
That Belpaire wanted to discuss the issue with Vermeylen indicates that
the literary innovations by Vermeylen and his colleagues were finally
being taken seriously by *DWB*. In addition, this controversy took place
at the precise moment when *DWB* was being confronted with heterodoxical actors from within the Catholic literary field itself, that is, with
young authors and other periodicals that challenged the basic principles
of *DWB* and Catholic literature in general. By taking a stand against
Vermeylen, Belpaire wanted to preserve the unity within the Catholic
literary field, and in this she temporarily succeeded, with young Catholic heterodoxical writers, who would normally have opposed *DWB*, sid-
ing with her.

Secondly, the debate was also a struggle between 'old' players (men)
and 'new' players who had recently entered the literary field (women).
It was not generally accepted that a woman critic could be involved
in a controversy with a prominent author and critic. That Vermeylen
wanted to discuss these issues with Belpaire meant that he valued her
as well as her views and that he thought she was influential in the literary field. Indeed, he wrote in his review that he had wanted to clarify
his and Belpaire's position precisely because Belpaire was the editor of
the most important Catholic review. Independently of the content of the
controversy, Belpaire herself was apparently satisfied that she has been
'attacked' by Vermeylen, as she had complained on an earlier occasion
that she was not taken seriously – as a writer, a critic, or as a woman.

That her gender nevertheless remained an important fact, is illustrated by the stereotypical responses to her debate with Vermeylen. Indeed no one doubted her authority in the matter – Cuppens, for instance, wrote: 'He [Vermeylen] tries to ridicule your theory, which is a simple truth, but he does not succeed' – but people did doubt whether she was 'manly' enough to defend herself. Cuppens promised to 'help' her in her response to Vermeylen.[22] Her nephew assured her that the Dutch priest, professor and poet Herman Schaepman, who had been one of Belpaire's teachers, would certainly have responded – had he still been alive.[23] Karel van den Oever, a young Catholic writer who was actually opposed to Belpaire and the conservative principles of *DWB*, nevertheless wrote an article in *De Groene Linde* in her defence. The most flagrant response came from Joris Eeckhout, who wrote to Belpaire saying that he would prove in the periodical *Jong Dietschland* that, far from being a 'beau geste' by Vermeylen, it was an indelicate, impudent gesture designed to disparage Belpaire after her article in *DWB* which had approved of Vermeylen's prose.[24] On this basis, Vermeylen's critique was considered to be not only unfounded but also a personal attack on Belpaire. Eeckhout considered that her delicacy had been damaged by this impudence and that she needed to be rehabilitated by some 'noble men'.

Within the same logic Emiel van der Straeten argued some years later that Van den Oever, who by then had completely turned against Belpaire, had not been gallant in his personal critique of Belpaire. Van der Straeten warned that if Van den Oever published his pamphlet 'Het Programma-Verraad in "Vlaamsche Arbeid"' (The programme betrayal in 'Vlaamsche Arbeid'), which contained this critique, he himself would respond. Then, he continued, Van den Oever would not only have to deal with a 53-year-old woman.[25] It suggests that Van der Straeten thought

---

[22] A. Cuppens to M.E. Belpaire, 6 April 1905. AMVC-Letterenhuis, B417/B2, n° 166196/472.

[23] Jules Persyn, *De wording van het tijdschrift Dietsche Warande en Belfort en zijn ontwikkeling onder de redactie van Em. Vliebergh en Jul. Persyn (1900–1924)* (Ghent, 1963), p. 169.

[24] J. Eeckhout to M.E. Belpaire, 17 May 1905. AMVC-Letterenhuis, B417/B2, n° 80755/34.

[25] E. Van der Straeten to J. Muls, s.d. [June 1912]. AMVC-Letterenhuis, A38115/B1, n° 28425/8.

Belpaire incapable of taking a powerful position. Apparently, her gender and her merits as a critic could not be disconnected.

*Belpaire's stubborn attempts to Christianize*

Belpaire's Catholic interpretation of literature also structured her relationships with other writers. As argued above, *DWB* in general, and Belpaire in particular, favoured authors whose work proved their high moral standards. Belpaire considered this important especially for women writers, because women functioned in society as transmitters of Catholic and pro-Flemish values. Therefore she was always attempting to convert women whose work she esteemed – and who would thus be an acquisition for *DWB* – but who were not practising Catholics.

For example, before 'recruiting' Anna Germonprez, who had mainly published in non-confessional periodicals, Belpaire made inquiries about her background and beliefs. After the local priest had guaranteed that her conduct and work were perfectly 'decent', Belpaire welcomed Germonprez to *DWB*. Belpaire also had lively discussions on religion with the Dutch Protestant Dina Logeman-van der Willigen, who would be responsible for the greater part of the articles on Scandinavia in *DWB* in the first decade of the twentieth century. Logeman-van der Willigen seems to have been receptive to Belpaire's views, and the latter, charmed by the thought that she could make another conversion, did not hesitate to pay Logeman-van der Willigen a higher honorarium than was customary. The same was the case for the Dutch writer Alida Wynanda Sanders van Loo, who manipulated Belpaire by stating that she was very sympathetic to Catholicism. Again convinced that she had converted someone to the 'right belief', Belpaire offered Sanders van Loo the position of principle art critic for *DWB* and paid her a high honorarium. When she discovered that Sanders van Loo's life was not as pious as she had suggested, Belpaire felt deceived and banned Sanders van Loo from *DWB*.

A final example is Virginie Loveling. Belpaire was impressed by Loveling's writings and charmed by her personality but thought that she had one weak point: Loveling was not religious. Thus Belpaire decided to 'broaden' Loveling's horizon and to convert her. However, unlike Logeman-van der Willigen and Sanders van Loo, who lived from their pens and would do anything for a new commission, Loveling did not depend on Belpaire and *DWB* for publications or money – as one of the most respected Flemish authors she had plenty of other opportunities available – and so she neither had to nor wanted to indulge Belpaire and her Catholic beliefs. In the end Belpaire reconciled herself to these facts and nevertheless published Loveling's *Oorlogsdagboek* (War diary) in *DWB*. Loveling, still as non-Catholic as ever, wrote to her nephew that *DWB* was ultra-Catholic but that it did not matter: 'I can freely publish whatever I like'.[26] When she met her match, Belpaire could actually be quite tolerant.

*Conclusion*

Before the First World War, *DWB* was one of the most favourable forums for women writers in Flanders. This can be explained by the orthodox position of the periodical in the Catholic literary field and its Catholic and pro-Flemish position. Moreover, the role played by Marie Elisabeth Belpaire has to be considered as an important reason for the success of *DWB*. As a woman, her central position and her authority in the periodical were exceptional. She used this position to propagate her Catholic principles but also to support women writers, whose role in transmitting the Catholic and pro-Flemish ideas she considered crucial. As such she functioned as a bridge between women writers and the generally male-dominated literary field.

---

[26] V. Loveling to A. and A. Buysse, 19 August 1922. Private archive of Livine Stevens.

# Decoding a Genius Mind –

## The French Philosopher Simone Weil (1909–1943) and the Swedish Critic Margit Abenius (1899–1970): a Case of Cultural Transmission

MARTA RONNE

'I cannot believe that more than a handful of the tens of thousands of readers she has won since the posthumous publication of her books and essays really share her ideas. Nor is it necessary …', Susan Sontag (1933–2004) wrote about the French philosopher Simone Weil while reviewing her *Selected Essays* in 1963. She concluded: 'We read writers of such scathing originality for their personal authority, for the example of their seriousness, for their manifest willingness to sacrifice themselves for their truths, and – only piecemeal – for their "views"'. First published in English translation in 1952, at the time of Sontag's review, Simone Weil was already an acknowledged contributor to Western philosophical thought, often compared to Kleist, Kierkegaard and even to Wittgenstein.[1] Nevertheless, since her first work appeared in print, her 'views' had been regarded as almost impossible to interpret. Twenty years earlier, at a time when Weil was still barely known outside France, the prominent Swedish critic Margit Abenius wrote:

> Simone Weil belongs to those great writers who cannot be rendered but with their own words. To paraphrase her would always be to obscure or to weaken something that itself is both naked and strong in its own spontaneity. The most important question is therefore how we should transfer her philosophical thought into the Swedish culture …[2]

---

[1] Susan Sontag, 'Simone Weil', 1963; Peter Winch, *Simone Weil* (Cambridge, 1989).

[2] Margit Abenius, 'Simone Weil', *Bonniers Litterära Magasin* 7 (1951), p. 511. All

This question was crucial to Margit Abenius' own efforts to introduce Simone Weil to Sweden. She did this by translating Weil's *La Pesanteur et la Grâce* from French in 1954, and by presenting Weil's thought to a Swedish audience in literary reviews and lectures.[3] In the 1950s, Abenius continued writing and lecturing on Weil's mysticism.[4] Finally, in 1961, she edited a selection of Weil's essays and letters.[5]

The question of how a thinker of Weil's dignity and complexity can be transferred from one language and culture to another is the starting point for this essay. My aim is to analyse Margit Abenius' introduction of Simone Weil's writings to Sweden as a case of cultural transmission. My focus is on the actual process of cultural transmission as well as on the role of the female culture transmitter. I examine the circumstances of Abenius' early work on Weil's writings, as well as possible motives for her decision to devote herself to understanding and transmitting Weil's philosophy to Swedish readers.

---

translations from Swedish into English are by the author.

[3] *La Pesanteur et la grâce* (Paris, 1947), *Gravity and Grace* (New York, 1952), *Tyngden och nåden* (Stockholm, 1954). For obvious reasons I use many Swedish sources, most of them also have a summary in English. When needed, I will provide my own translations of the titles and quotations. I will use the English titles of Weil's works in the text for convenience, but the original title is always given when the work is mentioned for the first time.

[4] Gunnel Vallquist, another acknowledged Swedish critic, writer and translator, and a member of the Swedish Academy, translated Weil's *L'Enracinement. Prélude à une déclaration des devoirs envers l'être humain* (Paris, 1949) (English translation: *The Need for Roots*, New York, 1952) into Swedish only a year after Abenius' translation of *La Pesanteur et la Grâce*. She also prefaced Weil's famous biography by Simone Pétrement in 1976 (*La vie de Simone Weil I-II*, Paris, 1973). Her role as a cultural transmitter might thus also be regarded as important in the context of introducing Weil to Sweden. However, Margit Abenius' contribution may be regarded as crucial, as it was she who completed the first Swedish translation of Weil and who worked on introducing her philosophical thought to a broader audience in a series of lectures.

[5] Swedish translation: *Personen och det heliga. Essäer och brev*, transl. by Karin Stolpe (Stockholm, 1961). The Swedish title was a translation of Weil's *La personne et le sacré*, as some of the essays came from her *La personne et le sacré*. *Écrits de Londre* (Paris, 1957).

Margit Abenius is mostly known for her academic research in stylistics, as a critic and an essayist, and – last but not least – for her literary reviews on Swedish Radio.[6] However, when it comes to her work on Simone Weil, she can also be regarded as a cultural transmitter, who both translated and introduced a thinker from a dominating language area to a peripheral one. According to a working definition by Petra Broomans:

A cultural transmitter basically works within a particular language and cultural area. She/he often takes on various roles in the field of cultural transmission: translator, reviewer, critic, journalist, literary historian, scholar, teacher, librarian, bookseller, collector, literary agent, scout, publisher, editor of a journal, writer, travel writer, or counsellor. Transmitting another national literature and its cultural context to her own national literature and cultural context is the central issue in the work of a cultural transmitter. Transmission often reflects a bilateral situation. The motivation can be aesthetically, ideologically and/or politically based.[7]

Internationally acknowledged shortly after her death as one of the foremost thinkers of the twentieth century, Simone Weil has been continuously republished throughout the Western world. A philosopher, theologian, agnostic, mystic, historian, both a Marxist and an anti-Marxist, a pacifist, trade unionist and a middle-class intellectual who

---

[6] Abenius is the subject of my current research project on gender and literary criticism in Sweden 1930 to 1970, financed in 2005–2007 by The Bank of Sweden Tercentenary Foundation.

[7] See Petra Broomans, 'The Concept of Ethnolinguistic Nationalism and Cultural Transfer. The reception of Scandinavian Literature in Flanders and The Netherlands', in P. Broomans et al., eds, *The Beloved Mothertongue. Ethnolinguistic Nationalism in Small Nations. Inventories and Reflections.* Groningen Studies in Cultural Change (Leuven, 2008), p. 40. I wish thereby to suggest a broader definition of the term, which involved more than translations. In my own project, I also regard Abenius as a cultural transmitter due to her work on reviewing women's literature on radio. She also led several private book circles for female readers, which I consider tantamount to the creation of an intellectual space for women readers.

mastered both ancient Greek and Sanskrit, she continues to occupy the-
ologians and philosophers. In Sweden, however, she does not seem to
appeal to a broader audience. Despite the initial interest in her writings
in the 1940s, and unlike Simone de Beauvoir, whose *The Second Sex* was
translated in the early 1970s and then rediscovered both by lay readers
and by Swedish feminist thought in the mid-1990s, Weil has almost exclusively been subject to scholarly research in philosophy, theology and
aesthetics.[8] To lay readers she remains rather anonymous. The reason
might be that she is mostly regarded as a mystic and remembered for her
purely religious writings. Both she and Margit Abenius deserve a short
introduction.

*The philosopher*

Born in 1909 in Paris into a secularized Jewish middle-class family and
brought up in a climate of agnosticism, Simone Weil developed an early
interest in a form of Christian socialism.[9] In *Attente de Dieu* (*Waiting for
God*), written in 1942 and first published posthumously in 1950, Weil
defined herself as Christian by birth, but wholly ambivalent regarding
the question of God's existence. To her, Christian philosophy was synonymous with an engagement in politics and social welfare, rather than
with purely theological matters.[10]

From her early years, Weil was always mentioned as being extraor-
dinarily brilliant. Despite that, she regarded herself as inferior to her
beloved elder brother André, who in her eyes was a genius. At the Lycée
Henri IV in Paris she was known as one of the most talented philosophy students and in 1928 she finished first in the entrance exam for the

---

[8] Catarina Stenqvist, *Simone Weil. Om livets tragik och dess skönhet* (Stockholm,
1984), passim; Staffan Bergsten, 'Simone Weils tragiska estetik', *Läskonst,
skrivkonst, diktkonst* (Stockholm, 1987), passim.

[9] Her parents were the physician Bernard Weil and Selma (Salomea) Reinhertz.
Simone's older brother was the famous mathematician André Weil (1906–1998).
Before marrying Bertrand Weil in 1905, Selma Weil intended to study medicine.
Later she transferred her own intellectual ambitions to her children. See David
McLellan, *Simone Weil – Utopian Pessimist* (London, 1989), p. 4; André Weil, *The
Apprenticeship of a Mathematician* (Basel/Boston, 1992), pp. 18-19.

[10] Stenqvist, *Simone Weil*, p. 12.

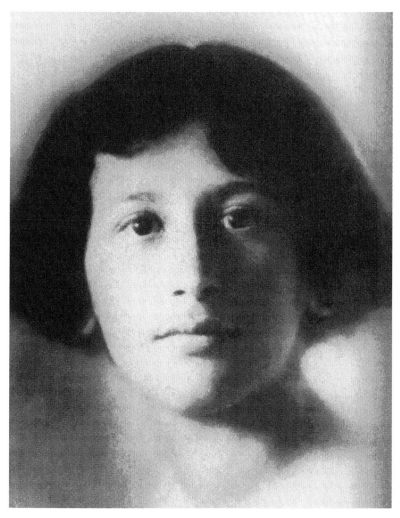

Simone Weil (1909-1943), aged thirteen.

École Normale Supérieure.[11] According to Simone de Beauvoir, Weil was considered an eccentric among the students, mostly because of her early interest in advanced philosophical research, but also for her ascetic

---

[11] Her peer, Simone de Beauvoir (1908–1986), actually finished second in the same examination, and thus could well have defined herself as 'second only to Weil' rather than 'second only to Sartre'; McLellan, *Utopian Pessimist*, p. 18.

and solitary lifestyle.[12] In 1931 she received her *Agrégation* diploma and from then on made a living teaching philosophy in schools, with her lesson notes from Roanne 1933–1934 being published by a former pupil several years later.[13] She was known for her radical opinions and for her involvement in political activities in support of unemployed and striking workers. In solidarity with the working class, she participated in the general strike in France in 1933 and in 1934 she worked incognito in two French factories. A declared pacifist, she nonetheless fought in the Spanish Civil War in 1936, before becoming a mystic in 1937, after a series of revelations during a stay in Assisi. She turned to Roman Catholicism but refused to be baptized, and from then on occupied herself with various religious issues, as was the case in the posthumously published *Attente de Dieu* (*Waiting for God*). She experienced the terror of war in Paris and escaped to New York with her family, but after a short stay returned to Europe on her own in 1942 and joined the French Resistance in England. Diagnosed with tuberculosis in 1943, she died in a sanatorium in Kent the same year at the age of thirty-four. Her ascetic lifestyle and self-starvation were believed to have hastened her physical deterioration.

## The critic

Margit Abenius, ten years Weil's senior, had been brought up under similar social conditions. Born in 1899 she was the eldest of four children of Wilhelm Abenius (1864–1956), associate professor of chemistry and high school principal, and Maria Westholm (1868–1935), a priest's daughter from the north of Sweden.[14] The Abenius family can be compared to that of Weil, not least regarding their literary and musical interests and their concern for their children's intellectual development. By

---

[12] Jean-Marie Perrin & Gustave Thibon, *Simone Weil, telle que nous l'avons connue*, p. 10; Simone de Beauvoir, *Mémoirs d'une jeune fille rangée*, pp. 236-237.

[13] Anne Reynaud, ed, *Leçons de philosophie de Simone Weil* (Paris, 1959); Simone Weil, *Lectures on Philosophy* (Cambridge, 2002).

[14] Similarly to Selma Weil, Abenius' mother did not have an academic education, though this would not have been impossible as Swedish universities accepted women students from 1873. To use a phrase from Pierre Bourdieu, she still had gained solid 'cultural capital' due to her own family background.

Margit Abenius (1899–1970). From Uppsala University Library.

her mid-teens Margit Abenius had decided to become an academic and a literary historian. Despite her brilliant results at school, Abenius was a persistent autodidact, who in her early teens made reading and literature studies her only goal in life. Multilingual, she consumed Scandinavian, English, German and French literature and handbooks in stylistics and literary studies, according to her own interests. At the age of nineteen, she took her final examination at Uppsala's most prestigious upper-secondary school, the coeducational Humanist Gymnasium. In 1921 she was admitted to the humanities faculty of Uppsala University where she studied Nordic languages, and in 1931 she received her doctoral degree in stylistics.

Although women had been allowed to take up employment in the academic sector since 1923, very few Swedish women academics had been given the chance to continue their research careers during the first decades of the twentieth century. This explains Abenius' choice to make her living writing book reviews and literary essays, though she never wrote for the daily press, only for a few of the most prestigious literary magazines in Sweden. Her origins meant that she did not experience the sufferings and the terror of war as Weil did. Nevertheless, from the late 1930s she was involved in the anti-Nazi debate and protested against Hitler's persecution of the Jews. From the early 1950s, she was an acknowledged member of the literary elite and one of the two best-paid contributors to *Bonniers Litterära Magasin* (Bonnier's Literary Magazine, commonly known as *BLM*), the most prestigious literary journal in Sweden. She was also in the position to accept or reject new writers submitting work to Bonnier's publishing house. In the words of Pierre Bourdieu, she had achieved enough symbolic capital to consecrate others in the literary field.[15] A member of one of the Swedish literary academies from 1949, she also wrote a biography of the famous Swedish modernist poet Karin Boye (1900–1941) in 1950. On her death in 1970, Abenius was remembered as one of the most prominent Swedish critics of the twentieth century. Today her name is rarely found in contemporary handbooks on literature and Swedish literary criticism.

---

[15] Despite her position in the literary field, as a female critic Abenius was probably regarded as an exception by many. The critic Sven Stolpe (1905–1996) attacked her, for example, for having refused a manuscript he sent to Bonniers. In one of his exceptionally misogynistic letters he informed Abenius that he would send the manuscript again, this time directly to the editor-in-chief, for what he called a professional evaluation. (A letter from Sven Stolpe to Margit Abenius, 11 November 1940. G 1n:14, Uppsala University Library). Even if Stolpe seems to have been unusually quarrelsome compared to others in Abenius' professional acquaintance, he was not the only one who treated her as less professional than her male colleagues.

*Discovering Weil*

Like many Swedish intellectuals, Abenius became interested in Simone
Weil's philosophy in the early 1950s. Though in a seemingly peripheral
position, Sweden was not unaffected by dramatic political imbalances
and by a growing intellectual discord within the Western world. The
Second World War was over and the Cold War had begun. In Sweden,
where the welfare state was born, the modernism movement of the
1940s was involved in at least three major literary debates. The issues
were pessimism in modern literature, the question of incomprehensibil-
ity and the issue of morality and immorality.[16] The literary magazine *40-
tal* (The 1940s) had been founded in 1944 and several women modernist
poets such as Rut Hillarp (1914–2003) and Elsa Grave (1918–2003) had
made their debut there. As well, critics Karl Vennberg (1910–1995) and
Erik Mesterton (1903–2004) participated in 1940's modernist literary
critique. At the same time, Margit Abenius was from time to time sent
'a reasonable package of the best among the latest ones' in order to review them, although her position was more that of a timeless arbiter of
taste.[17]

On the continent, politics, literature and philosophy seemed inseparable. In France, Jean Paul Sartre (1905–1980), Albert Camus (1913–
1960) and other existentialists were trying to extract a new philosophical
system by combining existentialism and socialism. Simone de Beauvoir
published *The Second Sex* in 1949, the same year NATO was founded
and the Soviet Union admitted being in possession of nuclear weapons.
Western intellectuals travelled east to explore the communist utopia
while Eastern Europe was closing its borders as the utopia became reality. Growing spirituality was in the air. To intellectuals who were seeking alternative philosophical systems, Weil's concept of the human self
seemed indispensable for the process of constructing a new and better
Europe. As she had published little during her lifetime, all her most important writings on mysticism, on moral philosophy and social justice
were now being edited one by one, published in haphazard collections

---

[16] Jenny Björklund, *Hoppets lyrik, Tre diktare och en ny bild av fyrtiotalismen. Ella
Hillbäck, Rut Hillarp, Ann Margret Dahlquist-Ljungberg* (Eslöv, 2004), pp. 33-84.

[17] A letter from Åke Runnquist to Margit Abenius, 27 June 1950. G 1n:14, Uppsala
University Library.

by her closest acquaintances.[18] *Gravity and Grace, Waiting for God* and *The Need for Roots* were read in French by European intellectuals, many of whom found them relevant during the period of recovery from the Second World War and the emerging Cold War. Albert Camus wrote in the early 1950s: 'One can hardly imagine a rebirth of Europe without paying regard to Simone Weil's claims'.[19]

The introduction of Weil to Sweden came at the right time but it was probably not Abenius' own idea. In 'On Human Need for Spirituality', a lecture held in 1956, Abenius described her first encounter with Weil's writings as a matter of total coincidence.[20] According to her own version, she had received the original French edition of *Gravity and Grace* from a friend:

> While I was glancing through it, I got that kind of premonition one sometimes gets, a foreboding that that book would become very important to me some day. ... It was only much later that I could devote myself to reading her posthumous works. In order to fully understand her I was finally forced to translate her La pesanteur et la grace [sic!] ...[21]

The spiritual vocabulary of the utterance, including terms such as 'premonition' and 'foreboding' was important to the context of the lecture. However, it also indicates that Abenius presented her discovery of Weil's writings in terms of a conversion or a vocation. In reality, the circumstances of Abenius' first meeting with Weil's works had probably been purely professional and a bit more trivial, even if it also made a very strong impression on her. 'Weil's books arrived today and were post-

---

[18] Although edited posthumously in 1949, *L'Enracinement* (*The Need for Roots*) was the only book that Weil managed to prepare for print. For a more detailed bibliography 1933–1989, including English translations, see McLellan, *Utopian Pessimist*.

[19] Quotation on the back cover of Abenius' edition of *Gravity and Grace* in 1954.

[20] Manuscripts concerning Simone Weil, Margit Abenius 13, Uppsala University Library.

[21] In Swedish: 'Om människans andliga behov', föredrag i Tylösand d. 25/9 1956, a lecture in Tylösand 25 September 1956, p. 4. Margit Abenius 13, Uppsala University Library.

ed today', *BLM*'s chief editor wrote to Abenius in June 1950. 'It would be nice if you could write something about her, as a couple of people have been talking about her recently'.[22] Abenius' introductory essay on Simone Weil was published in *Bonnier's Litterary Magazine* in 1951, together with her own choice of Weil's aphorisms from both *Gravity and Grace* and *The Need for Roots*.

As a transmitter of Weil's writings, Abenius addressed different kinds of audiences. The essay was certainly aimed at a high-brow academic reader, as it mainly analysed the development of Weil's philosophical system and its aesthetics. Thus, it addressed readers who possessed good skills in both theology and philosophy, as well as literature.

However, Abenius' translation of *Gravity and Grace* and her edition of *Waiting for God* were also accessible to a common reader, due to Abenius' very precise translations being free from borrowed terms. In her letter of 1957, the translator of the original version of *Waiting for God* into Swedish expressed her gratitude to Abenius for her having created a Swedish terminology for Weil's philosophical texts while translating *Gravity and Grace*, a terminology she promised to use herself. She also followed Abenius' advice to replace all of the borrowed French terms with very precise Swedish equivalents.[23] To Abenius, transferring Weil's mystical thought and her moral philosophy included the task of making it comprehensible to a lay reader.

The twelve lectures on Weil that Abenius gave all around the country and on the radio between 1953 and 1959 were of a more popular kind. It seems clear that Abenius strove to interest a more general audience and to transmit Weil's philosophical ideas as a system of universal moral values. The focus was often on Weil's philosophical thought in relation to her short and dramatic life, which also enabled Abenius to speak of ethics in more everyday terms. Some of the lectures were held in chapels and places intended for meditation or prayer. Whether the place was always chosen on the basis of the subject matter of the lecture or the opposite is uncertain, but it is hardly surprising that these lectures were explicitly devoted to the mysticism of Simone Weil, to her concept of

---

[22] A letter from Åke Runnquist to Margit Abenius, 27 June 1950. G 1n:14, Uppsala University Library.

[23] Letters from Karin Stolpe to Margit Abenius, 11 May 1955 and 1 January 1957. G 1n:14, Uppsala University Library.

social justice and human responsibility, as well as to spiritual matters in
general.

Considering different audiences, it might be of interest to discuss the
transmitter's possible motives. According to Broomans, the transmitter's
motivation 'can be aesthetically and/or ideologically or even politically
based'.[24] We might assume that when writing on demand for a highly
esteemed literary journal, Abenius was mostly concerned about presenting aspects of Weil's aesthetics which she found relevant to the Swedish
literary debate. On the contrary, in her lectures she strove to awaken
the audience's interest in Weil's concept of humanity and moral justice.
In other words, Abenius' motives seem to have been aesthetic on the
one hand, and ideological on the other. The very moment Abenius was
asked to present Weil's writings in *Bonnier's Literary Magazine*, the issue became an aesthetic matter, as the magazine expected a text that
would appeal to the literary elite. However, both the elite and a broader
middle-class audience showed a growing ideological interest in Weil's
mystical thought. Due to Abenius' introduction of her thought, Weil
became both a part of the Swedish literary field and of the growing exis-
tential debate in the early 1950s. From now on, her philosophical system
and her aesthetic doctrine, also known as her 'tragic aesthetics', would
be regarded as inseparable.[25] It is in this context that Abenius' translation work is of interest, since by combining her aesthetic and ideological
motives Abenius determined the way in which Weil would be perceived
from then on.

### Decoding a genius mind

Although multilingual and a philologist, Abenius hardly imagined the
result of becoming a translator. According to her own story, in order to
be able to fully understand the world of Simone Weil, '[she] was finally
forced to translate La pesanteur et la grace [sic!], which caused [her]
extreme difficulties, as [she] was not a trained translator and considered that translation work needed both natural qualities and intensive

---

[24] See Broomans' introduction to this volume.

[25] Simone Weil's 'tragic aesthetics' is synonymous to her seeking universal beauty
and universal laws in ancient tragedy and natural science; Bergsten 'Simone
Weils tragiska estetik', passim.

training'.[26] Despite her excellent language skills, she apparently did not perceive herself as equal to professional translators. Later on, she passed on the actual task of translating Weil's texts to professionals and was satisfied with prefacing them – and with reviewing others. On this point, the definition of a transmitter taking/obtaining various positions in the literary field might be modified. One and the same transmitter may obtain different positions in relation to the same object. Depending on the circumstances, it is possible to act as a translator, or as an editor of a single text/a whole *oeuvre*, or solemnly as a critic who revises other's editions of the same author.

Among Abenius' undated manuscripts and drafts concerning her work on Weil's writings in the early 1950s, we find biographical notes on Weil and a fragmentary bibliography, all of them typed in French. There are also a number of small cards on which Abenius wrote single words and expressions from *Gravity and Grace* and their possible Swedish equivalents, each card marked with a book page number. A black notebook, headed 'Notes on Simone Weil, Margit Abenius, 1950' is full of single French words, many of them returning haphazardly page after page, as if sketched mechanically by a very distracted person, or by someone desperately seeking for *le mot propre*.[27] A list of sources on Simone Weil and many chaotic reminder notes, as well as translations of single sentences from *Gravity and Grace* fill the rest of the notebook. The translations seem to have been a linguistic struggle.

## Margit Abenius as a cultural transmitter

Abenius did not primarily regard herself as a *female* critic who introduced a *female* philosopher, but as an intellectual dealing with another intellectual. Nevertheless, as Abenius and Weil were female exceptions in male-dominated professions, Abenius' work as a case of cultural transmission can hardly be understood without regard to the issues of religion, class, nationality and gender.

Despite very different life conditions, Abenius and Weil had much in common. Of similar social origins and education, their various similari-

---

[26] Abenius, 'Om människans andliga behov', a lecture in Tylösand on 25 September 1956, p. 4. Margit Abenius 13, Uppsala University Library.

[27] Margit Abenius 13, Uppsala University Library.

ties include both becoming religious through conversion, despite their shared critical attitude towards Christianity. Also, as women intellectuals concerned with questions of social justice and human rights, neither Weil nor Abenius ever expressed an explicit engagement with the women's movement.[28] Last but not least, both Weil's and Abenius' intellectual skills have traditionally been analysed in relation to their health.

Abenius' interest in understanding Weil as a mystic should probably be seen in the context of her own lifelong inner dispute with Christian dogma. As I have already mentioned, Weil's interest in the question of God's existence, while not consenting to be baptized, was in a sense similar to Abenius' oscillation between her total denial of the existence of God and her need for Christian ethics. Brought up in a family whose religious practice was traditional though of moderate intensity, Abenius declared she was an agnostic, or even an atheist early in life. However, at the age of 18–19, the question of God's presence continued to occupy her and her female friends, as can be seen in her diaries. During the Second

---

[28] As a philosopher, Weil was concerned with the idea of the human self, as well as with questions of social justice and responsibility, all of them regarded in a general human perspective. It is only recently that her philosophical system was acknowledged as a contribution to modern feminist thought. See Christopher Frost & Rebecca Bell-Metereau, *Simone Weil. On Politics, Religion and Society* (London, 1998). Abenius, for her part, never explicitly participated in the debate on women's rights, despite her lifelong literary promotion of female writers and intellectuals. This may seem surprising, considering the fact that she was only 22 when Swedish women finally obtained the right to vote, and that she was a very good friend of a number of prominent female intellectuals and pioneers within the Swedish suffrage movement. However, women only formally obtained access to the public sector in the mid-1920s. Their right to vote had also created an illusion of gender equality that might have influenced many from Abenius' generation. See Ulla Manns, *Den sanna frigörelsen. Fredrika – Bremer-förbundet 1884-1921* (Eslöv, 1997), p. 35; Birgitta Wistrand, *Elin Wägner i 1920-talet. Rörelseintellektuell och internationalist* (Uppsala, 2006), pp. 26-30. Last but not least, it is of course important to remember that the liberal women's movement did not involve all middle-class women, despite most of them being aware of the debate on women's rights and gender differences. Many of them probably simply defined themselves as intellectuals and did not feel the need to subscribe to the women's movement.

World War and in the late 1940s, Abenius had become very concerned
with moral and ethical issues, including the question of human good,
an interest that, according to her own statements, was partly generated
by her own inner crisis. As she claimed, finding Weil's mysticism in the
early 1950s made her 'discover the transcendence', or rather it had made
her rediscover what she had always known about God being more powerful than the struggle between good and evil.[29] In private she described
the process of discovering and understanding the thought of Weil as an
inner struggle and as exploring Weil's inner 'Inferno'. [30] It should be observed, however, that when lecturing on Weil in a professional context,
she chose to discuss both Weil's faith and spirituality in general terms of
responsibility, freedom, equality and truth, without using too much of
the explicitly religious vocabulary.[31]

Also, the question of Abenius alluding to her own health and mood,
an issue about which she was wholly explicit in private, needs to be
elaborated here as it concerns the image of both Weil and Abenius as
physically and mentally fragile. According to her family and her nearest acquaintants, Simone Weil had been extremely physically weak.[32]
As has been the case with many other women intellectuals in history,
the early image of Weil's lifelong struggle with her physical being soon
became inseparable from her philosophical genius. Not even Susan Sontag could analyse Weil's essays without mentioning her appendicitis, her

---

[29] Margit Abenius, *Memoarer från det inre* (Stockholm, 1963), p. 201.

[30] A letter from the Swedish theologian Emilia Fogelklou, 22 March 1953. G 1n:5,
Uppsala University Library.

[31] However, it should be noted here that Abenius' way of interpreting part of Weil's
vision of human suffering brought her into a deep conflict with some of her intellectual acquaintances. Both the philosopher Ingemar Hedenius (1908-1982) and
the critic Knut Jaensson (1893-1958) attacked Abenius for her acceptance of the
Catholic idea of Good and Evil as well as of meaningful human suffering, one of
the key ideas in Weil's philosophy. Svante Nordin, *Ingemar Hedenius. En filosof
och hans tid* (Stockholm, 2004), pp. 98-100 and 245-250.

[32] Both Simone Pétrément and others mention Weil's poor health as crucial to her
intellectual development but also as a hindrance to her contact with others. However, it seems that Simone Weil's inability to mix with others had to do with the
family's daily life. According to André Weil, his sister had 'a fear of germs' which
'she carried to an extreme as a child' (Weil, *The Apprenticeship*, p. 16).

almost pathological physical clumsiness and her legendary migraines, as well as her early death from tuberculosis. However, unlike many women writers who have been regarded as outsiders to literary movements, Weil was given a prominent position in Western philosophy.[33] Abenius, for her part, was regarded from her early years as being very sensitive and fragile.[34] At least from the age of 18, she suffered from an almost permanent insomnia, probably the first symptom of her lifelong manic depression. In her letters and autobiographical writings, she made no secret of her disease, and over long periods of time she would present herself as disabled by her depression – or as temporarily cured. As gender research points out, women writers' *oeuvres* are often analysed in the context of their physique and their private experiences.[35] According to Susan Bordo:

> ... mind/body dualism is no mere philosophical position, to be defended or dispensed with by clever argument. Rather, it is a practical metaphysics that has been deployed and socially embodied in medicine, law, literary and artistic representations, the psychological construction of self, interpersonal relationships, popular culture, and

---

[33] See Winch, *Simone Weil* (Cambridge, 1989); Richard Bell, *Simone Weil. The Way of Justice as Compassion* (Lanham, 1998); Henry Le Roy Finch, *Simone Weil and the Intellect of Grace. A Window on the World of Simone Weil* (New York, 1999); Rush Rhees & D.Z. Phillips, *Discussions on Simone Weil* (Albany NY, 2000); John Randolph LeBlanc, *Ethics and Creativity in the Political Thought of Simone Weil and Albert Camus* (New York, 2004).

[34] In her letters, Abenius mentioned her parents' concern about her fragility and their efforts to cure her before she went to university in 1921 (a letter to Olof Gjerdman, 30 October 1919. G 1n:19, Uppsala University Library). Her 'fragility' was also mentioned to me by her sister-in-law, Lisa Abenius, during our conversation on 18 October 2004.

[35] See Mary Ellman, *Thinking about Women* (New York, 1968). In Sweden: Boel Hackman, *Jag kan sjunga hur jag vill: tankevärld och konstsyn i Edith Södergrans diktning* (Helsingfors, 2000), pp. 20-31. On the feminist critique of biographical interpretations of women authors, see AnnaCarin Billing, 'Tänk den som vore en karl' in: Marta Ronne, ed, *Mot normen. Kvinnors skrivande under 1900-talet* (Uppsala, 2007), pp. 11-39, passim; and Margaretha Fahlgren, 'Från periferin' (Ronne, 2007), passim.

advertisements – a metaphysics which will be deconstructed only through concrete transformation of the institutions and practices that sustain it.[36]

The reason why I am bringing up the issue here is that the image of Weil as physically weak but intellectually outstanding was the one that Abenius met at an early stage of her work, due to Weil's family, friends and editors. She also used that image when presenting Weil to a general audience, both in relation to her own mental condition and in order to make the contrast between Weil's philosophical genius on the one hand, and her weak physique on the other. As the duality of body and mind is a classic motif in women's narratives of the intellectual, the issue, however problematic, is of importance when analysing the way Abenius approached Weil's writings.[37]

The task of bringing Simone Weil's writings to Sweden also included a piece of diplomatic work, as it often does when a literary heritage has to be negotiated in terms of copyrights and personal integrity. Weil had been written about – not to say canonized – shortly after her death by some of her nearest acquaintances (Perrin and Thibon in 1952, Pétrement in 1973 and others), among whom her mother Selma Weil seems to have been the most determined to guard both the literary heritage and the official image of her daughter. The copyright on Simone Weil's writings, as well as many of her letters and other documents, belonged exclusively to the Weil family, which allowed Selma Weil to interfere with both the translators and the editors, as well as to provide her own version of Simone Weil's life story to biographers. In her correspondence with Abenius, Selma Weil appears as an open-minded and social person, full of gratitude to those who contributed to the transmission of Simone Weil's *oeuvre*. Her first letters are full of practical information on places that Abenius should visit and people she should meet, all connected to Simone's life. Selma Weil also introduced Abenius to

---

[36] Susan Bordo, *Unbearable Weight: Feminism, Western Culture and the Body* (Berkeley, 2004), pp. 13-14.

[37] See Marta Ronne, "'The Mind and Body Problem": Academy, Gender and Power in Women's Contemporary Dissertation Novels', in: Åsa Johansson & Petra Ragnerstam, eds, *Limitation and Liberation: Women Writers and the Politics of Genre* (Uppsala, 2005).

those whom she herself regarded as important sources of information on her daughter, as well as to Weil's first English translator, A. Mills. However, after the initial personal contact during Abenius' journey to France in 1954, and the development of Selma Weil's understanding of Abenius' work, a slight conflict arose between the two as to the selection of writings in the Swedish edition of Weil's *La personne et le sacré*. As Selma Weil informed Abenius, she was not 'particularly fond of editions consisting of "selections" (morceaux choisis)' that in her opinion seldom do justice to the writer. She was thus against the project of publishing Simone Weil's selected letters, and especially those that had not yet been edited in France. With impressive diplomacy, Abenius managed to convince her that Weil's philosophical *oeuvre* could per se be regarded as 'morceaux choisis', and that her own choice of essays by no means would vulgarize Weil's writings:

> What has deeply influenced me in Simone Weil's writings was her request to *transmit* the truths in the right way to different audiences and on different levels. I have absolutely no intention whatsoever to popularize her thought. It would be a crime. To me, the most important thing is to knead the intellectual ferment ... into the dough ['que le levain ... soit incorporé à la pâte']. I suppose you can hardly imagine the difference between Sweden and France when it comes to social conditions and our tradition of education! I find it just to make some changes in my selection so that the material can be transferred in a way that suits Swedish readers.[38]

Finally, Weil's essay on Marxist doctrine was removed from the collection on Selma Weil's personal request; however, the remainder, including a number of her selected letters, was published as planned.

Due to her work on Weil's writings and her contact with the Weil family, Abenius became part of an international network of translators, editors and biographers, by whom she seems to have been regarded as an important transmitter of Weil's *oeuvre* to the northern part of Europe. Her correspondence with Selma Weil shows clearly that she became immediately accepted due to her social background, her academic merits

---

[38] A letter from Margit Abenius to Selma Weil, 26 July 1957. G 1n:19, Uppsala University Library. Original spelling.

and her age. Regarding the fact that she was one of the very few women within that network, the impact of gender as 'negative symbolic capital' in this particular case was probably less important than other forms of symbolic capital she possessed.[39] This makes her case as a cultural transmitter interesting when regarded in terms of gender and class, an issue that I discuss elsewhere.[40] As Toril Moi put it: 'When analysing the social position and habitus of one particular woman it is easy to overestimate the effects of one specific social factor such as femaleness, or to ascribe to gender alone the effects of a much more complex and interconnected web of factors such as sex, class, race and age'.[41]

## Conclusions

To Abenius, her work on understanding and introducing Simone Weil's philosophy and aesthetics was to become one of the most important stages of her professional career, although her interpretations of Weil's philosophy were also regarded as controversial by some influential Swedish intellectuals. At the same time, discovering Weil was a deeply personal and emotional experience. As a critic and a transmitter, she contributed to the introduction of Weil to Sweden shortly after Weil's work was published in France, during a time of her growing popularity and developing significance for the intellectual climate of the early 1950s. The contribution of Abenius in bringing Weil to Sweden may thus be regarded as substantial. My aim has been to discuss some of the aspects of cultural transmission, here exemplified by Abenius' work on the introduction of Weil's oeuvre to Sweden in the 1950s.

---

[39] Toril Moi, 'Appropriating Bourdieu: Feminist theory and Pierre Bourdieu's sociology of culture', *New Literary History* 22 (1991) 4, p. 1038.

[40] Marta Ronne, 'Teoretiska perspektiv på kön, klass och gränsöverskridanden i akademin. Margit Abenius som forskare och litteraturkritiker', *Utbildning och Demokrati* 2 (2006), p. 116f.

[41] Moi, 'Appropriating', p. 1037.

# About the authors

JOHAN BRAECKMAN is professor at Ghent University. He studied human ecology at Vrije Universiteit Brussel and philosophy at Ghent University, and wrote his doctoral dissertation on the philosophical implications of Darwin's evolutionary theory. He teaches courses on the history of philosophy, philosophical anthropology and the history and philosophy of biology at Ghent University.

PETRA BROOMANS is Associate Professor of Scandinavian Linguistics and Literatures at the University of Groningen. She is coordinator of the project 'Scandinavian Literature in Europe around 1900: the Influence of Language Politics, Gender and Aesthetics' (2004–2010) and is currently working on a new project, 'Cultural Transmission and Minor Language Areas'. She is also editor-in-chief of the series Studies in Cultural Transfer and Transmission (CTaT). For further information please visit her website: www.petrabroomans.net.

MARYSA DEMOOR is Professor of English Literature at Ghent University. She has published extensively on Victorian and Edwardian culture. Her most recent book publications include *Their Fair Share. Women, Power and Criticism in the* Athenaeum, *from Millicent Garrett Fawcett to Katherine Mansfield, 1870–1920* (Ashgate, 2000) and *Marketing the Author: Authorial Personae, Narrative Selves and Self-Fashioning, 1880– 1930* (Palgrave, 2004). She is also co-editor with Laurel Brake of the *Dictionary of Nineteenth-Century Journalism* (forthcoming, British Library, Academia Press, ProQuest) and the *Lure of Illustration in the Nineteenth Century: Picture and Press* (forthcoming, Palgrave).

ESTER JIRESCH has an MA in History and Scandinavian Studies and has studied in Vienna and Stockholm. She is currently conducting PhD research at the Groningen Research School for the Study of the Humanities (GRSSH) at the University of Groningen, on 'The role of networks in the work of female cultural transmitters of Scandinavian literature and culture in Europe around 1900. A comparative study of the Dutch/ Flemish and the Austrian/German-speaking regions'. She has published several articles and a monograph, *Die Österreichisch-schwedische*

*Gesellschaft. Ihre Geschichte, ideologische Hintergründe und kulturelle Konstruktion* (=Wechselbeziehungen Österreich – Norden, Vol 6, eds. Matthias Langheiter-Tutschek and Sven Hakon Rossel) (Vienna, 2004: Edition Praesens).

JANKE KLOK studied Scandinavian Literatures and Linguistics at the University of Groningen, where she is currently lecturing and completing her PhD on 'The literary representation of the city in the work of four Norwegian woman writers in the period 1880–1980 – case studies on the feminine imagination of the city'. She has published several articles on Scandinavian literature and in the field of gender studies, and is editor of *De ideologieën voorbij? Vijftig jaar na* Le deuxième sexe, co-editor of *Scandinavian Newsletter – a literary and cultural magazine* and of 'Wilde aardbeien', a book series for Scandinavian literature in the Netherlands.

GERALDINE REYMENANTS wrote her PhD thesis on the position of women in the literary field (Ghent University, 2005) and has published mainly on twentieth-century women authors. She is currently research coordinator at the Institute for the Equality of Women and Men (Belgium).

MARTA RONNE has a PhD in Comparative Literature from Uppsala University, Uppsala, Sweden. Her doctoral thesis was on gender and Swedish university novels published between 1903–1943. She is currently teaching and conducting research in comparative literature and gender studies at the Centre for Gender Studies and the Department of Literature in Uppsala. She has published several articles and is currently working on a professional biography of Margit Abenius (1899–1970), one of the most prominent Swedish literary critics of the twentieth century. Ronne is also a key figure in Uppsala for the project 'Peripheral autonomy? Longitudinal analyses of cultural transfer in the literary fields of small language communities', which is run in cooperation with the universities of Ghent and Groningen. See her website at www.littvet.uu.se.

LISELOTTE VANDENBUSSCHE studied English and Dutch Literature and Linguistics at Ghent University and Literary Theory at the Katholieke Universiteit Leuven. She wrote her doctoral dissertation on liberal women writers in literary and cultural magazines in Flanders (1870–1914), which will be published by the Royal Academy for Dutch Literature and Linguistics (KANTL, forthcoming). She has also published in *Nederlandse Letterkunde*, *Women's History Review*, *Spiegel der Letteren* and *Yang* and contributed to several books. She is currently a postdoctoral researcher at the Department of Translation Studies of University College Ghent and is affiliated with Ghent University. Her doctoral research focuses on literary translators in Flanders, 1830–1914.

GRIET VANDERMASSEN, studied philosophy and English and German literature and linguistics at Ghent University. She is the author of *Who's Afraid of Charles Darwin? Debating Feminism and Evolutionary Theory* (Rowman & Littlefield, 2005) and is currently a postdoctoral researcher at the Centre for Gender Studies at Ghent University. She has published articles in *Sex Roles*, the *Journal of Theoretical Biology* and the *European Journal of Women's Studies*, amongst other publications.

EBBA WITT-BRATTSTRÖM is Professor of Comparative Literature and Gender Studies at Södertörn University College, Stockholm. She has published numerous books, articles and anthologies, including 'Ediths jag. Edith Södergran och modernismens födelse' (Edith's self: Edith Södergran and the birth of modernism, 1997), 'Dekadensens kön. Ola Hansson och Laura Marholm' (The Gender of Decadence: Ola Hansson and Laura Marholm, 2007), 'The New Woman and the Aesthetic Opening. Unlocking Gender in Twentieth-Century Texts' (2004), and the essay collection *Ur könets mörker: Litteraturanalyser* (Out of the darkness of sex: Literary analyses, 2003). She is Swedish editor of volumes two and three of *Nordisk Kvinnolitteraturhistoria* (1800–1900; 1900–1960) (Nordic Women's Literary History, 1993 and 1996), and member of the editorial board for the publication of Nordic Women's Literary History on the web (in Swedish, Danish and English). She currently holds the Dag Hammarskjöld guest professorship at the Nordeuropa Institute, Humboldt University, Berlin (2008–2011).

# Bibliography

A.d.R., 'Lena en Roza van Louisa Duijkers', *Vlaamsche Arbeid* 3 (1907-1908) 5, pp. 152-153.

Abenius, M., 'Simone Weil', *Bonniers Litterära Magasin*, 7 (1951), pp. 511-517.

— *Memoarer från det inre* (Stockholm, 1963).

Adlersparre, K., and Huss, E., *Qvinnan inom svenska litteraturen; bibliografiskt försök af två damer* (Stockholm, 1873).

Alenius, M., 'Om alla slags berömvärda kvinnopersoner. Gynaeceum – en kvinnolitteraturhistoria' in: E. Møller Jensen et al., eds, *I Guds namn. 1000-1800*, (Höganäs, 1993), pp. 217-246.

Allphin, C., *Women in the Plays of Henrik Ibsen* (New York, 1975).

Anonymous [V. Loveling], [untitled], *La Flandre Libérale*, February 24, 1876.

Anonymous [V. Loveling], 'L'Infanticide en Chine', *La Flandre Libérale*, January 6, 1876.

Anonymous [V. Loveling], 'Le bon Dieu détrôné', *La Flandre Libérale*, February 7, 1876.

Anonymous, *Congrès de l'Association internationale pour le Progrès des Sciences Sociales, tenu à Gand, 1862-1863. Annales, portraits, letters* (Gent, s.d.), pp. 402-449.

Ardis, A., *New Women. New Novels* (London, 1990).

Armstrong, I., *The Radical Aesthetic* (Oxford, 2000).

Baekelmans, L., 'Skandinavische literatuur in vertalingen' in: *Dietsche Warande en Belfort* (1929), pp. 661-675.

Baers, M., 'Spreekbeurt door Mej. Senator Baers uit naam van de Vrouwen van het land', Annex to *Dietsche Warande en Belfort* 48 (1948) 3-4, pp. 6-9.

Basse, M., *Het Aandeel der Vrouw in de Nederlandsche Letterkunde II* (Gent, 1921).

Beer, G., *Darwin's Plots. Evolutionary Narrative in Darwin, George Eliot and Nineteenth-Century Fiction* (Cambridge, 1983, ²2000).

Bell, R. H., *Simone Weil: The Way of Justice as Compassion* (Lanham, 1998).

Belpaire, M.E., *Vrouweninvloed* (Antwerpen, 1903).

Benedictsson, V., 'Ur mörkret', in: Witt-Brattström, E., ed, *Ord på liv och död I-II, Kortprosa, dramatik, dagbok* (Stockholm, 2008), pp. 87-98.

Bergsten, S., 'Simone Weils tragiska estetik', *Läskonst, skrivkonst, diktkonst* (Vänersborg, 1987), pp. 231-255.

Bernheimer, C., *Decadent Subjects. The Idea of Decadence in Art, Literature, Philosophy, and Culture of the Fin de Siècle in Europe*, Kline, T.J. & Schor, N., eds (Baltimore, 2002).

Bernos, M., 'De l'influence salutaire ou pernicieuse de la femme dans la famille et la société, *Revue d'histoire moderne et contemporaine* 29 (1982), pp. 453-461.

Bienfait, C., 'Margaretha Meyboom', in: *Leven en Werken. Maandblad voor Meisjes en Vrouwen 12* (Amsterdam, 1927), pp. 831-838.

— ed, *In herinnering aan Margaretha Meyboom. Door haar vrienden* (s. l., [1930]).

Billing, AC., '"Tänk den som vore en karl." Diktjaget, fin-de-siècle och normernas spel i några dikter av Harriet Löwenhjelm', in: Ronne, M., ed, *Mot normen. Kvinnors skrivande under 1900-talet* (Uppsala, 2007), pp. 11-39.

Bjørhovde, G., *Rebellious Structures. Women Writers and the Crisis of the Novel 1880-1900* (Oslo, 1987).

Björklund, J., *Hoppets lyrik. Tre diktare och en ny bild av fyrtiotalismen. Ella Hillbäck, Rut Hillarp, Ann Margret Dahlquist-Ljungberg* (Eslöv, 2004).

Blau du Plessis, R., *Writing beyond the ending: narrative strategies of twentieth-century women writers* (Bloomington, 1987).

Bliksrud, L., ed, *Norske essayister. Camilla Collett* (Oslo, 1997 [1993]).

Bordo, S., *Unbearable Weight: Feminism, Western Culture and the Body* (Berkely, 2004).

Bosch, M., *Het geslacht van de wetenschap. Vrouwen en hoger onderwijs in Nederland 1878-1948* (Amsterdam, 1994).

Bourdieu, P., *The field of cultural production. Essays on art and literature* (Cambridge, 1999).

Bracke, N., 'Vrouw', in: De Schryver, R. et al., eds, *Nieuwe encyclopedie van de Vlaamse Beweging* III (Tielt, 1998), pp. 3604-3627.

Braeckman, J., *Darwins moordbekentenis. De ontwikkeling van het denken van Charles Darwin* (Amsterdam, 2001).

Brantly, S., *The life and writings of Laura Marholm* (= Beiträge zur nordischen Philologie. Schweizerische Gesellschaft für skandinavische Studien, ed) (Basel [et al.] 1991).

— *The Life and writings of Laura Marholm, UMI, diss., Yale University 1988* (also in Beiträge zur nordischen Philologie 21, Frankfurt/M, 1991).

Broomans, P., 'Hur skapas en litteraturhistorisk bild? Den nordiska litteraturens fräschhet i Nederländerna och Flandern?', in: Dahl, P. and Steinfeld, T., eds, *Videnskab og national opdragelse. Studier i nordisk litteraturhistorieskrivning 2* (København, 2001a), pp. 487-541.

— 'In the name of God and the Father. Scandinavian women's literary history from a meta-literary historical point of view', in: Van Dijk, S, Van Gemert, L. and Ottway, S., eds, *Writing the history of women's writing. Toward an international approach,* Koninklijke Nederlandse Akademie van Wetenschappen Verhandelingen, Afd. Letterkunde, Nieuwe Reeks, deel 182 (Amsterdam, 2001b), pp. 125-134

— 'Scandia i Nederländerna. Om Margaretha Meijboom och hennes nordiska tidskrifter', *Tijdschrift voor Skandinavistiek* Vol 22, Nr. 1 (Amsterdam, 2001c), pp. 155-167.

— 'Den nordiska litteraturens fälttåg i Europa i Europa kring 1900. Om Brandes och medresenärer, maktkamp och avfall', in: Harsløf, O., ed, *Georg Brandes og Europa* (København, 2004:a), pp. 163-176.

— '"The splendid literature of the North", Women translators and intermediaries of Scandinavian women writers around 1900', in: Dijk, S van, et al., eds, *I have heard about you', Foreign Women's Writing Crossing the Dutch Border: from Sappho to Selma Lagerlöf* (Hilversum, 2004:b), pp. 307-323.

— 'Mary Wollstonecraft in Scandinavia; her letters in the Netherlands', in: Van Dijk, S. et al., eds, *'I have heard about you', Foreign Women's Writing Crossing the Dutch Border: from Sappho to Selma Lagerlöf* (Hilversum, 2004:c), pp. 248-253.

— 'Om vårt sätt att forska i kulturförmedling. Exempel: Marie Herzfeld (1855-1940)', in: Rossel, S. H., et al., eds, *Der Norden im Ausland - das Ausland im Norden. Formung und Transformation von Konzepten und Bildern des Anderen vom Mittelalter bis heute* (= Wiener Studien zur Skandinavistik Vol. 15) (Wien, 2006:a), pp. 201-209.

— 'The Self-Fashioning of Hedvig Charlotta Nordenflycht', in: Inger M. Olsen and Sven H. Rossel, eds, *Female Voices of the North II. An Anthology.* Wiener Texte zur Skandinavistik (WTS). Band 3 (Wien, 2006:b), pp. 27-51.

— and Jiresch, E., 'Philippine Wijsman: een selfmade vertaalster', in: *Filter. Tijdschrift over vertalen*, 13, nr. 3 (2006), pp. 31-41.

— 'The Inexpressible of the Nature of Woman. Women Cultural Transmitters and Ibsen's Writing About How Women Love', in: Helland, F. et al., eds, *The Living Ibsen.* Proceedings - The 11th International Ibsen Conference, 21 - 27 August 2006. Acta Ibseniana, Centre for Ibsen Studies, University of Oslo (Oslo, 2007), pp. 399-405.

— 'The Concept of Ethnolinguistic Nationalism and Cultural Transfer. The Reception of Scandinavian Literature in Flanders and the Netherlands', in: Broomans, P. et al., eds, *The Beloved Mothertongue. Ethnolinguistic Nationalism in Small Nations. Inventories and Reflections.* Groningen Studies in Cultural Change (Leuven, 2008), pp. 37-47.

Buchten, D., Christensen, E.S. et al., eds, *"Jeg har en koffert i Berlin". Nordmenn i Berlin rundt 1900 og 2000* (Oslo, 2007).

Burke, P., *Lost (and Found) in Translation: A Cultural History of Translators and Translating in Early Modern Europe* (Wassenaar, 2005).

Cannegieter, H.G., 'Karakterschets. Margaretha Meyboom', in: *Morks-Magazijn* 27 (1925), pp. 3-4.

Chamberlain, L., 'Gender and the Metaphorics of Translation', in: Venuti, L., ed, *The Translation Studies Reader* (London/New York, 2000), pp. 314-329.

Claes, D., 'Het Davids-fonds en de vrouwen', *Dietsche Warande en Belfort* 2 (1901), 3, pp. 274-292.

Collett, C., *I de lange Nætter* (Christiania, 1863).

— *Sidste Blade* (Christiania, 1873).

— *Fra de Stummes Leir* (Christiania, 1877).

— *Fra de Stummes Leir. Samlede verker. Mindeutgave. Andet Bind* (Kristiania/ Kjøbenhavn, 1913).

— *Samlede verker. Mindeutgave. Andet Bind* (Kristiania/Kjøbenhavn, 1913).

— *Samlede verker. Mindeutgave. Tredje Bind* (Kristiania/Kjøbenhavn, 1913).

Crols, F., *Katholieke Vlaamsche vrouwenbeweging* (Brugge, 1913).

Cronin, H., *The Ant and the Peacock: Altruism and Sexual Selection from Darwin to Today* (New York, 1991, [2]1994).

Dahlerup, P., *Det moderne gennembruds kvinder* (dissertation) (Köpenhamn, 1983).

Dahlgren, L., ed, *Dagny* (1898).

Darwin, C., *The Descent of Man, and Selection in Relation to Sex*, Barrett, P. and R.B. Freeman, eds, vols. 21 and 22 of *The Works of Charles Darwin* (London, [2]1989).

'Darwin & Co. Dubbelnummer over taal, evolutie en literatuur', special issue of *Armada. Tijdschrift voor wereldliteratuur* 8/9 (2002/2003).

Dassen, P. and Kemperink, M., eds, *The many faces of human evolution in Europe, c. 1860-1914* (Leuven/Paris/Dudley, 2005).

De Baar, M., '"God has chosen you to be a crown of glory for all women!" The international network of learned women surrounding Anna Maria van Schurman', in: S. van Dijk et al., eds, *'I have heard about you', Foreign Women's Writing Crossing the Dutch Border: from Sappho to Selma Lagerlöf* (Hilversum, 2004), pp. 108-135.

— 'Prophetess of God and prolific writer. Antoinette Bourignon and the reception of her writings', in: Suzan van Dijk et al., eds, *'I have heard about you', Foreign Women's Writing Crossing the Dutch Border: from Sappho to Selma Lagerlöf* (Hilversum, 2004), pp. 136-149.

De Beauvoir, S., *Memoirs d'une jeune fille rangée* (Paris, 1958).

'De biologisering van het wereldbeeld: de doorwerking van Darwins evolutietheorie in de Nederlandse cultuur', special issue of *Negentiende eeuw* 17 (1993).

De Bont, R., *Darwins kleinkinderen. De evolutietheorie in België 1865-1945* (Nijmegen, 2008).

De Giorgio, M., 'Het katholieke model', in: Fraisse, G. and Perrot, M., eds, *Geschiedenis van de vrouw. De negentiende eeuw* (Amsterdam, 1993), pp. 125-156.

De Vrieze, S., 'Selma Lagerlöf och Margaretha Meyboom', in: Lagerlöfsällskapet (Ek, B. et al., eds), *Lagerlöfstudier 6* (Lund, 1979), pp. 101-114.

Derks, M., 'Vrouwen, confessionalisering en biografie. Catharina Alberdingk Thijm of de eigenaardigheid van een karakter', in: van Heijst, A. and Derks, M., eds, *Terra Incognita. Historisch onderzoek naar katholicisme en vrouwelijkheid* (Kampen, 1994), pp. 109-128.

Dolan, B., *Ladies of the Grand Tour* (London, 2001).

Drachmann, H., *En bok om Strindberg* (Karlstad, 1894).

Dudley, J., *A Man's Game. Masculinity and the Anti-Aesthetics of American Literary Naturalism* (Alabama, 2004).

Duyvendak, L., *Het Haags Damesleesmuseum: 1894-1994* ('s-Gravenhage, 1994).

— 'Meijboom, Margaretha Anna Sophia', in: *Biographisch woordenboek van Nederland 5,* (Den Haag, 2001), pp. 332-334.

Eeckhout, J., 'Juffrouw Maria, Elisa Belpaire', *Dietsche Warande en Belfort* 26 (1926), 1, pp. 28-34.

Eeden van, F., 'Westerbro', in: *De Pionier. Weekblad ter bespreking van binnenlandsche Kolonisatie,* 16 June, 1906, p. 1.

Elias, H.J., *Geschiedenis van de Vlaamse gedachte IV, Taalbeweging en cultuurflamingantisme. De groei van het Vlaamse bewustzijn, 1883-1914* (Antwerpen, 1965).

Ellmann, M., *Thinking about Women* (New York, 1968).

Espagne, M. and Werner, M., 'Deutsch-französischer Kulturtransfer im 18. und 19. Jahrhundert. Zu einem neuen interdisziplinären Forschungsprogramm des C.N.R.S', *Francia* 13 (1985), pp. 502-510.

— 'La construction d'une référence culturelle Allemande en France genèse et histoire (1750-1914)', *Annales: Economies, Sociétés, Civilisations* 4 (1987), pp. 969-992.

Ezell, M.J.M., *Writing Women's Literary History* (Baltimore, 1993).

Fahlgren, M., 'Från periferin till centrum. Edith Södergran och kvinnorna i 1940-talets litteraturhistoriska seminarierum', Ronne, M., ed, *Mot normen. Kvinnors skrivande under 1900-talet* (Uppsala, 2007), pp. 113-128.

Felski, R., *The Gender of Modernity* (Cambridge, Mass, 1995).

Finch, H. LeRoy, *Simone Weil and the Intellect of Grace. A Window on the World of Simone Weil* (London, 2001).

Frost, C., and Bell-Meterau, R., *Simone Weil On Politics, Religion and Society* (London, 1998).

Gedin, D., *Fältets herrar. Framväxten av en modern författarroll. Artonhundraåttitalet* (Stockholm, 2004).

Gentikow, B., *Skandinavien als präkapitalistische Idylle. Rezeption gesellschaftskritischer Literatur in deutschen Zeitschriften 1870 bis 1914* (Neumünster, 1978).

Gilbert, S.M., and Gubar, S, *The madwoman in the attic. The woman writer and the nineteenth-century literary imagination* (New Haven/London, 1979).

Goekoop-de Jong van Beek en Donk, C., *Hilda van Suylenburg* (Amsterdam, 1897).

Grave, J., 2001, *Zulk vertalen is een werk van liefde. Bemiddelaars van Nederlandstalige literatuur in Duitsland 1890-1914* (Nijmegen, 2001).

Grit, D., *Dansk skønlitteratur i Nederland og Flandern 1731-1982. Bibliografi over oversættelser og studier* (Ballerup, 1986).

Hackman, B., *Jag kan sjunga hur jag vill: tankevärld och konstsyn i Edith Södergrans diktning* (Helsingfors, 2001).

Hannay, M. P., ed, *Silent but for the Word. Tudor Women as Patrons, Translators, and Writers of Religious Works* (Kent, 1985).

Hareide, J., ed, *Skrift, kropp og selv: nytt lys på Camilla Collett* (Oslo, 1998).

Hendershot, C., *The Animal Within. Masculinity and the Gothic* (Michigan, 1998).

Herzfeld, M., *Die Skandinavische litteratur und ihre tendenzen. Nebst anderen essays* (Berlin/Leipzig, 1898).

Jiresch, E., *Die Rolle von Netzwerken in der Arbeit von weiblichen Vermittlern skandinavischer Literatur und Kultur und das von ihnen vermittelte Bild in Europa um 1900. Eine vergleichende Studie des niederländischen/flämischen und deutschen/österreichischen Sprachraums* (Groningen, in progress).

Kemperink M. and Krul, W., eds, 'De gedeelde werkelijkheid van wetenschap, cultuur en literatuur', special issue of *Spiegel der letteren* 42 (2000).

Kemperink, M., '"Excelsior" is het devies van de natuur: Darwinisme in de Nederlandse roman (1860-1885)', in: *Nederlandse letterkunde* 3 (1998), pp. 97-126.

—  'Als je voor een dubbeltje geboren bent... Representatie van het lagere volk in de Noord-Nederlandse literatuur van het fin de siècle', in: *Spiegel der Letteren* 42 (2000), pp. 134-155.

—  'Evolution and utopianism in Dutch literature around 1900. An early polemic', in: Dassen, P. and Kemperink, M., eds, *The many faces of human evolution in Europe, c. 1860-1914* (Leuven/Paris/Dudley, 2005), pp. 115-128.

— 'Jungle en paradijs: Darwinisme in de Nederlandse roman (1885-1910)', in: *Nederlandse letterkunde* 4 (1999), pp. 1-36.

— *Het verloren paradijs: de Nederlandse literatuur en cultuur van het fin de siècle* (Amsterdam, 2001).

Key, E., *Lifslinjer I* (Stockholm, 1903).

— *Missbrukad kvinnokraft* (Stockholm, 1896).

Krontiris, T., *Oppositional Voices: Women as Writers and Translators of Literature in the English Renaissance* (London, 1992).

Lagerlöf, S., *Gösta Berlings saga* (Stockholm, 1891).

— *Liljecronas hem* (Stockholm, 1911).

LeBlanc, J. R., *Ethics and Creativity in the Political Thought of Simone Weil and Albert Camus* (New York, 2004).

Ledger, S., *The New Woman. Fiction and Feminism at the Fin de Siècle* (Manchester, 1997).

Ledwon, L., 'Darwin's Ghosts: The Influence of Darwinism on the Nineteenth-century Ghost story', in: *Proteus* 6 (1989), pp. 10-16.

Leijonhufvud, S. och Brithelli, S, *Kvinnan inom svenska litteraturen intill år 1893. En bibliografi: utarbetad med anledning af världsutställningen i Chicago* (Stockholm, 1978).

Lie, J., *Lindelin* (Kopenhagen, 1897).

Loveling, R. and V., *Gedichten* (Groningen, 1870).

— *Nieuwe Novellen* (Gent, 1876).

— *Novellen* (Gent, 1874).

Loveling, R., 'Iets over het onderwijs der vrouw', *De Toekomst* 15 (1871), pp. 411-415.

— 'Onbehendige troostwoorden', *De Toekomst* 18 (1874), pp. 216-222.

— 'Trina', *Het Letterkundig Zondagsblad* 7 (1864), pp. 11-24.

Loveling, V., 'De kwellende gedachte', in: Loveling, R. & V., *Nieuwe Novellen* (Gent, 1876, ²1887), reprinted in *De Hollandsche Lelie* (1892) and *de Toekomst*.

— 'Anton', *Het Nederduitsch Tijdschrift* (1866), pp. 47-85.

— 'Boekbeoordeling van *De schriftlezing. Handschrift en karakter* door H.W. Cornelis', *Tijdschrift van het Willemsfonds* 3 (1898), pp. 190-192.

— 'Boekbeoordeling. *Studiën over Calderon en zijne geschriften*, door J.J. Putman', *Nederlandsch Museum* 8 (1881), pp. 340-367.

— 'Boekbeoordelingen. *Amazone* door C. Vosmaer', *Nederlandsch Museum* 8 (1881), pp. 245-247.

— 'Boekbespreking van Louwerse "Voor de kinderkamer, een geïllustreerd maandblad voor het kleine volkje"', *De Toekomst* 28 (1884), pp. 152-154.

— 'C. Vosmaer, *Amazone*', *Atheneum belge* 4 (1882), p. 233.
— 'De keus eener kostschool', *De Toekomst* 18 (1874), pp. 183-184.
— 'De l'Enseignement Populaire dans les trois pays scandinaves', *Revue de Belgique* 3 (1871), pp. 143-149, pp. 213-224, pp. 68-81 and pp. 213-223.
— 'Detel', *Het Nederduitsch Tijdschrift* (1866), pp. 27-64.
— 'Een Holsteinsche jongen', *Nederlandsch Museum* 6 (1880), pp. 174-268.
— 'Een soirée bij Busken Huet en een Receptie bij Victor Hugo', *Groot Nederland* 6 (1908), pp. 467-482.
— 'Een stierengevecht', *Nederland* 34 (1893), pp. 377-398.
— 'Een wereldlijk hospitaal', *Nederlandsch Museum* 14 (1887), pp. 47-66.
— 'Eene catholieke processie in Hannover', *Nederlandsch Museum* 15 (1888), pp. 5-13.
— 'Eenige bemerkingen op sommige strofen van Ledegancks gedicht "De Hut in 't Woud"', *De Toekomst* 18 (1874), pp. 117-121.
— 'Iets over Andersens vertellingen', *De Toekomst* 18 (1874), pp. 318-321.
— 'J.J. Cremer, *Romantische werken*', *Atheneum belge* 5 (1882), pp. 14-16.
— 'J.J. Putman, *Studiën over Calderon en zijne geschriften*', *Atheneum belge* 5 (1882), pp. 102-103.
— 'Klaus Groth, *Drei plattdeutsche Erzählungen*', *Atheneum belge* 4 (1881), pp. 51-52.
— '*Lelie- en rozeknoppen. Weekblad voor meisjes*', *Nederlandsch Museum* 8 (1882), pp. 243-249.
— 'Meesterschap', in: *Jonggezellenlevens en andere novellen* (Aalst, 1907, repr. Antwerpen, 1934).
— 'Moederlijk gezag', *De Toekomst* 16 (1872), pp. 93-94.
— 'Stonehenge', *Leeskabinet* 67 (1902), pp. 127-131.
— 'Teirlinck-Stijns, *Six nouvelles, traduit du flamand par J. Elseni et F. Gueury*', *Atheneum belge* 4 (1881), pp. 109-110.
— 'The Conferring of Degrees te Cambridge', *Nederlandsch Museum* 18 (1892), pp. 313-320; reprinted in *De Toekomst* 37 (1893), pp. 144-149.
— 'Witen Slachters', *Nederlandsch Museum* 8 (1882), pp. 316-348.
— *Een dure Eed* (Gent, s.d. [1892]).
— *Een Idylle* (Amsterdam, 1893, repr. Antwerpen, 1934).
— *Een Revolverschot* (Antwerpen, 1911).
— *Erfelijk belast* (Rotterdam, 1906).
— *In onze Vlaamsche gewesten: politieke schetsen* (Gent, 1877).
— *Sophie* (Gent, 1884).

— 'Het doel van Middelbaar Onderwijs voor meisjes door A.M. De Cock', *De Toe-komst* 15 (1871), pp. 385-387.

MacCanell, J. F., *The Regime of the Brother. After Patriarchy* (London, 1991).

Mai, A-M., 'Det danska språkets innerliga älskarinna. Om Anna Margrethe Lasson', in: Møller Jensen, E. et al., eds, *I Guds namn. 1000-1800* (Höganäs, 1993), pp. 341-347.

Månesköld-Öberg, I., *Att spegla tiden – eller forma den. Ola Hanssons introduktion av nordisk litteratur i Tyskland 1889-1895* (Göteborg, 1984).

Manns, U., *Den sanna frigörelsen. Fredrika—Bremer-förbundet 1884-1921* (Eslöv, 1997).

Marholm, L., *Das Buch der Frauen. Zeitpsychologische Portraits* (Paris/Leipzig, 1895).

— *Der Weg nach Altötting und andere Novellen*, 1900.

— *Frau Lilly als Jungfrau, Gattin, und Mutter* (Berlin, 1897).

— *Karla Bührung. Ein Frauendrama in 4 Akten* (München, 1895).

— *Six modern women. Psychological Sketches*, transl. Hermione Ramsden (Boston, 1896).

— *Studies in the Psychology of Woman*, transl. Georgia A. Etchison (New York, 1906).

— *Wir Frauen und unsere Dichter* (Wien, 1895).

— *Zur Psychologie der Frau I-II* (Berlin, 1903).

— *Zur Psychologie der Frau* (Berlin, 1897).

— *Zwei Frauenerlebnisse*, Novellen (Berlin, 1895).

Marks, S., *Margaretha Meyboom (1856-1927). En eldsjäl för den nordiska litteraturen i Nederländerna. En inventering av Meybooms litterära aktiviteter* (Groningen, 2000) (unpublished masterthesis).

McFadden, M., H., *Golden Cables of Sympathy. The Transatlantic Sources of Nine-teenth-Century Feminism* (Lexington, 1999).

McLellan, D., *Simone Weil – Utopian Pessimist* (London, 1989).

Meyboom, L. S. P., *De godsdienst der oude Noormannen* (Haarlem, 1868).

Meyboom, M., *Bjørnstjerne Bjørnson* (= Mannen en vrouwen van beteekenis in onze dagen 41, no. 7) (Haarlem, 1911b).

— 'De Scandinavische Bibliotheek', in: *Eigen haard Vol 34* (Amsterdam, 1908), pp. 822-824.

— ed, *Scandinavië-Nederland. Tijdschrift voor Nederlandsche en Scandinavische Taal, Letteren en Kultuur* (Amsterdam, 1905-1906).

— 'Open brief aan Freule Anna De Savornin Lohman naar aanleiding van haar brochure "De liefde in de vrouwenkwestie"' (Amsterdam, 1899).

— 'Skandinavische litteratuur in Nederland', in: *De Boekzaal 5* (Zwolle, 1911a), 45-49.

— *Vrouwenwerk. Schetsen* (Leiden, 1895).

— *Selma Lagerlöf* (= Skandinavische Bibliotheek, Logeman H., ed, volume missing) (Leiden, 1919).

— et al., eds, *Scandia. Maandblad voor Scandinavische Taal en Letteren* (Groningen, 1904).

— 'Henrik Ibsen en het huwelijk', *De Gids* (1909), pp. 274-297.

— 'Een Ibsen-Enquête', *De Nederlandsche Spectator* (1898), pp. 214-217.

Moi, T., 'Appropriating Bourdieu: Feminist theory and Pierre Bourdieu's sociology of culture', in: *New Literary History* 22 (1991), 4, pp. 1017-1049.

Mral, B., *Talande kvinnor. Kvinnliga retoriker från Aspasia till Ellen Key* (Falun, 1999).

Muls, J., 'Toespraak van Prof. Dr Jozef Muls namens het Belpaire-Teichmann Fonds, de Kunstwereld en de Koninklijke Vlaamsche Academie voor Taal en Letterkunde', Annex to *Dietsche Warande en Belfort* 48 (1948), 3-4, pp. 2-6.

Musschoot, A.M. and Parys, J. van, eds, 'Correspondentie van de gezusters Loveling. Brieven van en aan Frans de Cort', *Mededelingen van het Cyriel Buyssegenootschap* 20 (2004).

Nilsson, R. and Westman Berg, K., 'Studier i den första svenska bibliografin över kvinnliga författare', in: Hermelin, C., Lewandowski, J., Lönnqvist, H., eds, *Kvinnliga författare 1893-1899. Biobibliografi över svensk och finlandssvensk skönlitteratur* (Stockholm, 1892), pp. 13-25.

Pataky, S., *Lexikon deutscher Frauen der Feder. Eine Zusammenstellung der seit dem Jahre 1840 erschienenen Werke weiblicher Autoren, nebst Biographien der Lebenden und einem Verzeichnis der Pseudonyme* (Berlin, 1898).

Paul, A., *Strindberg – minnen och brev* (Stockholm, 1915).

Nordenstam, A., *Begynnelser. Litteraturforskningens pionjärkvinnor 1850-1930* (Stockholm, 2001).

Nordin, S., and Hedenius, I., *En filosof och hans tid* (Stockholm, 2004).

Perrin, J-M., and Thibon, G., *Simone Weil, telle que nous l'avons connue* (Paris, 1952).

Persyn, J., 'Lena, door Louisa Duykers. – Duimpjes uitgave, Victor Delille, Maldeghem, 1906', *Dietsche Warande en Belfort* 8 (1907), 1, pp. 101-103.

— 'Over letterkunde / Clara Viebig', *Dietsche Warande en Belfort* 9 (1908), 6, p. 551.

— *De wording van het tijdschrift Dietsche Warande en Belfort en zijn ontwikkeling onder de redactie van Em. Vliebergh en Jul. Persyn (1900-1924)* (Gent, 1963).

Pétrement, S., *La vie de Simone Weil I-II* (Paris, 1973) / *Simone Weil* (Stockholm, 1976).

Poldervaart, S., 'Margaretha Meijboom en Westerbro. Coöperatieve huishouding als feministisch ideaal', in: *Jaarboek voor Vrouwengeschiedenis 14* (Amsterdam, 1994), pp. 46-60.

— *Tegen conventioneel fatsoen en zekerheid. Het uitdagende feminisme van de utopisch socialisten* (Amsterdam, 1993).

Reynaud, A., ed, *Leçons de philosophie de Simone Weil* (Paris, 1959).

Rhees, R., et al., eds, *Discussions on Simone Weil* (Albany NY, 2000).

Ronne, M., "'The Mind and Body Problem": Academy, Gender and Power in Women's Contemporary Dissertation Novels', in: Johansson, Å. and Ragnerstam, P., eds, *Limitation and Liberation: Women Writers and the Politics of Genre* (Uppsala, 2005), pp. 59-69.

— 'Teoretiska perspektiv på kön, klass och gränsöverskridanden i akademin. Margit Abenius som forskare och litteraturkritiker', in: *Utbildning och Demokrati 2* (2006), pp. 111-128.

Rossbach, A., 'Nieuwe Duitsche Boeken / Die vor den Toren, roman van Clara Viebig', *Vlaamsche Arbeid 6* (1910-1911), 4, pp. 157-158.

Rossel, S.H., ed, *A History of Danish literature* (= Vol. 1 of A History of Scandinavian literature) (Nebraska, 1992), pp. 261-316.

Rydell, R.W. and Gwinn, N., eds, *Fair Representations. World's Fairs and the Modern World* (Amsterdam, 1994).

Savornin-Lohman de, A., *De liefde in de vrouwenkwestie. Laura Marholm: Das Buch der Frauen en Mevrouw Goekoop: Hilda van Suylenburg* (Amsterdam, 1899).

Schilt, J., *100 jaar H. J. W. Becht uitgever 1892-1992. Impressie van een eeuw boeken maken en verkopen* (Haarlem, 1992).

Schenkenveld-Van der Dussen, R. et al., eds, *Met en zonder lauwerkrans. Schrijvende vrouwen uit de vroegmoderne tijd 1550-1850: van Anna Bijns tot Elise van Calcar* (Amsterdam, 1997).

Schmook, G., *Onze Rensen* (Antwerpen/Brussel/Gent/Leuven, 1950).

Scott Sørensen, A., 'Taste, manners and attitudes – the *bel esprit* and literary salon in the Nordic countries c. 1800', in: Von der Fehr, D. et al., eds, *Is there a Nordic feminism? Nordic feminist thought on culture and society* (London, 1998) pp. 121-145.

— ed, *Nordisk salonkultur. Et studie i nordiske skønånder og salonmiljøer 1780-1850* (Odense, 1998).

Selboe, T., *Litterære vaganter. Byens betydning hos kvinnelige forfattere* (Oslo, 2003).

Showalter, E., *A literature of their own. British women novelists from Brontë to Lessing* (Princeton, 1977).

— 'Towards a feminist poetics', in: Showalter, ed, *The New Feminist Criticism. Essays on women, literature and theory* (London, 1986).

Smith, B. G., *The Gender of History. Men, Women, and Historical Practice* (Cambridge/Massachusetts/London, 1998).

Smith, J., '"The Cock of Lordly Plume": Sexual Selection and *The Egoist*', *Nineteenth-Century Literature* 50 (1995: 1), pp. 51-77.

Sontag, S., 'Simone Weil', in: *The New York Review of Books*, February1, 1963.

Stark, S., *"Behind inverted commas". Translation and Anglo-German Cultural Relations in the Nineteenth Century* (Clevedon, 1999). Also available as e-book: http://books.google.nl/books?id=601RPGkVmqwC&pg=PA60&lpg=PA60&dq=Susanne+Stark+1993&source=bl&ots=NOZq79FIBH&sig=xYrQZkrGv44_mfMZiSnguvVRd74&hl=nl&ei=4PajS7WWFomD4Qam4JnzCQ&sa=X&oi=book_result&ct=result&resnum=1&ved=0CAYQ6AEwAA#v=onepage&q=&f=false

Steen, E., *Den lange strid. Camilla Collett og hennes senere forfatterskap* (Oslo, 1954).

— *Camilla Collett om seg selv* (Oslo, 1985).

Steensen Blicher, S., *Brudstykker af en Landsbydegns Dagbog* (Kjøbenhavn, 1824).

Steinfeld, T., *Den unge Camilla Collett. Et kvinnehjertes historie* (Oslo, 1996).

— 'Fra salmeoversettelser til det borgerlige familiedrama', *Norsk kvinnelitteraturhistorie. Bind 1 1600-1900* (Oslo, 1988) pp. 28-40.

Stenqvist, C., *Simone Weil. Om livets tragik – och dess skönhet* (Stockholm, 1984).

Todd, J., *Mary Wollstonecraft, a revolutionary life* (London, 2000).

Tuohela, K., 'Feeling sick: on change and gender in the cultural history or illness', in: Lahtinen, A. and Vainio-Koohonen, K., eds, *History and Change* (Helsinki, 2004), pp. 46-556.

Van Berkel, K., 'Over het ontstaan van de twee culturen in het negentiende-eeuws Europa', *Spiegel der Letteren* 42 (2000), pp. 83-96.

Van Boven, E., *Een hoofdstuk apart. 'Vrouwenromans' in de literaire kritiek 1898-1930* (Amsterdam, 1992).

— 'Ver van de literatuur. Het schrijverschap van Ina Boudier-Bakker', *Nederlandse Letterkunde* 2 (1997), pp. 242-257.

Van Dijk, H., *'In het liefdeleven ligt gansch het leven'. Het beeld van de vrouw in het Nederlands realistisch proza, 1885-1930* (Assen, 2001).

Van Dijk, S. et al., eds, *'I have heard about you', Foreign Women's Writing Crossing the Dutch Border: from Sappho to Selma Lagerlöf* (Hilversum, 2004).

— 'Foreword: Foreign women's writing as read in the Netherlands', in: *'I have heard about you'*, *Foreign Women's Writing Crossing the Dutch Border: from Sappho to Selma Lagerlöf* (Hilversum, 2004), pp. 9-33.

Van der Hallen, O., *Vijftig jaar katholieke letterkunde in Vlaanderen (1885-1937)* (Leuven, 1938).

Van Elslander, A. and Musschoot, A. M., eds, 'Correspondentie van de Gezusters Loveling. Brieven van en aan Paul Fredericq I', *Mededelingen van het Cyriel Buysse Genootschap* 9 (1993), pp. 76-175.

Van Elslander, A. and Musschoot, A. M., eds, 'Correspondentie van de gezusters Loveling. Brieven van en aan Paul Fredericq II', *Mededelingen van het Cyriel Buyssegenootschap* 10 (1994), pp. 31-156.

Van Elslander, A., ed, *De 'biografie' van Virginie Loveling* (Gent, 1963).

Van Hoeck, M., 'Louisa Duykers', *Boekengids* 1 (1924) 5-6, pp. 129-131.

Van Itallie-van Embden, W., 'Margaretha Meyboom.' in: *Vrouwenjaarboek Vol. 1* (Amsterdam, 1929), pp. 183-189.

Vanacker, D., ed, *Virginie Loveling. Sophie* (Gent, 1990).

Vandenbussche, L., "Dat ik de broek aanheb, ziet gij'. Het 'androgyne' schrijverschap van Virginie Loveling', *Nederlandse Letterkunde* 13 (2008), pp. 69-89.

Vandermassen, G., Demoor M. and Braeckman, M. 'Close Encounters with a New Species: Darwin's Clash with the Feminists at the End of the Nineteenth Century', in: *Unmapped Countries: Biological Visions in Nineteenth-Century Literature and Culture*, Zwierlein, A.J., ed (Londen, 2005), pp. 71-81.

Verschaeve, C., *Aan de Vlaamsche vrouwen. Feestrede uitgesproken door E.H. Cyriel Verschaeve op de Landdagen der Christene Vlaamsche Meisjes te Oostacker, (16 September 1913) en te Gent (11 Augustus 1919)* (Tielt, 1920).

Vervliet, R., *De literaire manifesten van het fin de siècle in de Zuidnederlandse periodieken 1878-1914* (Gent, 1982).

Vinje, A. O., *A Norseman's Views of Britain and the British* (Edinburgh, 1863).

— *Bretland og Britarne* (Kristiania, 1873).

Visser, I., 'American women writers in the Dutch literary world 1824-1900', in: Van Dijk, S., et al., eds, *'I have heard about you'*, *Foreign Women's Writing Crossing the Dutch Border: from Sappho to Selma Lagerlöf* (Hilversum, 2004), pp. 281-299.

Von Flotow, L., *Translating and gender. Translating in the 'Era of Feminism'* (Manchester/Ottowa,1997).

— 'Dis-Unity and Diversity. Feminist Approaches to Translation Studies', in: Bowker, L., Cronin, M., Kenny, D. and Pearson, J., eds, *Unity in Diversity? Current Trends in Translation Studies* (Manchester, 1998), pp. 3-13.

W. [V. Loveling], 'L'école de l'armée', *La Flandre Libérale*, January 18, 1881.

— 'Le dernier ami', *La Flandre Libérale*, September 20, 1880.

— 'On nous écrit d'A', *La Flandre Libérale*, March 2, 1880.

— 'On nous écrit de M. petit village dans la Flandre Orientale', *La Flandre Libérale*, February 3, 1880.

— 'On nous écrit de Nevele', *La Flandre Libérale*, August 12, 1880.

— 'Voltaire au Paradis', *La Flandre Libérale*, May 23, 1876.

Weil, A., *The Apprenticeship of a Mathematician* (Basel, Boston, Berlin, 1992).

Weil, S., *La Pesanteur et la grâce* (Paris, 1947)/ *Gravity and Grace* (New York, 1952) / *Tyngden och nåden* (Stockholm, 1954).

— *L'Enracinement. Prélude à une déclaration des devoirs envers l'être humain* (Paris, 1949)/ *The Need for Roots* (New York, 1952).

— *Attente de Dieu* (Paris, 1950)/ *Waiting for God* (New York, 1951).

— *La personne et le sacré. Ècrits de Londre* (Paris, 1957)/ *Personen och det heliga. Essäer och brev* (Stockholm, 1961).

Whitford, M., *Luce Irigaray: philosophy in the feminine* (London, 1991).

Winch, P., *Simone Weil: "The Just Balance"* (Cambridge,1989).

Wistrand, B., *Elin Wägner i 1920-talet* (Uppsala, 2006).

Witt-Brattström, E., *Dekadensens kön. Ola Hansson och Laura Marholm* (Stockholm, 2007).

— *Ediths jag. Edith Södergran och modernismens födelse* (Stockholm, 1997).

— ed, *The New Woman and the Aesthetic Opening. Unlocking Gender in Twentieth-Century Texts* (Stockholm, 2004).

Wolf, M., 'The Creation of A "Room of One's Own". Feminist Translators as Mediators Between Cultures and Genders', in: Santaemilia, J., *Gender, Sex and Translation. The Manipulations of Identities* (Manchester (UK)/Northampton (USA), 2005), pp. 15-25.

Wollstonecraft, M., *Letters written during a short residence in Sweden, Norway and Denmark* (Wilmington, Del., 1796).


http://www.buchmesse.de/en/fbf/general/ , November 8 th, 2009.

http://www.hetutrechtsarchief.nl/thema/tijdbalk/1745, December 2th 2009.

http://www.christiansfeldcentret.dk/00038/, December 2th, 2009.

http://www.slideshine.de/9102, December 2th, 2009.

http://www.projekte.kunstgeschichte.uni-muenchen.de/dt_frz_malerei/41-dt-franz-malerei/studieneinheiten/1848_1860_d/6a/gruppe_1/b.htm, December 2th, 2009.

# Index

# D

# E

# F